First World War
and Army of Occupation
War Diary
France, Belgium and Germany

29 DIVISION
Headquarters, Branches and Services
General Staff
1 June 1916 - 30 June 1916

WO95/2280/3

The Naval & Military Press Ltd
www.nmarchive.com
Published in association with The National Archives

Published by

The Naval & Military Press Ltd

Unit 10 Ridgewood Industrial Park,

Uckfield, East Sussex,

TN22 5QE England

Tel: +44 (0) 1825 749494

www.naval-military-press.com

www.nmarchive.com

This diary has been reprinted in facsimile from the original. Any imperfections are inevitably reproduced and the quality may fall short of modern type and cartographic standards.

© Crown Copyright
Images reproduced by permission of The National Archives, London, England, 2015.

Contents

Document type	Place/Title	Date From	Date To
Heading	General Staff 29th Division June 1916		
Heading	War Diary General Staff 29th Division For The Month Of June-1916 Volume XVI		
War Diary		01/06/1916	30/06/1916
Miscellaneous	Appendix 1.		
Miscellaneous	Report On Raid Carried Out On Enemy's Trenches By 1st Lancashire Fusiliers On Night 3/4th June 1916. Appendix 1 (a)	03/06/1916	03/06/1916
Miscellaneous	Headquarters, 86th Brigade. Raids.	03/06/1916	03/06/1916
Miscellaneous	87th Brigade (for information)	02/06/1916	02/06/1916
Miscellaneous	31st Division (for information) 36th Division	02/06/1916	02/06/1916
Operation(al) Order(s)	Operation Order No. 11 By Brigadier General D.E. Cayley, C.M.G. Commanding 88th Brigade.	22/06/1916	22/06/1916
Miscellaneous	Headquarters, 29th Division.	27/06/1916	27/06/1916
Miscellaneous	86th Brigade.	26/06/1916	26/06/1916
Miscellaneous	C.R.A. App 1 (C).	27/06/1916	27/06/1916
Miscellaneous	Report on Raids by 86th Brigade on night of 27/28th June, 1916.	27/06/1916	27/06/1916
Miscellaneous	Report On Raid By 87th Brigade.	27/06/1916	27/06/1916
Miscellaneous	Report On Raid By 88th Brigade. Point of Entry Q.10.d.85.35.		
Miscellaneous	H.Q. 88th Inf. Bde. B. 344.	29/06/1916	29/06/1916
Miscellaneous	Headquarters, 29th Division.	28/06/1916	28/06/1916
Miscellaneous	Party Left Our Trenches at 2325 and formed up in front of hedge in Q 16 b.		
Miscellaneous	VIII Corps. G. 1716. 29th Division.	27/06/1916	27/06/1916
Miscellaneous	C Form (Duplicate). Messages And Signals.		
Miscellaneous	87th Brigade. App 1 (d)	28/06/1916	28/06/1916
Miscellaneous	Headquarters, VIIIth Corps.	29/06/1916	29/06/1916
Miscellaneous	Messages And Signals.	29/06/1916	29/06/1916
Miscellaneous	Be Brigade Major 86th Brigade.	29/06/1916	29/06/1916
Miscellaneous	86th Brigade. App 1 (C)	29/06/1916	29/06/1916
Miscellaneous	Messages And Signals.	29/06/1916	29/06/1916
Miscellaneous	86th Brigade.	28/06/1916	28/06/1916
Map	Order of Battle of Enemy's Forces Opposite. VIII Cp. on 27.6.16.		
Miscellaneous	Headquarters, 29th Division.	30/06/1916	30/06/1916
Miscellaneous	Report on Raid On Night June 29/30 Carried Out Against The German Front Line at point 60	29/06/1916	29/06/1916
Heading	The Staff Copy 84th D Qlc		
Miscellaneous	87th Bde.	30/06/1916	30/06/1916
Miscellaneous	Report On Patrol.	30/06/1916	30/06/1916
Miscellaneous	VIIIth Corps. 86th Brigade.	30/06/1916	30/06/1916
Operation(al) Order(s)	29th Division Order No. 36 Appendix 2 (d)	14/06/1916	14/06/1916
Miscellaneous	Raid on Y.1/Y.2 Night (29th) Programme Of Heavy Artillery Bombardment	29/06/1916	29/06/1916
Miscellaneous	Appendix 2.		
Miscellaneous	86th Brigade.	01/06/1916	01/06/1916
Operation(al) Order(s)	29th Division Order No. 34 Appendix 2 (a).	04/06/1916	04/06/1916
Operation(al) Order(s)	29th Division Order No. 35. Appendix 2 (b)	10/06/1916	10/06/1916

Type	Description	Date 1	Date 2
Miscellaneous			
Miscellaneous	Amendment To Division Order No. 36.	30/06/1916	30/06/1916
Miscellaneous	86th Brigade.	21/06/1916	21/06/1916
Miscellaneous	Headquarters, 86th Brigade.	16/06/1916	16/06/1916
Miscellaneous	Divisional Signal Communications.		
Miscellaneous	Artillery Communications.		
Operation(al) Order(s)	VIII Corps Operation Order No. 3. Appendix 2 (e)	15/06/1916	15/06/1916
Operation(al) Order(s)	29th Division Order No. 38. Appendix 2 (f)	18/06/1916	18/06/1916
Miscellaneous	March Table A		
Miscellaneous	March Table "B"		
Operation(al) Order(s)	29th Division Order No. 39. Appendix 2 (9)	18/06/1916	18/06/1916
Miscellaneous	Appendix "A" Arrangements for Gas Discharge.		
Miscellaneous	Appendix "B". Arrangements for Smoke Discharge.		
Miscellaneous	Appendix "C". Programme Of Infantry Advance And Artillery Bombardment.		
Miscellaneous	G.S.	19/06/1916	19/06/1916
Miscellaneous	Time. Moves of Infantry Trench Mortars. Divisional Heavy Artillery.		
Miscellaneous	Appendix "B". Arrangements for Smoke Discharge.	21/06/1916	21/06/1916
Miscellaneous	2/Lieut Stevens, Special Brigade. R.E. 2/Lieut. Pheasey. Special Brigade. R.E.	21/06/1916	21/06/1916
Miscellaneous	Appendix "C". Programme Of Infantry Advance And Artillery Bombardment.		
Miscellaneous	Smoke Discharge.		
Miscellaneous	C Form (Duplicate). Messages And Signals.		
Map	German Lines Opposite 29th Division Front.		
Miscellaneous	86th Brigade.	24/06/1916	24/06/1916
Operation(al) Order(s)	29th Tactical Exercise. Operation Order No. 40 App. 2 (h)	21/06/1916	21/06/1916
Miscellaneous	Time Table. 29th Divisional Exercise June 22nd.	22/06/1916	22/06/1916
Map	Training Area 29th Div.		
Miscellaneous	Headquarters, VIII Corps. B.E.F. France. June 21st, 1916	21/06/1916	21/06/1916
Miscellaneous	VIII Corps G. 1583.	21/06/1916	21/06/1916
Operation(al) Order(s)	29th Division Order No. 41. Appendix 2 (i)	28/06/1916	28/06/1916
Miscellaneous	Corrigendum.	29/06/1916	29/06/1916
Miscellaneous	R.A. VIII Corps R.A. 395/49.	28/06/1916	28/06/1916
Miscellaneous	Right Group, 29th Divl Artillery 26th June 1916.	26/06/1916	26/06/1916
Operation(al) Order(s)	Operation Order No. 1 by Brigadier General Malcolm Peake C.M.G., Commanding 29th Divisional Artillery. App 2 (j)	25/06/1916	25/06/1916
Miscellaneous	Headquarters, 29th Division.	30/06/1916	30/06/1916
Miscellaneous	Programme Of Heavy Artillery.		
Miscellaneous	Action of 29th D.A. Z day before Zero.	30/06/1916	30/06/1916
Miscellaneous	Headquarters 29th Divl. Artillery, 28th June 1916.	28/06/1916	28/06/1916
Miscellaneous	29th Div. G.S.	27/06/1916	27/06/1916
Miscellaneous	G.O.C., R.A. VIII Corps R.A. 395/77.	27/04/1916	27/04/1916
Miscellaneous	Instructions for 29th Divisional Artillery	18/06/1916	18/06/1916
Miscellaneous	29th Divisional Artillery-Instructions. Appendix 'A'.		
Miscellaneous	Supplementary Instructions-29th Divisional Artillery.	20/06/1916	20/06/1916
Miscellaneous	Further Instructions for 29th Divisional Artillery.	20/05/1916	20/05/1916
Miscellaneous	Right Group Left Group	26/06/1916	26/06/1916
Miscellaneous	29th Divisional Artillery	21/06/1916	21/06/1916
Miscellaneous	Right Group.	22/06/1916	22/06/1916
Miscellaneous	Headquarters 29th Divisional Artillery, 23rd June 1916.	23/06/1916	23/06/1916
Miscellaneous	Appendix 3. Comprises the following.		

Miscellaneous	VIII Corps. G. 1365. App 3	13/06/1916	13/06/1916
Miscellaneous	Headquarters, VIIIth Corps.	15/06/1916	15/06/1916
Miscellaneous	VIII Corps. G. 1365	13/06/1916	13/06/1916
Miscellaneous	VIII Corps. G. 1396	14/06/1916	14/06/1916
Miscellaneous	C.G.S. 53. O.C. Special Brigade VIII Corps.	15/06/1916	15/06/1916
Miscellaneous	C.G.S. 53 86th Brigade.	15/06/1916	15/06/1916
Miscellaneous	VIII Corps G. 1414 4th Division.	15/06/1916	15/06/1916
Miscellaneous	Lieut. Stevens, R.E., Special Brigade. Lieut. Pheasey, R.E., Special Brigade.	18/06/1916	18/06/1916
Miscellaneous	86th Brigade.	16/06/1916	16/06/1916
Miscellaneous	Code		
Miscellaneous	VIII Corps. G. 1476	18/06/1916	18/06/1916
Miscellaneous	86th Brigade.	19/06/1916	19/06/1916
Miscellaneous	VIII Corps. G. 1683	25/06/1916	25/06/1916
Miscellaneous	Lieut. Stevens, Special Brigade, R.E.	25/06/1916	25/06/1916
Miscellaneous	4th Division GGG 766/14	25/06/1916	25/06/1916
Miscellaneous	C.G.S. 35/3	26/06/1916	26/06/1916
Miscellaneous	VIII Corps G. 1693.	25/06/1916	25/06/1916
Miscellaneous	VIII Corps. G. 1693.	26/06/1916	26/06/1916
Miscellaneous	Report on Gas discharged on 29th Division front between Q.10.2 and Q.10.12.	27/06/1916	27/06/1916
Miscellaneous	VIII Corps G. 1368.	13/06/1916	13/06/1916
Miscellaneous	VIII Corps G. 1383	14/06/1916	14/06/1916
Miscellaneous	VIII Corps. G. 1421.	15/06/1916	15/06/1916
Miscellaneous	VIII Corps. G. 1416.	15/06/1916	15/06/1916
Miscellaneous	From Capt. Slater. R.E. To. G.S. 29th Div.	17/06/1916	17/06/1916
Miscellaneous	Capt. Slater, Special Brigade, VIIIth Corps.	16/06/1916	16/06/1916
Miscellaneous	G.S. 29th Division.	17/06/1916	17/06/1916
Miscellaneous	VIII Corps. G1465	17/06/1916	17/06/1916
Miscellaneous	Gen. Staff.	18/06/1916	18/06/1916
Miscellaneous	VIII Corps No. 976.Q.	17/06/1916	17/06/1916
Miscellaneous	Table Shewing Arrangements Made For Delivering Candles And P Bombs To Divisions On June 20th 1916.	20/06/1916	20/06/1916
Miscellaneous	VIII Corps. G. 1478	18/06/1916	18/06/1916
Miscellaneous	VIII Corps. G. 1493.	18/06/1916	18/06/1916
Miscellaneous	VIII Corps No. 976/Q.	22/06/1916	22/06/1916
Miscellaneous	VIII Corps. G. 1615	23/06/1916	23/06/1916
Miscellaneous	Appendix 4. Comprises the following.		
Miscellaneous	Notes For Conference On 20/6/16. Appendix 4 (a)	20/06/1916	20/06/1916
Miscellaneous	29th Division. Reserves Of Ammunition, Grenades, & C. App 4		
Miscellaneous	Divisional Signal Communications. App 4 (c)		
Miscellaneous	Artillery Communications.		
Miscellaneous	Artillery Ammunition. Approximate Expenditure. App. 4 (d)		
Miscellaneous	86th Brigade. App 4 (e)	24/06/1916	24/06/1916
Miscellaneous	Carrying And Working Parties. 86th Brigade. App. 4 (f)	13/06/1916	13/06/1916
Miscellaneous	Carrying And Working Parties. 87th Brigade.	13/06/1916	13/06/1916
Miscellaneous	Major Hardress Lloyd. Lieut C.T. Ball, Divisional Grenadier Officer. App 4 (g)	22/06/1916	22/06/1916
Miscellaneous	Appendix "A".		
Miscellaneous	Orders For Northern And Southern Observation Posts.		
Miscellaneous	Appendix "C". Programme Of Infantry Advance And Artillery Bombardment.		

Miscellaneous	Time. Moves of Infantry. Trench Mortars. Divl. Artillery. Heavy Artillery.		
Miscellaneous	Programme Of Preliminary Bombardment 29th Division. Divisional Artillery.		
Miscellaneous	Preliminary Divisional Artillery Bombardment. Times for Night Firing.		
Miscellaneous	Heavy Artillery Preliminary Bombardment.		
Miscellaneous	Smoke.		
Miscellaneous	Gas.		
Miscellaneous	Orders For N.C.O. In Charge Of 29th Divisional O.P. Auchonvillers.	22/06/1916	22/06/1916
Miscellaneous	Appendix "A".		
Miscellaneous	Appendix 5. Comprises the following.		
Miscellaneous	29th Division Daily Summary. for Period From 6.a.m 31/5/16 to 6.a.m. 1/6/16	31/05/1916	31/05/1916
Miscellaneous	29th Division Daily Summary. for Period From 6.a.m. 1/6/16. to 6. a.m. 2/6/16.	01/06/1916	01/06/1916
Miscellaneous	29th Division Daily Summary for Period From 6. a.m. 2/6/16 to 6. a.m. 3/6/16.	02/06/1916	02/06/1916
Miscellaneous		03/06/1916	03/06/1916
Miscellaneous	29th Division Daily Summary for Period From 6. a.m. 3/6/16 to 6. a.m. 4/6/16.	03/06/1916	03/06/1916
Miscellaneous	29th Division Daily Summary for Period From 6. a.m. 4/6/16 to 6. a.m. 5/6/16	04/06/1916	04/06/1916
Miscellaneous	29th Division Daily Summary for Period From 6. a.m. 5/6/16 to 6. a.m. 6/6/16	05/06/1916	05/06/1916
Miscellaneous	Daily Summary. Period from 6.O a.m. 7/6/16 to 6.O a.m. 8/6/16.	07/06/1916	07/06/1916
Miscellaneous	29th Division Daily Summary. for Period From 6. a.m. 8/6/16 to 6. a.m. 9/6/16.	08/06/1916	08/06/1916
Miscellaneous	29th Division Daily Summary. for Period From 6. a.m. 9/6/16 to 6. a.m. 10/6/16.	09/06/1916	09/06/1916
Miscellaneous	29th Division Daily Summary for Period From 6. a.m. 10/6/16 to 6. a.m. 11/6/16.	10/06/1916	10/06/1916
Miscellaneous	29th Division Daily Summary for Period from 6. a.m. 11/6/16 to 6. a.m. 12/6/16	11/06/1916	11/06/1916
Miscellaneous	29th Division Daily Summary. for Period from 6 a.m. 12/6/16. to 6 a.m. 13/6/16	12/06/1916	12/06/1916
Miscellaneous	29th Division Daily Summary Period from 6.O a.m. 13/6/16 to 6.O a.m. 14/6/16	13/06/1916	13/06/1916
Miscellaneous	29th Division Daily Summary for period from 6 a.m. 14/6/16. to 6 a.m. 15/6/16.	14/06/1916	14/06/1916
Miscellaneous	29th Divisional Daily Summary. from 6 a.m. 15/6/16. to 6 a.m. 16/6/16.	15/06/1916	15/06/1916
Miscellaneous	29th Division Daily Summary. Period from 6. a.m. 16/6/16 to 6. a.m. 17/6/16.	16/06/1916	16/06/1916
Miscellaneous	29th Division Daily Summary. Period from 17/6/16 (6. a.m.) to 6. a.m. 18/6/16.	17/06/1916	17/06/1916
Miscellaneous	29th Division Daily Summary. Period from 6 a.m. 18.6.16. to 6 a.m. 19.6.16.	18/06/1916	18/06/1916
Miscellaneous	29th Division Daily Summary for Period from 6. a.m. 19/6/16 to 6. a.m. 20/6/16.	19/06/1916	19/06/1916
Miscellaneous	29th Division Daily Summary. Period from 6 a.m. 20.6.16. to 6 a.m. 21.6.16.	20/06/1916	20/06/1916
Miscellaneous	29th Division Daily Summary. Period from 6. a.m. 21st/6/16 to 6. a.m. 22/6/16.	21/06/1916	21/06/1916

Miscellaneous	29th Division Daily Summary. Period from 6 a.m. 22.6.16. to 6 a.m. 23.6.16.	22/06/1916	22/06/1916
Miscellaneous	29th Division Daily Summary. Period from 6 a.m. 23.6.16. to a.m. 24.6.16.	23/06/1916	23/06/1916
Miscellaneous	29th Division Daily Summary. Period from 6 a.m. 24.6.16. to 6 a.m. 25.6.16.	24/06/1916	24/06/1916
Miscellaneous	29th Division Daily Summary from 6 a.m. 25.6.16. to 6 a.m. 26.6.16.	25/06/1916	25/06/1916
Miscellaneous	29th Division Daily Summary. From 6 a.m. 26.6.16. to 6 a.m. 27.6.16.	26/06/1916	26/06/1916
Miscellaneous	Appendix 6. Comprises the following.		
Miscellaneous	Casualties to 12 noon, June 25th 1916	25/06/1916	25/06/1916
Miscellaneous	Casualties During 24 Hrs Ending noon 24th June.	25/06/1916	25/06/1916
Miscellaneous	Casualties to 12 noon June 27th 1916.	27/06/1916	27/06/1916
Miscellaneous	Casualties to 12 noon 26th June. 1916.	26/06/1916	26/06/1916
Miscellaneous	Casualties to 12 noon June 29th 1916.	29/06/1916	29/06/1916
Miscellaneous	Casualties to 12 noon 28th June. 1916	28/06/1916	28/06/1916
Miscellaneous	Casualties to 12 noon June 30th. 1916.	30/06/1916	30/06/1916
Miscellaneous	Appendix 7. Comprises the following.	16/06/1916	16/06/1916
Miscellaneous	29th Division Dispositions. at 10. a.m. on June. 16th. Appendix 7	16/06/1916	16/06/1916
Miscellaneous	29th Division Dispositions at 10 a.m. on June 24th.	24/06/1916	24/06/1916

GENERAL STAFF

29th DIVISION

JUNE 1916

Appendices attached :-

1. Reports on Raids.
2. Operation Orders & Instructions.
3. Gas.
4. Conferences; Correspondence etc.
5. Daily Intelligence Summaries.
6. Casualty Returns.
7. Dispositions.

SECRET

AND

CONFIDENTIAL.

WAR   DIARY

GENERAL STAFF

29TH DIVISION

FOR THE MONTH OF

JUNE - 1916

- - - - - - - - - - -

VOLUME XVI

= = = = = = = = = =

Army Form C. 2118.

WAR DIARY - GENERAL STAFF, 29th DIVISION.

INTELLIGENCE SUMMARY.
(Erase heading not required.)

June 1916.

1916.

Instructions regarding War Diaries and Intelligence Summaries are contained in F. S. Regs., Part II. and the Staff Manual respectively. Title pages will be prepared in manuscript.

Place	Date	Hour	Summary of Events and Information	Remarks and references to Appendices
	1st June.		The G.O.C. visited the Right Sector in the morning. G.S.O.3 visited the trenches in the afternoon. The G.S.O.2 visited the training ground in the morning and the G.S.O.1 in the afternoon. The G.O.C. went to see the Corps Commander in the middle of the day.	
	2nd June.		The G.O.C. visited the Right Sector in the morning. The G.S.O.1 went to YVRENCHES to witness an attack practice by the 4th Division. The G.S.O.3 arranged about the boundaries of the training area between BUS and LOUVENCOURT, the German trenches having been marked out too far West. G.O.C. witnessed a raid practice at night erected by the 86th Bde on the training ground. G.S.O.III visited the Left Sector trenches at night with G.S.O. III of VIII Corps.	

T2134. Wt. W708—776. 500000. 4/15. Sir J. C. & S.

Army Form C. 2118.

WAR DIARY GENERAL STAFF. 29th Division.
or
INTELLIGENCE SUMMARY.
(Erase heading not required.)

Instructions regarding War Diaries and Intelligence Summaries are contained in F. S. Regs., Part II. and the Staff Manual respectively. Title pages will be prepared in manuscript.

1916.

Place	Date	Hour	Summary of Events and Information	Remarks and references to Appendices
	3rd June		There was a demonstration of Light Trench Mortars at VALHEUREUX 11 officers and men from each Battalion attended. A Raid was carried out on the enemy's trenches at Q.4.d.88.00. by the 86th Brigade at midnight 3/4th June and identifications were obtained but no prisoners were taken. There was only 1 casualty amongst the raiding party; Lieut. Colonel Kelly (Commanding Essex Regt.) was severely wounded. A report on the raid is attached to (Appendix I (a).) G.S.O. 1 inspected Medium Trench Mortar emplacements in the trenches.	Appendix I(a)
	4th June		The G.O.C. visited the Corps Commander at midday; in the morning he inspected the 86th Brigade carrying out an attack practice on the training area at LOUVENCOURT. Captain Fulton, Lancs. Fusiliers was attached to the General Staff vice Capt Gee, who returned to the 86th Brigade Staff. G.S.O. 1 and O.C Pioneers inspected work done on the "Yellow Line."	

Army Form C. 2118.

WAR DIARY GENERAL STAFF. 29th DIVISION.

or

INTELLIGENCE SUMMARY.

(Erase heading not required.)

Instructions regarding War Diaries and Intelligence
Summaries are contained in F. S. Regs., Part II.
and the Staff Manual respectively. Title pages
will be prepared in manuscript.

1916.

Place	Date	Hour	Summary of Events and Information	Remarks and references to Appendices
	5th June.		The G.O.C. visited the 86th Brigade at training. The G.S.O.11 visited the Left Sector trenches. At 3.p.m. there was a demonstration of firing of Medium and Light Trench Mortars. Wire cutting Torpedoes and of the use of smoke as a protective screen. 86th Brigade witnessed it.	
	6th June.		The G.O.C. visited the 87th and 88th Brigade Headquarters in the morning and an attack practice by the 86th Brigade at LOUVENCOURT in the afternoon. G.S.Os II and III visited the Left Sector trenches in the morning. Some hostile shelling about 1st AVENUE but quiet otherwise.	

Army Form C. 2118.

WAR DIARY GENERAL STAFF 29th DIVISION.

or

~~INTELLIGENCE SUMMARY.~~

(Erase heading not required.)

Instructions regarding War Diaries and Intelligence
Summaries are contained in F. S. Regs., Part II.
and the Staff Manual respectively. Title pages
will be prepared in manuscript.

1916.

Place	Date	Hour	Summary of Events and Information	Remarks and references to Appendices
	7th June.		The G.O.C. and A.D.C. proceeded on leave. The G.S.O.1 went to Corps Headquarters at 10.30 a.m. to explain our attack dispositions. The G.S.O.II and III went to the Right Sector to put up dump boards. Lieut Stephens of the "Special Brigade" arrived. 86th Brigade relieved the 88th Brigade in the Left Sector on the night 7/8th (App. 2(a))	Appendices (a)
	8th June.		The G.S.O.1 visited the Left Sector and selected positions for dumps and marked them with boards. The G.S.O.3 took D.A.QM.G. round dumps in the Right Sector and in the afternoon he visited a Stokes Mortar demonstration held by 31st Division at GEZAINCOURT. A quiet day, rain at night.	

T2134. Wt. W708-776. 500000. 4/15. Sir J.C. & S.

Army Form C. 2118.

WAR DIARY GENERAL STAFF 29th DIVISION.
or
INTELLIGENCE SUMMARY.

(Erase heading not required.)

Instructions regarding War Diaries and Intelligence Summaries are contained in F. S. Regs., Part II. and the Staff Manual respectively. Title pages will be prepared in manuscript.

1916.

Place	Date	Hour	Summary of Events and Information	Remarks and references to Appendices
	9th June.		G.S.O.II visited Fort Jackson and Southern Observation Post. G.S.O.1 visited the Model Stokes Mortar Emplacements at LOUVENCOURT. Hostile Artillery was very active during the day especially against our Left Sector. During the night Lieut Davies R. Dublin Fusrs. and 3 men went out on patrol from ROONEY'S Sap. One man was brought in later wounded, the patrol having been surprised, the remainder were wounded and presumably captured.	
	10th June.		Lieut. Colonel Biddulph was appointed C.R.E. and took over duties from Lieut. Colonel PYNE. G.S.O.III visited the 2 Divisional Observation Posts. A very wet day; evening enemy shelled our Left Sector rather heavily during the afternoon and again at 11.30 p.m. when they attempted a raid about Sap 7.(Point Q.4.d.22.75) but failed to enter our trenches. We had 19 killed and 37 wounded in this Sector and one killed and 7 wounded in MARY REDAN.	

T2134. Wt. W708-776. 500000. 4/15. Sir J. C. & S.

Army Form C. 2118.

WAR DIARY - GENERAL STAFF, 29TH DIVISION.

or

INTELLIGENCE SUMMARY

(Erase heading not required.)

Instructions regarding War Diaries and Intelligence Summaries are contained in F. S. Regs., Part II. and the Staff Manual respectively. Title pages will be prepared in manuscript.

1916.

Place	Date	Hour	Summary of Events and Information	Remarks and references to Appendices
	11th June		The G.O.C. returned from leave 12 midnight 11/12th bringing with him 2nd Lieut. NICHOLLS as A.D.C. The G.S.Os. I and II visited the Left Sector trenches in the afternoon. Copy No. 5 of VIIIth Corps G.1340 giving preliminary orders for the offensive operations was received.	M. NICKALLS, Notts & Derby
	12th June		The G.S.O. II and G.S.O. III visited the Right and Left Sectors respectively and inspected the dumps. The G.O.C. visited 88th Brigade at training in the morning and went to see the Corps Commander in the afternoon. A quiet day.	

WAR DIARY - GENERAL STAFF, 29TH DIVISION

1916.

Army Form C. 2118.

Instructions regarding War Diaries and Intelligence Summaries are contained in F. S. Regs., Part II. and the Staff Manual respectively. Title pages will be prepared in manuscript.

INTELLIGENCE SUMMARY.
(Erase heading not required.)

Place	Date	Hour	Summary of Events and Information	Remarks and references to Appendices
	13th June		The G.O.C. visited the 88th Brigade at training in the morning. There was a Divisional Conference in the afternoon attended by Brigadiers and Brigade Majors, C.R.A., C.R.E.M., A.A. & Q.M.G., the preliminary orders for the forthcoming offensive were discussed, the new date for the commencement of the bombardment (the 20th June) was given out. A copy of a list showing the various working parties required to be found by the two forward Brigades for carrying M up stores and ammunition to the forward dumps etc. is attached to Appendix, also a memo. detailing carrying parties from the 86th Brigade for 2" Trench Mortar Bombs &c. Divisional Operation Order No. 37 (Reference Relief of 87th Brigade by 88th in the Right Sector) was issued vide Appendix. 2(c)	Appendix (b) Appendix 2(c)
	14th June		The G.S.O.II visited the YELLOW LINE. The G.S.O.I inspected routes for the 86th Brigade to follow out of MAILLY WOOD to their forming-up places. The G.O.C. visited the 88th Brigade at training in the afternoon. The Corps Commander also inspected the training. Large carrying parties were employed by Brigades night and day in getting up supplies, water, ammunition, etc. Work was done on the gas cylinder emplacements, in the front line. Operation Order No. 36 giving preliminary instructions for the attack was issued at 10 a.m., Map attached vide Appendix. 2(d) 4th Division took over the portion of our front line from Q.4.d.2.9 to Q.4.b.5.4 on this date vide Appendix 2 (b). All clocks were altered to Summer time, i.e. one hour in advance, at 11/2 pm.	Appendix 2(d) Appendix 2(e)

WAR DIARY - GENERAL STAFF, 29TH DIVISION.

or

INTELLIGENCE SUMMARY.

(Erase heading not required.)

Army Form C. 2118.

1916.

Place	Date	Hour	Summary of Events and Information	Remarks and references to Appendices
	15th June		The G.O.C. visited the 88th Brigade at training early. The G.S.O.II visited the Centre Sector, and inspected FIRST AVENUE tunnel and the gas cylinders emplacements which are being constructed between Q.10.2 and Q.10.16. The Army Commander visited the G.O.C. at 5.0p.m. at Divisional Headquarters. G.S.O.I visited Corps HQrs at 1/2 p.m. In the evening the 88th Brigade relieved the 87th Brigade in the Right Sector. Two extra 2" Trench Mortar Batteries with personnel arrived and were sent to MAILLY. C.G.S.53 reference the installation of 400 gas cylinders in the Division Sector is attached to Appendix. (3) VIIIth Corps Operation Order No.3 (copy No.2) is attached to Appendix. 2 (e) 88th relieved 87 the in the right sector.	Appendices 3 ,, 2(e)
	16th June		The G.O.C. visited the 86th and 88th Brigade Headquarters during the morning. The G.S.O.I inspected MARY TUNNEL and Dumps in the Right Sector. The Corps Commander visited the G.O.C. in the evening. Work is being continued in filling dumps, filling in Cable trenches, digging deep dugouts, etc.	

Instructions regarding War Diaries and Intelligence
Summaries are contained in F. S. Regs., Part II.
and the Staff Manual respectively. Title pages
will be prepared in manuscript.

WAR DIARY - GENERAL STAFF, 29TH DIVISION.

or

INTELLIGENCE SUMMARY.

(Erase heading not required.)

Army Form C. 2118.

1916.

Place	Date	Hour	Summary of Events and Information	Remarks and references to Appendices
	17th June		The G.O.C. inspected the 2nd Class of the Divisional School at 8.30 a.m. In the afternoon he held a conference with the 86th Brigade C.Os. at MAILLY. The G.S.O.II visited the advanced Headquarters and Dumps in the Right Sector. The Corps Commander visited Divisional Headquarters at 5.30 p.m. Work on Dumps is nearly completed, ROTTEN ROW (the New Road from ACHEUX WOOD to ENGLEBELMER) is again in good condition owing to the dry weather. Lieut-Colonel GUISE-MOORE the new A.D.M.S. arrived, vice Colonel Kelly, invalided.	
	18th June		The G.O.C. visited the 87th Brigade training at LOUVENCOURT, in the morning. He visited the 88th Brigade Headquarters in the afternoon. The G.S.O.III visited the trenches of the Centre and Left Sectors. The G.S.O.I visited the 86th Brigade Headquarters in the evening. A quiet day. "U" Day is postponed till 24th June. 29th Division Order No. 38 was issued at 9 a.m.(vide Appendix 2(f)) with March Tables "A" and "B" attached. 29th Division Order No. 39 was issued at 10 p.m. with Appendices "A" and "C". Instructions for 29th Divisional Artillery and subsequent amendments are attached to Appendix 2(g) also/maps shewing lifts etc of Divisional Artillery. and Heavy Artillery.	Appendix 2(f) Appendix 2(g)

WAR DIARY – GENERAL STAFF, 29TH DIVISION.

Army Form C. 2118.

Instructions regarding War Diaries and Intelligence Summaries are contained in F.S. Regs., Part II. and the Staff Manual respectively. Title pages will be prepared in manuscript.

1916.

Place	Date	Hour	Summary of Events and Information	Remarks and references to Appendices
	19th June		The G.O.C. and G.S.O.II visited the 87th Brigade training at LOUVENCOURT. The G.S.O.I visited the trenches in the Right Sector and inspected the Medium Trench Mortar emplacements. The G.O.C. visited the trenches in the afternoon; Appendix "B" 29th Division Order No. 39, referring to gas and smoke arrangements, is amended and issued.	Appendix 2 (g)
	20th June		The G.O.C. visited the 87th Brigade training at LOUVENCOURT. The G.S.O.II visited the Left Sector trenches. The Corps Commander came to see the G.O.C. at 4.45 p.m. A Divisional Conference was held at 5 p.m. (points discussed are attached to Appendix 4(a).) Brigadiers, Brigade Majors, Machine Gun and Stokes Mortar Officers, C.R.A. and G.S.Os. attended. Preparations for the offensive continued. The weather is fine and roads dry.	Appendix 4(a)

Army Form C. 2118.

WAR DIARY — GENERAL STAFF, 29TH DIVISION.

or

~~INTELLIGENCE SUMMARY~~

(Erase heading not required.)

Instructions regarding War Diaries and Intelligence
Summaries are contained in F. S. Regs., Part II.
and the Staff Manual respectively. Title pages
will be prepared in manuscript.

1916.

Place	Date	Hour	Summary of Events and Information	Remarks and references to Appendices
	21st June		The G.O.C. visited the right of the line. The training area was marked out for a Divisional Tactical Exercise to be carried out to-morrow. 400 gas cylinders were carried up to the front trenches during the night 21/22nd. There was a Corps Conference at 4 p.m., attended by G.O.C, G.S.O.I and all Brigadiers and B.G.R.A. An amendment to revised Table "B" re gas was issued.	
	22nd June		A Divisional Tactical Exercise was carried out on the LOUVENCOURT Training Ground, the 87th Brigade and 2 Companies Royal Fusiliers and 2 Companies Royal Dublin Fusiliers taking part. The scheme and Operation Orders are attached.(vide Appendix2 (h)). The G.S.O.II went round the extreme right trenches, in the evening.	Appendix 2(h)

Army Form C. 2118.

WAR DIARY - GENERAL STAFF, 29TH DIVISION,

or

~~INTELLIGENCE SUMMARY~~

(Erase heading not required.)

Instructions regarding War Diaries and Intelligence Summaries are contained in F. S. Regs., Part II. and the Staff Manual respectively. Title pages will be prepared in manuscript.

1916.

Place	Date	Hour	Summary of Events and Information	Remarks and references to Appendices
	23rd June		Two Battalions of the 86th Brigade and Two Battalions of the 87th Brigade moved from MAILLY WOOD and LOUVENCOURT respectively to ACHEUX WOOD. Two Battalions 87th Brigade moved to trenches and ENGLEBELMER to relieve the 88th Brigade who moved to LOUVENCOURT. The G.O.C. visited 86th and 88th Brigade Headquarters in the morning. The G.S.O.I visited the Left Sector trenches. The G.S.O.II the right sector in order to site Machine Gun emplacements in FORT JACKSON and WITHINGTON AVENUE. A Corps Conference was held at 4 p.m., and was attended by the G.O.C., G.S.O.I, Brigadiers, and B.G.R.A. Our Artillery were active all day, but there was little retaliation. There was a very heavy thunderstorm at 4 p.m. and rain later in the evening, making the roads heavy. Major Hardress Lloyd and Lieut. Ball occupied the Southern Observation Post, and Capt. Fulton and Lieut. Ross occupied the Northern O.P. in the evening. Amendments to Division Orders Nos. ~~MY~~ 36, 38, 39, were issued. VIIIth Corps G.1615 and previous correspondence re gas and smoke is attached to Appendix. (3) The troops in the firing line were relieved very considerably.	Appendix 3
	24th June.		'U' day. The Divisional Artillery commenced wire cutting in front of enemy's first and second line trenches at 6 a.m. and continued all day. The morning was rather misty and the fire was mostly reserved till the afternoon which was bright and clear. It had been arranged to emit gas at 10 p.m. but the Westerly wind died down in the late evening to a dead calm causing it to be postponed. No heavy artillery fired to-day. The enemy deposited a shell on our metre gauge railway but damage was quickly repaired.	

WAR DIARY - GENERAL STAFF, 29TH DIVISION.

or

INTELLIGENCE SUMMARY

(Erase heading not required.)

Army Form C. 2118.

1916.

Instructions regarding War Diaries and Intelligence Summaries are contained in F. S. Regs., Part II. and the Staff Manual respectively. Title pages will be prepared in manuscript.

Place	Date	Hour	Summary of Events and Information	Remarks and references to Appendices
	25th June		**"V" DAY.** Wire cutting bombardment by the Divisional Artillery continued. Many gaps were cut in the wire of the front and second lines, also in the wire in front of BEAUCOURT REDGE. Our Heavy Artillery did not fire. Three enemy balloons were destroyed on our front by means of bombs from aeroplanes. Our centre O.P. at AUCHONVILLERS reported at 8 p.m. that COURCELLETTE Village was on fire, having been set alight by heavy shells. The G.O.C. visited the 4th Division in the morning. The G.S.Os. II and III visited the North and Centre O.Ps. and the second line trenches. The enemy did very little retaliation, but succeeding in breaking the water pipe leading from the SUCRERIE. A 5.9" shell pitched direct on one of our buried cable trenches without causing a break in the line.	
	26th June		**"W" DAY.** The bombardment continued. The Heavy Artillery and Heavy and 2" Trench Mortars commenced firing. BEAUMONT HAMEL was much knocked about especially by our Heavy Trench Mortars firing from TENDERLOIN. More gaps in the enemy's wire were cut, the 2" Trench Mortars firing very accurately. The enemy obtained a direct hit on our Northern Divisional O.P. at 2.15 p.m., killing a telephonist and destroying the O.P. Gas was discharged on our front at 10.45 a.m. and 11.20 a.m., the wind was favourable and the gas appeared to be blown down to the STATION ROAD and the Southern portion of BEAUMONT HAMEL. After three minutes the enemy put a barrage on our front and support trenches and shrapnelled SECOND AVENUE, but there did not appear to be more than one battery firing. There were two or three showers during the day but not sufficient to make the roads or trenches very wet. 29th Divisional Artillery Operation Order No.1 was received. (app. 2 J)	Appendix 2(J)

WAR DIARY — 29TH DIVISION GENERAL STAFF.   Army Form C. 2118.

1916.

Instructions regarding War Diaries and Intelligence Summaries are contained in F. S. Regs., Part II. and the Staff Manual respectively. Title pages will be prepared in manuscript.

INTELLIGENCE SUMMARY.
or
(Erase heading not required.)

Place	Date	Hour	Summary of Events and Information	Remarks and references to Appendices
	27th June		"X" DAY. G.S.O.I visited the Northern O.P. A Raid was attempted by the 88th Brigade (Newfoundland Regt.) on point Q.10.d.90.85 during the night 26(27th 1st) was held up by the wire. One Bangalore Torpedo was fired, but one failed to explode. The bombardment continued on the enemy's wire and front trenches. BEAUMONT HAMEL was entirely destroyed by Heavy Trench Mortar Shells. 107 of these shells were fired to-day. Some heavy shells were also put into BEAUCOURT. The remaining 18 gas cylinders were discharged at 2 a.m. We suffered very few casualties. Smoke was discharged at 10.15 a.m. and 7.15 p.m. but the enemy did not retaliate to any great extent. A great deal of rain fell during the day. The Corps Commander visited the G.O.C. at 3 p.m. The G.O.C. inspected and addressed the Dublin Fusiliers and 16th Middlesex Regt. at 9 a.m. and 9.15 a.m. respectively. The Northern O.P. was again shelled during the morning but no further damage was done. A new O.P. was constructed during the night 26/27th thirty yards South of the original one. The Southern O.P. was not shelled. It was observed by patrols that the enemy were holding their front line trenches strongly. The G.S.C.I visited ENGLEBELMER and arranged for a new O.P. there and at AUCHONVILLERS.	Appendices I(b)
	28th June		"Y" DAY. During the night 27/28th five attempts were made between the hours of 12 midnight and 1 a.m. to raid the enemy's trenches, three by the 86th Brigade and one by the 87th and 88th Brigades respectively; in no place were any prisoners taken but an officer and two men got into the enemy's trenches at point Q.4.d.90.30 and the enemy's parapet was reached at Q.10.d.85.35 and Q.10.b.80.85. The wire at Q.5.c.10.75 and Q.17.a.85.80 was too thick and the raiding parties were held up. All parties reported the enemy's front trench strongly held.(Appx.1c.) Special parties were told off all along our front to cut the wire. Heavy rain commenced at 9 a.m. and continued till 11 a.m. There was a dense mist in the early morning and up till 8 a.m. Smoke was discharged at 7.15 am.; it drew very little fire. BEAUMONT HAMEL was further destroyed. The artillery paid more attention to the enemy's front and support lines. Several heavy shells were put into BEAUCOURT. Owing to the rain "Z" Day was postponed	Appendix I(c)

T2134. Wt. W708-776. 500000. 4/15. Sir J.C. & S.

WAR DIARY - GENERAL STAFF, 29TH DIVISION.   Army Form C. 2118.

INTELLIGENCE SUMMARY
(Erase heading not required.)

1916.

Instructions regarding War Diaries and Intelligence Summaries are contained in F.S. Regs., Part II. and the Staff Manual respectively. Title pages will be prepared in manuscript.

Place	Date	Hour	Summary of Events and Information	Remarks and references to Appendices
			"Y" Day continued.	
			Postponed 48 hours: the 29th is to be termed "Y.1" day, the 30th "Y.2" day and July 1st "Z" Day. The afternoon and evening were fine. The Corps Commander visited Divisional Headquarters at 5 p.m. The G.O.C. inspected the Monmouth (Pioneers) at 9 A.M.	Appendix 2(c)
	June 29th		**"Y.1" Day.** During the night 28/29th a raid was carried out by a party of 3 officers and 80 men of the 1st Royal Dublin Fusiliers, but it failed owing to machine gun and rifle fire (vide Appendix 1d.) There were 30 casualties. The normal bombardment programme was carried out during the day, a special bombardment of 40 minutes taking place at 4.40 p.m., the last 10 minutes being intense. The Germans evidently feared an attack and placed a heavy barrage on our support and communication trenches and along TENDERLOIN. One of our Medium Trench Mortars blew up probably through a faulty charge and the three men working the gun were killed. The enemy's wire is reported destroyed almost entirely along his front trench and badly damaged in front of his support and reserve trenches. BEAUMONT HAMEL is now completely demolished. The weather is fine, and the roads and trenches have already dried considerably. Telephone connection with the new O.Ps. at ENGLEBELMER and AUCHONVILLERS was arranged. A Statement shewing artillery and trench mortar expenditure is attached to Appendix 4(d)	Appendix 1(d) Appendix 1(d) Appendix 4(d)

WAR DIARY - GENERAL STAFF, 29TH DIVISION.

Army Form C. 2118.

SUMMARY

(Erase heading not required.)

Place	Date	Hour	Summary of Events and Information	Remarks and references to Appendices
	1916.		"Y.2B DAY.	
	30th June		During the night a successful raid was carried out by the 1st Essex Regiment who entered the German trenches at point (60), vide Appendix 1(e) and searched five bays, they killed one German and brought back his helmet but unfortunately obtained no identification. Casualties one man slightly wounded. An officers patrol of the S.W.Bs. also killed a German by lying up on the enemy's parapet South of point (89) and waiting for him. (Appx.1(e)) The bombardment continued, an intense period taking place at 8.40 a.m. for 40 minutes. From an examination of our trenches in the early morning it appears that little damage has been done. Our casualties have been very slight. The enemy's wire has been almost completely destroyed along the whole front. The weather continues fine except for a small shower about 5 a.m. Capt. Hawes (Dublin Fusiliers) went to the 36th Division Headquarters to act as Liaison Officer. Capt. Maffett (Dublin Fusiliers) went to the Observation Tree at AUCHONVILLERS (Q.25.a.5.6). A Corps Conference took place at 8.30 a.m. The G.O.C., G.S.O.I and Capt. Hardress Lloyd (who had examined the state of the trenches during the early morning) attended. The enemy retaliated by twice shelling SECOND AVENUE, WHITE CITY, 88th TRENCH, CRIPPS CUT and our front line trench in front of CRIPPS CUT with 60 or 70 heavy shells each time. From 9.30 p.m. onwards the 88th Brigade and the two Battalions of the 86th and 87th Brigades respectively, commenced moving up from LOUVENCOURT and ACHEUX WOOD to their forming-up places in the trenches. The Northern O.P. was closed, and the officers there (Capt, Fulton and Lieut, Ross) were transferred to the Central O.P. at AUCHONVILLERS. The G.S.O.I visited the Southern O.P. in the afternoon. At 11 p.m. the 86th Bde adv. HQrs. were established in Essex St. At 9.20 p.m. the 87th Brigade Advanced Headquarters were established at PRAED STREET. At 10 p.m. the 88th Brigade Advanced Headquarters were established at PRAED STREET. The G.S.O.II was posted with the 87th and 88th Brigade Headquarters. Signal Communication between all Brigades and Divisional Headquarters is established. Daily Intelligence Summaries for the month of June are attached as Appendix 5. Casualties during the preliminary bombardment i.e. 24th to 30th June attached as Appendix 6. Disposition of the Division on the 16th and 24th June attached as Appendix 7.	Appendix 1(e) Appendix 1(e) Appendix 5 " 6 " 7

24/7/16

H. de B. de Lisle
Major General
Commanding 29th Division

APPENDIX 1.

Comprises the following :-

(a) Raid by 1st Lancashire Fusiliers on night 3rd/4th June, and correspondence relating thereto.

(b) Raid by 1st Newfoundland Regiment on night 26th/27th June, and correspondence relating thereto.

(c) Raids by 2nd Royal Fusiliers, 16th Middlesex Regiment, 1st Lancashire Fusiliers, 1st Border Regiment, 1st Newfoundland Regiment, on night 27th/28th June, and correspondence relating thereto.

(d) Raid by 1st Royal Dublin Fusiliers on night 28th/29th June, and correspondence relating thereto.

(e) Raid by 1st Essex Regiment on night 29/30th June, and correspondence relating thereto. Also report on officers' patrol carried out by the 2nd South Wales Borderers.

===============

Appendix 1(a).

REPORT ON RAID CARRIED OUT ON ENEMY'S TRENCHES BY 1st LANCASHIRE FUSILIERS ON NIGHT 3/4th June 1916.

The raiding party, consisting of 3 Officers and 48 Other Ranks, left our trenchs at 11.30.p.m., and assembled at a place 200^x from the enemy's trench. From 0000 to 0030 there was an Artillery bombardment. On the opening of this bombardment, the enemy sent up numerous flares all along his line, and turned on a serchlight, but the position of assembly was not disclosed by the light. At 0030 the Artillery bombardment lifted on to the second line, and the wire-cutting party and Bangalore Torpedo men went forward to the point of entry. This point was just North of a hedge, but owing to the smoke etc was hard to locate, and a point was struck in the wire about 50^x South, which had not been cut by artillery fire. The Bangalore Torpedo was inserted and exploded, but by this time it was 0038 and as the artillery bombardment was due to return on the front line at 0040 the party was ordered back, the officer and two men remaining and continuing to cut the wire after the guns had returned to the front line.

At 0045 the raiding party advanced, although the wire had not been completely cut through, and entered the trench, which was found to be vacated by the Germans. The Dug-outs under the parapet were entered and about 50^x of trench searched on either side, but not a single German was seen. Some papers, notice boards etc were collected. These have already been forwarded. After remaining ten minutes the raiders withdrew in accordance with the time table. Two rifle grenades were fired into the trench from the enemy support line, but did no damage to the raiders. During the retirement Machine Gun fire and rifle fire was opened on the party and one private was wounded. The German trench was found to be from 9 to 10 feet deep, 3 feet wide at the bottom, and 10 to 12 feet wide at the top with gradual sloping sides. The firestep was made of wood, about four feet above the bottom of the trench. No bomb or other stores were seen. The trench was for the most part revetted with brushwood, and was in excellent repair and scrupulously clean. The traverses were very large and the parados very high. Dug-outs were about 20 feet deep and connected. Communication trenches had the same profile as the firing line but without fire step. The wire was 40 to 50 yards wide, very strong and breast high.

Headquarters,
    86th Brigade.

RAIDS.

The G.O.C. wishes attention drawn to the following points, most of which no doubt have already received consideration.

1. When raids are arranged by time it is very necessary that watches of all concerned, raiding party, R.A. batteries, including trench mortars, should be checked very carefully with Corps time on the day in question. The failure of one battery might turn success into disaster.

2. The inspection of the raiding party, to see that all men have proper distinguishing marks, possess no papers or identifications, are suitably dressed and properly equipped, must be made with the greatest care.

3. A telephone connection with the field battery covering the point of entry is recommended. In case opposition is met and a retirement becomes necessary in face of rifle and machine gun fire, the covering fire of a field battery would then become of the greatest value, and the retirement to a sheltered spot become possible; otherwise severe losses might be sustained.

4. Two minutes before the expiration of the time allotted for wire cutting, the wire cutting party must be brought back. If wire still remains to be cut a Bangalore Torpedo can then be used to save time.

5. Although rapidity in gaining trenches, both to cut wire and at the point of entry, is desirable, any hurry induces undue fatigue and sometimes coughing, which may interfere with success.

6. It is very necessary that a report be made on the profile of the German trenches, i.e., depth, width, if covered in etc.

7. Entry must be made with the least possible noise.

8.   To block the ends of trenches, a short roll of French wire round a traverse may be found very effective, but this must be practised beforehand to be of any value. Torches should be used sparingly, and when the signal for retirement is given, trenches must be evacuated as rapidly as possible consistent with safety.

(signed) C. G. Fuller, Lieut. Colonel, G.S.
29th Division.

3rd June 1916.

SECRET.

87th Brigade (for information)

88th Brigade (for information)

----

1.   A raid will be carried out by the 86th Brigade on the night of June 3/4th.

2.   Point of entry into the German trenches will be Q.4.d.87.00.

3.   The time table will be as follows:-

- 00.00 - 00.30   Intense bombardment by artillery and trench mortars on wire and front trenches at point to be raided.

- 00.30 - 00.40   Artillery lift to second line. Trench Mortars cease fire on point of entry. Wire cut by Bangalore Torpedoes.

- 00.40 - 00.45   Artillery returns to front line. Trench Mortars again fire on point of entry in order to catch unawares any Germans who may have left their dug-outs on hearing the noise of the explosion of the torpedo.

- 00.45 - 01.00   Artillery lifts again to second line and remains there till end of bombardment. Trench Mortars cease fire, except the four on pt. 8863. Raiding party enters enemy's trenches.

- 01.00   Raiding party leaves trenches.

- 01.20   Bombardment ceases.

4.   00.00 will be 12.00 midnight 3/4th June.

5.   It is very important to keep this as SECRET as possible: it is therefore undesirable to inform those concerned before it is absolutely necessary.

(signed) D. Ovey, Major,
29th Division.

2nd June 1916.

SECRET.

31st Division (for information)

36th Division

1. A raid will be carried out by this Division on the night June 3/4th.
2. Point of entry into German trenches will be Q.4.d.87.00.
3. The bombardment will commence at 12 midnight and finish at 1.20 a.m. 4th June.

(signed) D. Ovey, Major.
for Major General Commanding 29th Division.

2/6/16.

SECRET.

App 1 (b)

COPY No......

OPERATION ORDER No. 11

By

Brigadier General D.E. Cayley, C.M.G. Commanding 88th Brigade.

ENGLEBELMER,

22nd June, 1916.

Reference
Trench Map 1/10,000 BEAUMONT
57d S.E. 1 & 2 (parts of)

(1) It is intended to carry out a raid on the German trenches on the night W/X.

(2) <u>Point of Entry</u>. Between point 7347 (Q.10 D 7.45) and Q.11 C 1.35.

(3) <u>Time Table</u>. 2330. Raiding party leaves our trenches and forms up in NO MAN'S LAND 150ˣ from enemy's wire.

2400 Special bombardment by 29th Divisional Artillery on enemy's front line trench between these two points. The ravine in rear of this trench also to be bombarded.

00.15 Divisional Artillery switch to each flank (points 89 x 54) leaving part of trench to be raided clear for bangalore torpedoes party to come up and cut the wire. After doing this they retire to forming up place.

00.25 Divisional Artillery again shell front line trench opposite where wire has been cut.

00.30 Divisional Artillery again switch to flanks and raiding party enter trench. They will bomb outwards along the trench and block the trench this side of communication trench at Q.11 C. 1.3. They will also bomb along the trench to point 7347 where they will block the trench just past point 7347. If no Germans are met with in the front line fire trench, a party will bomb up the communication trench which leads back to the Ravine from point 7347. On reaching the Ravine they will bomb any "dug-outs" they may find, and will if possible bring back a prisoner or some identification. A Stokes Mortar bomb or two will be carried for bombing dug-outs.

01.00 Raiding party leave the German trenches and go back to our own trenches if they can. If they cannot do this owing to enemy's fire, they will lie up in "NO MAN'S LAND", at their original forming up place until such a time as they can return to our trenches.

01.05 Divisional Artillery return to trench which has just been raided.

01.15 Cease fire.

(4) <u>Heavy Artillery</u>. 6" and 8" Howitzers fire salvoes between 2400 and 0015 and again at 0027 they fire a salvo. Another salvo is fired at 0108. These salvoes will be fired at point (17) (89), and at point (54) and at T.11.c. 55.75.

(5) <u>Machine Guns</u>. Machine Guns will place a barrage across NO MAN'S LAND between our trenches and point 89, and between our trenches and point 54 in order to prevent any Germans leaving their trenches and taking the raiding party in flank.

Issued at... 2000

[signature] Captain,
Brigade Major, 88th Brigade.

Copy No. 1   Staff
"   "   2   Newfoundland Regt.
"   "   3   87th Brigade
"   "   4   87th Bde. Machine Gun Coy.
"   "   5   29th Division.
"   "   6   O.C. Right Group R.A.

Headquarters,
29th Division.

        I regret to report that the raid last night carried out by the Newfoundland Regt. was a failure.

        The raiders went out at the appointed time and the artillery commenced according to programme. After a quarter of an hours bombardment, a Bangalore Torpedoe was placed in position in the enemy's wire and exploded. This did not cut all the wire, so another Torpedoe was placed in position. In spite of many efforts, this party could not make this Torpedoe explode, and after a good deal of time had been wasted over this, Captain Butler decided to try and cut through the wire. The artillery programme was put back a quarter of an hour on the telephone to give the raiders extra time. They, however, did not succeed in cutting through the enemy's wire.

        Captain Butler reports being fired on from the enemy's front line trench.

27th June, 1916.

Brigadier General,
Commanding 88th Brigade.

S E C R E T.   U R G E N T.

> HEADQUARTERS,
> 29th DIVISION.
> GENERAL STAFF.
> No.
> Date

86th Brigade.
87th Brigade.
88th Brigade. (for information)
VIIIth Corps.   -"-,

---

1. The 88th Brigade will carry out a raid on the German trenches to-night. The point of entry is between point 7347 (Q.10.d.73.47) and Q.11.c.1.35.

2. The time table will be as follows :-

11.30 p.m. The raiding party leaves our trenches and forms up in "No Man's Land" 150 yards from enemy's wire.

12 midnight. Special bombardment by Divisional Artillery on enemy's front line trenches between above two points.

12.15 a.m. The Divisional Artillery switch to flanks and raiders cut wire.

12.25 a.m. Raiders retire and Divisional Artillery again shell front line till 12.30 a.m.

12.30 a.m. Divisional Artillery switch to flanks and raiders enter trenches.

1.0 a.m. Raiders leave German trenches and return to ours if they can. If heavy barrage prevents their returning they lie up in "No Man's Land".

1.5 a.m. Divisional Artillery returns to enemy's front trench.

1.15 a.m. Ceases fire.

The quiet period to-night extends from 10.30 p.m. to 11.30 p.m. Machine Gun, Lewis and Rifle fire will be opened on the enemy's front line to prevent any repairs to his wire, but the 86th and 87th Brigades will ensure that all Machine Guns etc whether in the front line system or the Redoubt line are kept clear of the section of trench which the raiding party propose to enter. These Brigades will arrange for barrages of Machine Gun fire to be placed North of an East and West line through point 89 and South and East of a line drawn from Q.17.a.0.5 to point 54

/In

- 2 -

In order to prevent any Germans taking the raiding party in flank. In this connection it should be noted that the raiding party intend if no Germans are met with in the front line of the fire trench to bomb up the communication trench which leads back to the "Y" Ravine from point 7347 (Q.10.d.73.47)

4. Kindly acknowledge receipt by wire.

(Signed) C. G. FULLER,
Lieut-Colonel, G.S.,
29th Division.

26.6.16.

G.R.A.
86th Brigade.
87th Brigade.
88th Brigade.

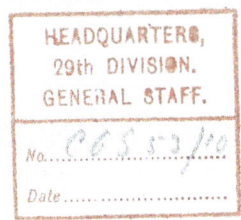

SECRET.

app 1 (c)

1. Raids on the enemy's trenches will be carried out to-night during the period of quiet from 12 midnight to 1 a.m. (vide para. 5 (a) of 29th Division Order No. 39) by the 86th, 87th and 88th Brigades.

2. The points of entry for the four raiding parties will be as follows :-

    87th Brigade about Q.17.a.85.80.

    88th Brigade about Q.10.d.85.35.

    86th Brigade about Q.10.b.75.15. and at point (27).

3. The Divisional Artillery will lift off the front line at 12 midnight precisely, and will not return to it till 1 a.m. During this period, both the Heavy and Divisional Artillery will fire on the enemy's reserve trenches. The support trenches will not be fired on during the period of quiet, since the raiding parties may have to enter the support trenches in order to obtain prisoners or identifications. All Machine gun, Lewis gun and Rifle fire on the enemy's front and support lines, will cease during the period of quiet.

4. It is most important that each raiding party should secure at least one prisoner.

5. The 36th Division carried out a successful raid from the THIEPVAL WOOD last night, and secured 1 officer and   men prisoners. They found that our shelling had in many instances completely cowed the men, and that they came out of their dug-outs quite quietly, on being told to do so in German. The following German sentence is useful for this purpose, and should be committed to memory by raiding

/parties.

parties.

ERGEBT EUCH ! ALLE DIE SICH JETZT ERGEBEN WERDEN
Surrender !   All who surrender at once will be
GUT BEHANDELT.
well treated.

From some dug-outs, the Germans refused to move, and Stokes Mortar bombs were thrown into them by the raiders. All raiding parties should carry bombs for this purpose.

6. In addition to the raids above mentioned, reconnoitring patrols will be sent out by the 86th and 87th Brigades to-night during the interval of quiet to report on the condition of the enemy's wire.

W. M. Armstrong Capt.
for Lieut-Colonel, G.S.,
29th Division.

27th June, 1916.

Report on Raids by 86th Brigade on night of 27/28th June, 1916.

2nd Royal Fusiliers.   Point of entry Q.10.b.80.85.

A party of 16 men under 2nd Lieut. Hurle went out from BRIDGE END under a guide from the Lancashire Fusiliers to shew the gap cut the previous night. The guide led them to the gap, but they found there was a further row of wire that had not been touched. After searching for gap and not finding one the order to retire was given. After seeing men back through the first gap 2nd Lieut. Hurle and Sergt. Turner, crept through the wire to edge of enemy's parapet and were challenged by the enemy. Rifle fire and Machine gun fire was opened. The trench was about 8 feet deep with firestep. The officer considers that the sentries are doubled and that there are sentry groups about every three bays. Machine guns were very active and the officer reports that he saw at least five firing. Casualties 1 man wounded and Sergt. Turner and 1 man missing.

16th Middlesex Regt.   Point of entry Q.4.d.90.30.

Lieut. Cleghorn and 12 men went out from South of HORSESHOE with guide from Lancashire Fusiliers to the supposed gap in enemy's wire. The guide left and the officer and two men got through the wire and entered enemy's trench. They waited for rest of patrol and the enemy at once threw bombs from about 2 traverses North, and sent over what appeared to be rifle grenades. Machine gun fire was opened and a barrage of shrapnel over the SUNKEN ROAD and our front line. The machine gun appeared to fire from about 30 yards behind their front line. The officer threw two bombs in direction of Machine gun and gave the order to retire. All the party came in safely, the last two coming in at 3.20. Two men were slightly wounded. The wire was not very well cut and a large body of men would have great difficulty in getting through. The signal for the barrage was apparently two red rockets at 12.25 a.m.

1st Lancashire Fusiliers.   Point of entry Q.5.c.10.75.

2nd Lieut. Sheppard and 2nd Lieut. Rudd and 18 men went out of Sap 7 to point 27. The wire was found insufficiently cut to allow the passage of a large party. When the officers and first 3 men were half way through the wire flares were sent up and rifle and machine gun fire was opened. The party tried to get through the wire and failed, and lay down from which position they threw bombs into the trench. Eventually the party was compelled to withdraw to SUNKEN ROAD, in the meantime the enemy opened a barrage of shrapnel behind the SUNKEN ROAD and our front line. Casualties 1 killed 5 wounded 2nd Lieut. Rudd and 1 man missing. The wire is not sufficiently cut to allow of the passage of a large number of men, at any rate at night, and it appears the line is strongly held at night.

Copies to CRA, 87th & 88th Bdes, and VIII Corps

REPORT ON RAID BY 87TH BRIGADE.

Point of entry Q.17.a.85.80.   27/28 June

The 1st Border Regiment carried out a raid on the German trenches last night. The raiding party found a thick belt of wire uncut and were fired on by machine guns in rear of enemy's front line. Bangalore torpedoes failed to work and the wire was too thick to cut in time. The party returned at 1.20 a.m. There were no casualties.

Copies to 86", 88" Bdes & CRA. and VIII Corps.

REPORT ON RAID BY 88TH BRIGADE.

Point of entry Q.10.d.85.35.

27/28

The Newfoundland Regiment carried out a raid on the German trenches last night. The raiding party under Captain Butler left our trenches at 11.30 p.m. and formed up in "No Man's Land". From 11.30 p.m. to 12 midnight there was an artillery bombardment on enemy's front line trench, and also in rear of his support line. At 12 - o - clock the bombardment was entirely directed at his support line and the raiding party commenced moving forward from forming-up place. No Bangalore torpedo was necessary to cut the wire, as this was from all accounts practically non-existent. The raiding party got as far as the enemy's parapet and report that they could see the enemy's parapet thickly lined with men. The raiders claimed to have caused several casualties as evidenced by groans coming from the German trenches, but suffered rather heavily themselves in doing so. The three officers who took part in the raid were wounded. Total casualties are as follows :- 2 killed, 3 officers wounded, 10 other ranks wounded, 7 missing.

Copies to C.R.A, 86: & 87: Bdes, and VIII Corps.

H.Q. 88th Inf. Bde. B. 344.

Headquarters,
    29th Division.

    Herewith report by Lieut-Colonel HADOW on raid carried out by the Newfoundland Regiment on the night of 27th June 1916.

    I concur in Lieut-Colonel HADOW'S recommendations, and would especially bring to notice the services performed by Captain BUTLER and No. 1164 Pte. PHILLIPS.

    The latter undoubtedly got into the German trench single handed, and from his account I feel confident that he personally killed at least two Germans.

    As a result of the raid, I believe that pretty heavy casualties were caused to the enemy.

                      (Signed) D. E. CAYLEY,
                            Brigadier-General,

29.6.16.   Commanding 88th Infantry Brigade.

- 2 -

88th Brigade.

    I am glad to read in this report such good accounts of the conduct of officers and men.

    All recommendations for recognition will be called for later.

                      (Signed) H. de B. de LISLE,
                            Major-General.

30.6.16.

Headquarters,
29th Division.

Herewith Capt. Butler's report on raid on German trenches during night 27/28th instant.

Captain,
for/Brigadier General,
Commanding 88th Brigade.

28th June 1916.

"Party left our trenches at 2325 and formed up in front of hedge in Q 16 b.

2335. Moved in three lines in file towards enemy trenches, halting at a point about 150 yds from enemy wire, four scouts going ahead to a point about 50 yds further waiting there until midnight.

00.03 Left forming up place and proceeded to a point about 60 yards from wire and waited. In the meantime bangalore torpedo men carried torpedoes forward & NCO reconnoitred wire. Bombers went up with this party.

0020 As torpedo had not been heard to explode. O.C. party moved up to torpedo men who were going along a large gap practically straight through enemy wire(which was about 15 yds in width at this

2

The wire was reconnoitred and the gap was found to be complete, hardly a strand being in the way. The gap would be about 5 yards wide, but all the wire in the vicinity was badly cut up and, in daylight ought not to present any difficulty to infantry getting through with ease.

At 0030, a man was sent back to main party, with the order to advance, ~~the bombers remaining~~ in the wire & the scouts laying tape was advancing.

At 0037 ~~party~~ Head of party arrived at entrance of gap. (Progress had been slow owing to the numerous flares which were being sent up all along enemy front. (Most of these flares were sent up from his support trench). The party was fired on from the front trench by a burst of rifle fire and bombs coming from directly in front of gap.

3

We immediately extended to single rank and faced enemy trench, every man throwing bombs which were very effective & many landing direct into enemy trench. This continued for about 5 minutes two of the officers being hit by bombs and fell in front of enemy wire. Some of our men (about four) were on enemy parapet and one German was bayoneted and another shot by them.

Owing to the number of bombs thrown by us, the supply was getting rather low and as the German trenches were heavily manned it was deemed inadvisable to go further. Our casualties were increasing rapidly, and it was decided to retire with the wounded back to the hedge, the gap in wire being held by our bombers and riflemen

The fight lasted about 25 minutes the covering party being withdrawn at 01.15.

The enemy used bombs & rifle fire mostly but machine guns were busy on either flank. Most of their fire was wild but their bombs were very effective. Trench mortars also placed a few bombs in their own wire, whilst their artillery put several lachrymatory shells in no mans land about 100 yds from their wire. Three of our men were gassed but recovered soon afterwards. These shells were sent over about 0105.

The wounded were got back to the trees in hedge at 0166 and several cases of exemplary conduct were observed. the men going back to enemy wire 3 or 4 times for wounded comrades.

Covering party returned to trees about 1.25 reporting that the only men that were still out had been examined and found dead. As they were in enemy wire it was thought inadvisable to send out for them.

The party returned to our trenches and were found to be 21 short.

This deficit was made up as follows.

Killed 2. Missing ~~believed killed~~ Missing 8 Wounded 11.

Later information gives:- Killed 3 Missing believed killed 3 Missing 1 Wounded 13.

P.T.O.

At least three of our men penetrated into enemy trench. Two were apparently bayonetted & fell in trench. The third & returned to our line just before daylight.

His story is as follows:

He was a wire cutter and consequently well to the front with three or four more men. As soon as fire was opened from enemy trench he rushed forward to enemy parapet. He stabbed two men with his bayonet — one had a round cap on with a badge like two buttons in front. The other wore a helmet with spike.

He lay on parapet for a while apparently undetected and, as enemy fire directly in front of him had subsided, he entered the trench. This bay was unoccupied, and was blocked with sandbags at either end, apparently very recent work.

In this bay there was a dugout entrance which might have led to other bays. His last bomb was thrown in here

He was unable to find any identification, as there was nothing in this place & the bays on either side were occupied.

He cannot say how long he was in the trench, but when he left it he had to cut a way through with his wirecutters. (His appearance on return looked as if he had been through a lot of barbed wire, his clothes being torn very badly) On arriving on side wire he lay in some tall nettles & fired all his ammunition 120 rounds at enemy parapet where flashes were seen. By the light of the flares he got some good shots in and thinks he accounted for some of the enemy. While he was in German trench & afterwards he heard many groans and he says the bombs from our men must have done considerable damage. He retired to a shell hole about 100 yards from enemy wire and lay there with two other until machine gun fire had subsided.

B. Butler Capt
Nfld Regt

SECRET

VIII Corps.
G. 1716.

~~4th Division.~~
29th Division.
~~31st Division.~~
~~48th Division.~~
~~G.O.C., R.A.~~
~~B.G.R.A., C.H.A.~~

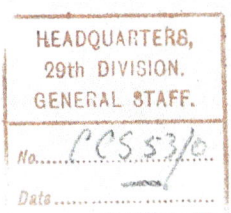
HEADQUARTERS,
29th DIVENION.
GENERAL STAFF.

No. CCS 53/6
Date.

With reference to arrangements for tonight.

(1). Reconnaissance of wire will be carried out between 12 midnight and 1.0 a.m. Reports as to the state of the wire will be forwarded to Corps Headquarters as soon as possible after return of raiders.

(2). RAIDS.- All raids tonight will take place simultaneously, the procedure will be as follows :-

    (a). At 1.45 a.m. Divisional artillery (18-prs) will open a heavy barrage on enemy's front trench.

    (b). At 2.0 a.m. raiders will enter enemy's trench.

    (c). By 2.30 a.m. raiders will have returned to their own lines, and at that hour Divisional artillery will resume night bombardment.

(3). (a). Divisions will arrange direct with Corps Heavy Artillery as to any special points they wish bombarded.

    (b). Divisions will inform Corps Heavy Artillery of the exact point of entry of each raid.

H.Q. VIII Corps.
27th June, 1916.

W. Ruthven
B.G., G.S.
VIII Corps.

"C" Form (Duplicate)
MESSAGES AND SIGNALS.

Handed in at: 8 Corps   Office: 19·3 m.   Received: 19·3 m.

TO: 29th Div

Sender's Number	Day of Month	In reply to Number	AAA
G676	24		

Reference my G.1416 the 29th Div commences at midnight and ends at 1 am aaa No other change aaa Attached 31st Div Corps Heavy Arty and 10th Corps reptd 29th Div

FROM PLACE & TIME: 8th Corps 7.20 pm

App 1 (d)

SECRET.

th Brigade.
87th Brigade.
88th Brigade.
C.R.A.

HEADQUARTERS,
29th DIVISION.
GENERAL STAFF,

No. C.G.S.53/10
Date 28/6/16

1. A raid on the enemy's trenches to-night will be carried out by the 1st Royal Dublin Fusiliers between the hours of 1.30 a.m. and 2.30 a.m.

2. The point of entry for the raiding party will be point 89 in Q.10.d.

3. The Divisional and Heavy Artillery will carry out a preliminary bombardment of the front near the point of entry commencing at 1 a.m.

The Heavy Artillery will lift to the reserve line at 1.25 a.m, and the Divisional Artillery will lift to this line at 1.30 a.m.

4. All Machine gun, Lewis gun and rifle fire on the enemy's front will cease from 1 a.m. to 2.45 a.m. between an East and West line through Q.10.b.8.2 on the North, and an East and West line through Q.10.d.95.30 on the South.

5. Every endeavour should be made by the raiding party to secure a prisoner or an identification.

The raiding party, however, will not enter the enemy's second line O1 to 17 for this purpose, but will confine themselves to the front line and the western end of the "Y" RAVINE.

28th June, 1916.

Lieut-Colonel, G.S.,
29th Division.

Headquarters,

    VIIIth Corps.

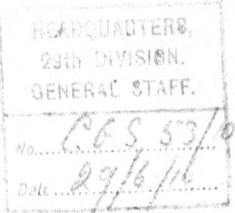

    The following report on a raid carried out by the 1st Royal Dublin Fusiliers is forwarded for information :-

    Point of entry point 89.

    Lieut. Gunn Cunningham (in command) 2nd Lieut. de Voy 2nd Lieut. Pearson and a party of 80 men went out from the point where 1st AVENUE cuts the front line. They found the enemy's wire difficult to get through and while cutting it they were fired on by rifles and machine guns, some bombs were also thrown at them. They report that the machine guns were firing from the enemy's wire. The party then retired, and the enemy commenced barrage fire with trench mortars, shrapnel and heavy artillery. Casualties, officers wounded Lieut. Gunn Cunningham and 2nd Lieut. de Voy, other ranks killed 4, wounded 14, missing believed killed 3, missing 3.

                                            Lieut-Colonel, G.S.,

                                               for Major-General,

29th June, 1916.   Commanding 29th Division.

MESSAGES AND SIGNALS.
Army Form C. 2121.

TO: HQ 29 Div

Sender's Number: 1.P.194
Day of Month: 29 June

Herewith I forward a report from 1/R Dub Fus on this raid of last night. I understand that the GOC has personally seen the OC & received full details. I have not seen the OC myself & have nothing to add to the report. By day the enemy line appears empty, doubtless it is well held by machine guns but these do not fire. Arty F.O O's in the front line show head & shoulders over the parapet for hours at a time & are not fired at. By night the line is undoubtedly strongly held.

W.J. Williams?
Brig Gen'l

From / Place / Time:
HEADQUARTERS,
29th DIVISION
GENERAL STAFF.

No. G.G.S. 15

The Brigade Major
86th Brigade.

I have the honour to report on the raid attempted by this Battalion on night of 28th/29 June.

The party consisted of Two officers Lieut Gunn Cunningham + Lt Devoy + 80 O.R. the object being to enter the German trenches, secure an identification, + also cut wire as far as possible, near point (89). The party was divided into two portions, the front to enter the enemy trenches, + the rear to support + cut wire.

Lieut Devoy, whilst laying the tape, at about 1.20 was slightly wounded in the hand – which delayed operations somewhat, + the men did not commence to leave our trenches until 1.30. Owing to this officer being wounded I placed Lieut Gunn Cunningham in charge of the front party, + Lieut Pearson who had come with me as intelligence officer in charge of the support. Owing to both Lieut Gunn Cunningham (slightly) + Lieut Devoy (slight), as well as other leaders being wounded, it has not been possible to hear from them what actually occurred.

from statement of other NCOs & men. It appears that

(i) At the point S of (89) the wire is completely "cut". Elsewhere a considerable amount of cutting has yet to be done – 15ˣ in some places.

(ii) That the advanced parties reached the enemy's wire without difficulty.

(iii) An enemy patrol was seen crawling into trench near the point.

(iv) Bombs were thrown from enemy's front line as soon as the party reached the wire – followed at once by rifle & machine gun fire from a trench close behind the front trench – again followed by a heavy bombardment by trench mortars of their own wire & of no man's land.

(v) Several men in front being killed, & both officers wounded, the remainder of the party also being subjected to heavy fire from mortars which caused many casualties, the retirement was difficult & slow: some men only getting back at daybreak.

(vi) Flares were put up continuously by the Germans & the party must have been spotted.

my own conclusion is that

(1) Though the German front line may be badly smashed in places, fire from a line or lines in rear very effectively sweeps the ground in front of their first line : + that the troops holding this line or lines were able to fire despite our artillery bombardment.

(2) The Germans are very carefully watching their line at point 89, + can bring mortar fire to bear on an attacking line in a very short space of time.

(3) In this particular instance, the size of the front was too large : + its approach was seen.

I regret that the casualties are very heavy – principally caused by mortars. The N.C.O.s report the men behaved with coolness, + I am glad to say that their spirit is not in the least affected by this check. A list of names of officers + men who did specially good work in attack will be forwarded tomorrow

N Nelson Lt Col

29/6/16   Comd 1st Royal Dublin Fusiliers

App 1 (e)   SECRET.

86th Brigade.
87th Brigade.
88th Brigade.
C.R.A.

HEADQUARTERS,
29th DIVISION.
GENERAL STAFF.
No. C.G.S.53/10
Date 29/6/16

1. A raid on the enemy's trenches will be carried out by the 1st Essex Regiment between the hours of 12.30 a.m. and 1.30 a.m. to-night.

2. The point of entry will be point 60.

3. The Divisional and Heavy Artillery will carry out a preliminary bombardment of the front near the point of entry commencing at 12 midnight.

The Heavy Artillery will lift to the reserve line at 12.25 a.m., and the Divisional Artillery will lift to this line at 12.30 a.m., both returning to the front line at 2.30 a.m.

The Heavy Artillery will also bombard points 89 and 96 between the hours of 12 midnight and 12.30 a.m.

4. All machine gun, Lewis gun and rifle fire on the enemy's front between an East and West line through points 63 and 54 will cease from 12 midnight to 1.45 a.m.

5. The raiding party will not go beyond the enemy's front line; every endeavour should be made to obtain a prisoner or identification.

D. Wey. Major
for Lieut-Colonel, G.S.,
29th Division.

29th June, 1916.

MESSAGES AND SIGNALS.

No. C. 2121.

TO	86th Brigade CRA	
	87th " "	
	88th " "	

Sender's Number.	Day of Month	In reply to Number	
* GC 313	29/6	C	A A A

Reference para 3 of CGS 53/9 of even date the action of the Heavy artillery will be as follows and not as stated in the above paragraph aaa Fire on point 60 from 12 midnight till 12.25 am then lift to reverse line till 2.30 am. Also fire on points 53, 54, 85, 89 from 12 midnight till 2.30 am aaa addressed all Bdes & CRA.

1.

From: 29th Div
Time: 1.35 pm

S E C R E T.

86th Brigade.
~~87th Brigade.~~
~~88th Brigade.~~
~~C.R.A.~~

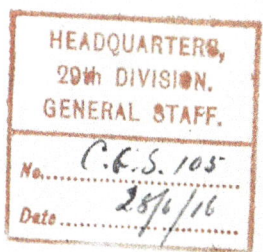

The attached diagram shewing "Order of Battle of enemy's forces opposite VIIIth Corps front on 27.6.16." is forwarded for your information and retention.

W. M. Armstrong.

Captain, G.S.,
29th Division.

28th June, 1916.

"A" Form

SECRET.

[Stamp: ARMY HEADQUARTERS, 29th DIVISION. GENERAL STAFF.
C. GS. 53/3
28.6.16]

86th Brigade.
~~87th Brigade.~~
~~88th Brigade.~~

Owing to the heavy rains rendering observation difficult, there appears to be little likelihood of the wire on the enemy's front line being properly cut. ~~Divisions~~ You will therefore arrange to complete the cutting of the wire to-night by means of Bangalore Torpedoes and parties provided with wire cutters.

The success of to-morrow's operations depend in a great measure on the efforts of these parties.

C.S. Fuller
Lieut. Colonel, G.S.
29th Division.

28th June 1916.

ORDER of BATTLE of ENEMY'S FORCES
OPPOSITE VIII Cp. on 27.6.16.
6TH ARMY

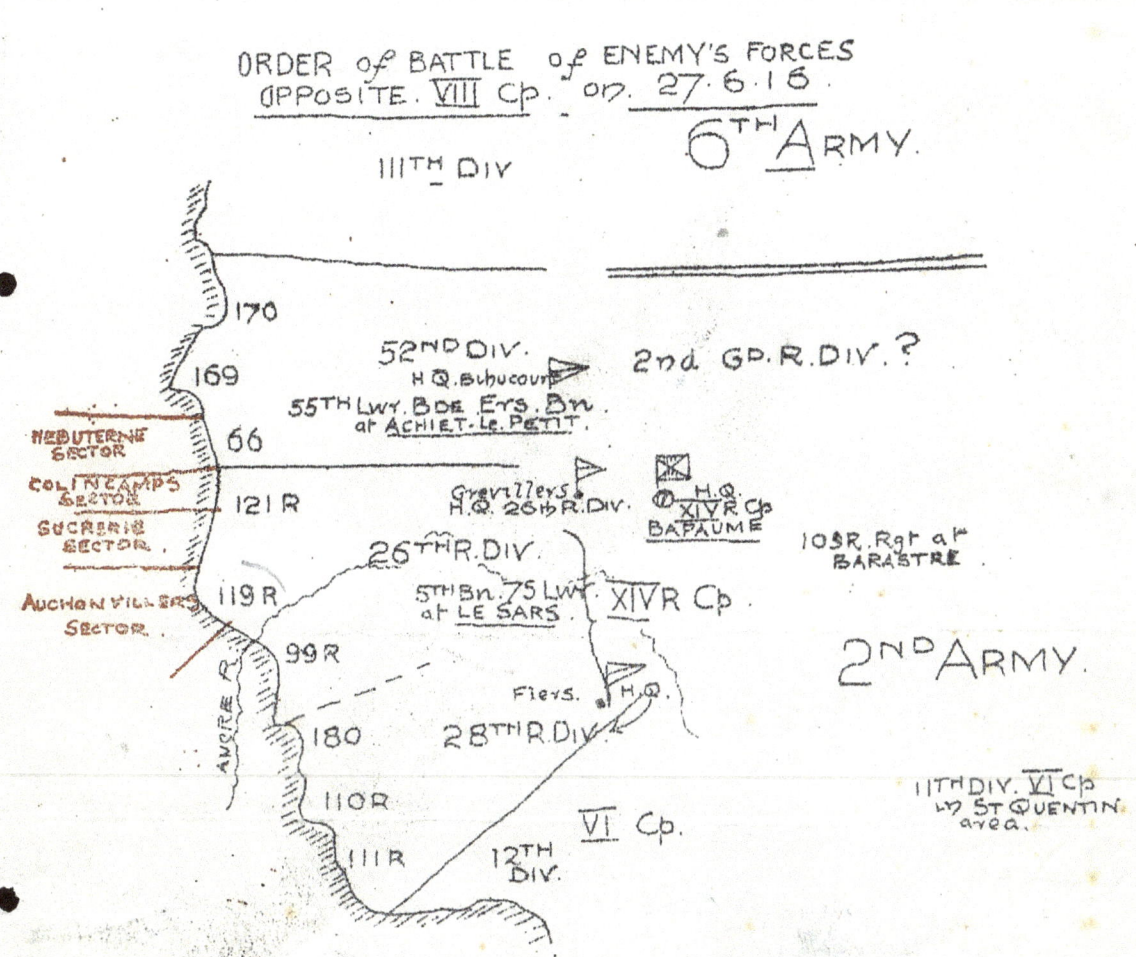

2ND ARMY

11TH DIV. VI Cp
in ST QUENTIN area.

PORCES WHICH MAY POSSIBLY BE MET WITH.

10th Bav. Div.
2nd " " (I Bav. Cp) from VERDUN.
V R. Cp.
III Cp. in CHARLEROI area.
1 Unidentified Div.
VII R Cp at CAMBRAI.

Headquarters,

29th Division.

      Herewith report of Lieut. H.B. RUSSELL, 1st Essex Regt. on the raid carried out last night.

30/6/16.

                      For Brigadier General,
                      Commanding, 88th Infantry Bde.

Report on Raid on night June 29/30 carried out against the German ~~first~~ line at point 60.

At 2230 I proceeded with 2 N.C.O's from sap near Charing Cross for the purpose of laying the white directing tape. We layed this to within 20 yds of German trench in front of point 60. The wire was very well cut by artillery fire. We returned at 2330

At 0025 the whole party ~~~~ advanced in single file to the end of the tape and then halted forming up in three parties in lines of files. The wire cutting party going forward. We found that there was no need to use a Bangalor torpedo. On the signal all clear ~~beings~~ given, the whole party rushed through the gap in the wire, one party going to the right, and the one to the left and the remaining party held the communication trench other men being detailed as a covering party. We entered the trench at 8·00·50. The bay that we entered had a fire step about 3'6" from the parapet, the trench being about 5' deep. There was therefore no need for the trench ladder.

The party going to the right was held up by a barricade 3 bays from the point of entrance. Over which they were bombed. and therefore

The left hand party found one man presumably a sentry, he would not halt and was therefore shot. There were no marks of identification on him. They also bombed a dug out but were unable to investigate it owing to its being partially fallen in. The enemy sent up a large number of flares and threw over bombs from somewhere in rear. They also fired with a machine gun from the support line and from our right and left. We left the trench at 0105. The whole party returned to our own trenches, there being no casualties except grazes from bombs etc.

We brought back one notice board from the head of communication trench and the helmet of the dead German.

H B Russell
Lieut
1st Essex Regt

Loovencourt
30/6/16

To staff cafe

87th Bde

I forward herewith report by
2nd Lieut Karran who went out
to the German parapet last
night for your information.

G D Parker Maj
30/6/16
Brig

29 Div G.

Forwarded for your information

30/6/16

Bland Capt
Bde Major
87 Bde
for GOC

Report on Patrol.

I left our lines near Sap 3 at 10.20 P.M. on the 29th of June with a party of 1 Sergeant and 5 other men. We moved forward to about Q 10 D. 90.20 while it was still dusk and waited in the sunken road about half an hour until it was properly dark and then crept up to enemy's wire. I left three men here to keep a look-out and the Sergeant and I crept forward followed by the other two men at about 5 paces distance. I arrived on the parapet immediately over the entrance to a dug-out where there was no fire step. Almost as soon as I arrived a German appeared out of the darkness about 10 yds to my left and passed immediately below me. When he was about 2 yds from me and turned to go round the traverse I fired at him with my pistol and he fell with a grunt.

Page 2.

I moved along the parapet to find a way down into the trench and heard sounds of the occupants coming out. As the rest of the script and party where outside the wire, I retired and the whole party moved off before the Germans could spot us. We got back to our own trench about 12 midnight.

The German appeared to be wearing a British Warm but it was too dark to distinguish other details. He was not carrying a rifle. The trench was about 7 ft broad at the top and from 8-10 ft deep. The fire step appeared to be made with long strips of wood along the top and also along the side. The parapet was much knocked about by our shells but the bay did not appear to be much damaged. The dug-out I saw was in the right hand corner of the bay, looking at it from my direction

Page 3.

and was under the parapet. The entrance appeared to be larger than those of our deep dug-outs. The trench appeared to be quite dry. I went in through a good gap in the wire about 4 yds wide. The rest of the wire at this point appeared fairly strong.

J. B. Kanan
2/Lt
2nd South Wales Borderers.

30/6/16.

SECRET.

VIIIth Corps.
86th Brigade.
87th Brigade.
88th Brigade.

HEADQUARTERS,
29th DIVISION.
GENERAL STAFF.

      Last night a raid was carried out by the 1st Essex Regiment, point of entry point 60, no difficulty was encountered in getting through the enemy's wire, and the trench was entered. Five bays were thoroughly searched and one dug-out was bombed. A German who was found in the front trench held up his hands and surrendered, but ran away and was shot close to a barricade which was found blocking a communication trench; there were two communication trenches in the sector raided forming an "Island", the party went about 20 yards down these trenches but were then stopped by a strong German bombing party. After a brisk grenade fight lasting for 15 minutes the party withdrew taking with them the helmet of the dead German and a Notice Board. Casualties - one man slightly wounded.

      Last night also, the South Wales Borderers sent out a small patrol of one officer, one Sergeant, and four men to lie up on the enemy's parapet just South of point 89. On seeing a German walking along the trench towards them the officer shot him with his revolver. He then tried to get down into the trench to obtain an identification, but while doing so, other Germans came up from a dug-out; the party then withdrew.

Lieut-Colonel, G.S.,
29th Division.

30th June, 1916.

SECRET.   COPY NO..... 1 ....

Appendix 2(d).
U.M. Armstrong

29th DIVISION ORDER NO. 36.

Reference.   15th June 1916.
1/20,000 57 D S.E.
1/10,000 Trench Map
Sheet 57 D S.E.
BEAUMONT, 1 & 2,
parts of.

The following preliminary instructions are issued for information and guidance in framing orders to formations and units.

1. The 29th Division has been ordered to attack the German positions on the line Q.17.b.15.4. to Q.5.c.2.8., on a date to be notified later, which will be indicated in these orders by the letter "Z". This attack will take place in conjunction with attacks by the Divisions on both flanks.

OBJECTIVES OF DIVISION.
2. The objectives allotted to this Division are :-
(a). German front line system of trenches from point 03 (Q.17.b.15.4) to point 27 (Q.5.c.2.8), including the village of BEAUMONT HAMEL.
(b). German second line trenches from R.7.c.9.4. to point 41 (Q.6.d.4.0)
(c). German third line trenches from R.8.b.8.2. and point (o9) to point 20 (R.2.b.4.0)

OBJECTIVES OF 36th DIVISION.
3. The 36th Division will advance simultaneously on our Southern flank, its objectives being :-
(a). German trenches from Point 03 to the RIVER ANCRE, and from the RIVER ANCRE to R.20.a.
(b). German trenches from R.8.d. Southwards.
The Battalions of the 36th Division, which will attack the enemy's front system of trenches immediately South of the 29th Division, will occupy and consolidate the trenches from point 03 to the STATION BUILDINGS, Q.18.b.7.6. inclusive. They will not advance further North than this line, but they will be responsible for seizing and holding the Bridge and Mill at R.13.a.2.7.

OBJECTIVES OF 4th DIVISION.
4. On our Northern flank the 4th Division will attack :-
(a). The German front line system of trenches and second line trenches, its right directed on Point 53. On reaching point 53 (timed 35 minutes before our troops reach point 41) they will commence bombing down the trench to point 41.
(b). The German third line of trenches its right directed on point 20.

BOMBARDMENT.
5. A steady bombardment by all available guns will take place day and night for several days preparatory to the infantry attack.

GAS.
6. It is intended to use gas at intervals during the bombardment, if the wind is favourable. Further instructions on this subject will be issued later.

[Handwritten at top:] 7. A smoke barrage will be attempted... on both sides of the River Ancre by 36th Div. will... the attacks of the 29th and 36th Div. from the high ground on the north side of the river. This barrage will continue from...

(2)

SMOKE BARRAGE.	7. It is intended to form a smoke barrage on the Southern flank of the advance by means of 4" Stokes Mortars pushed forward to Q.18.a., immediately behind the two leading battalions of the 87th Brigade. This barrage will commence about 0.55, and will be directed up the Valley of the RIVER ANCRE, a short distance North of the RAILWAY ROAD, so as to cover the flank of the attack on the BEAUCOURT RIDGE from the high ground in R 19 and 20.
IMPORTANCE OF THIS ATTACK.	8. It is most important that the attack of the Division should be successful. The assault will be carried out with the utmost vigour, and all Commanders will exert their maximum effort in driving the enemy from his positions.
PRELIMINARY MOVES OF TROOPS.	9. During the night previous to the commencement of the bombardment, the troops holding our front system of trenches will be reduced to three Battalions. One Battalion will be in reserve in MAILLY WOOD. The 87th Brigade will have two Battalions in the front line, and the 86th Brigade one Battalion in the front line, and one in reserve in MAILLY WOOD. The 87th and 86th Brigade Headquarters will remain at ENGLEBELMER and the Cafe JOURDAIN, MAILLY respectively. The remainder of these Brigades and the 2nd Monmouths will be withdrawn to ACHEUX, under instructions to be issued later. The 88th Brigade will be at LOUVENCOURT
FORMING-UP PLACES.	10. On Y/Z night the troops will move to their Forming-Up Places. The trenches and Areas allotted to Brigades for forming up, and the positions of the Brigade Battle Headquarters, are shewn on the attached map. The following routes will be available for Brigades for this move as under :- 87th Brigade - GABION, WITHINGTON and TIPPERARY AVENUES, and the ground South and East of the AUCHONVILLERS - ENGLEBELMER Road as far North as the Brigade Boundary. 86th Brigade - BROADWAY, 2ND and 3RD AVENUES, and the ground between the above road and the 4th Division Boundary. The line of demarcation between the 87th and 86th Brigades in ENGLEBELMER will be the Northern Road via Q.19.b.5.3. - Q.19.b.5.5. - Q.19.c.2.6 - R.24.b. 85.15. (all inclusive to the 86th Brigade). The 87th and 86th Brigades will be clear of the REDOUBT LINE by 12.0 pm. on Y/Z night. The 88th Brigade will use GABION, WITHINGTON and TIPPERARY AVENUES for their advance.
PREPARING WIRE.	11. The 86th and 87th Brigades will be responsible for cutting the wire of our front, support and reserve trenches during the three nights (W/X - X/Y - Y/Z) preceding the day of assault. The wire will be cut diagonally, pathways being made at intervals of about 20 yards. Rifle and Lewis gun fire from our trenches must be kept up on the German wire each

(3).

night during the bombardment to prevent the enemy repairing the gaps in it caused by our artillery and trench mortar fire.

ARTILLERY LIFTS.

12. The following is the programme of artillery lifts.

0.0   No artillery fire West of the German front line.
0.20. No artillery fire West of the STATION and WAGON ROADS.
1.20. No artillery fire West of the BEAUCOURT RIDGE, i.e., R.7.c.9.4., R.7.a.3.1., Q.6.c.4.0.
1.38 No artillery fire West of the line R.7.a.5.2. to R.1.c.25.50.
2.40. No artillery fire West of the PUISIEUX ROAD, R.7.b.8.1. to R.1.d.6.9.
3.30. No artillery fire West of the final objective, GRANDCOURT - SERRE Ridge, R.8.b.5.7., R.2.b.3.0.

The above times are those noted for the Divisional Artillery lifts.
The Heavy Artillery will in all cases lift five minutes beforehand, except on the final objective when they will maintain their fire up to the moment of assault, at 3.30.
At the commencement of each Infantry attack the Divisional artillery will lift 100 yards, and they will continue lifting at the rate of 50 yards per minute to the next objective.
The Heavy Artillery will lift straight on to the next objective.
Infantry must not arrive at their objectives before the times above noted, as the artillery will still be firing on those points. The Infantry must therefore make their pace conform to the rate of artillery lifts, and if they find themselves checked by our own barrage, they must halt and wait until the barrage again moves forward.
The success of the assault depends largely on the close co-operation of the artillery. Infantry should realise that it is better for them to be occasionally checked, than for the artillery to lift from the objective too early.
At 2.30 the Divisional Artillery will begin to creep forward from the line of wire (R.7.a.5.2. to R.1.c.25.50) towards the PUISIEUX Road and the Infantry should be prepared to follow as closely as possible.

TIME OF ASSAULT.

13. The exact time of the assault will be notified later.

ASSAULTING COLUMNS.

14. (a). The assault on the first and second objectives will be delivered by the 86th and 87th Brigades. Each Brigade will have two Battalions in front line and two in reserve. The reserve Battalions will move through the leading Battalions for the attack on the second objective.
The 88th Brigade will be in Divisional Reserve, and will be used for the attack on the 3rd objective.
(b). The objectives assigned to the Brigades are as follows :-

(4).

87th Infantry Brigade.

1st Objective. The front system of trenches from Point 03 (Q.17.b.15.4) (incl) to Point 89 (Q.10.d.55.70) (excl), back to the STATION Road, the boundary on the right being the line Q.17.b.2.35 Point 83 - STATION BLDGS. (Q.18.b.7.6) (all excl), and on the left the Y RAVINE (incl).

2nd Objective. Second line trenches from Point R.7.c.9.4. to Q.12.b.70.50 (incl).

86th Infantry Brigade.

1st Objective. The front system of trenches from Q.10.d.55.70 (incl) to Point 27 (Q.5.c.2.8) (incl) back to the STATION and WAGON Roads, including the village of BEAUMONT HAMEL, the boundary on the right being the Y RAVINE (excl) and on the left the trench Q.5.c.2.8 - Point 59 - 88 - 04 (all incl).

2nd Objective. Second line trenches from point Q.12.b.70.50 (excl) to point 41 (Q.6.c.4.0) (incl) For the attack on the second objective, the STATION Road as far South as STATION ALLEY (incl) will be allotted to the 86th Brigade.

88th Infantry Brigade.

German third line trenches from R.8.b.8.2. and point 09 to point 20 (R.2.b.4.0)

ATTACK ON FIRST OBJECTIVE.

15. (a). For the attack on the first objective the leading Battalions will be formed up in depth on a three Company front, except the left Battalion of the 86th Brigade, which will have two Companies in the front line, the third Company being specially told off to clear the Northern edge of BEAUMONT HAMEL.
(b). Battalions detailed to carry the first system of trenches will advance at such time as will bring them about 100 yards short of, but parallel to the enemy's trench at the time fixed for the assault.
At this hour the leading troops will move straight forward to their final objective (STATION and WAGON Roads) across the enemy's trenches, but will not enter the enemy's front trenches, as these will be cleared by special parties detailed for this purpose, who will move in rear of the attacking waves.
"Strong points" will be selected at suitable places at the junction of the enemy's main and communication trenches, and will be consolidated. They should be designed for a garrison of about a platoon. On no account are troops to stop because formations on their flanks are held up. Experience has proved that the best way to assist troops, who are being held up, is to push forward, and to outflank the enemy.
(c). On arriving at their objective the leading troops of the 87th and 86th Brigades will

(5).

strong patrols and
immediately send/bombing parties up the RAILWAY,
STATION, and BEAUMONT ALLEYS.

ATTACK ON 2ND OBJECTIVE.

16. (a). The leading troops of the four reserve Battalions of the 86th and 87th Brigades will leave our trenches, as soon as the last wave of the leading Battalions has reached the enemy's wire. They will then move through the leading Battalions, and over the three lines of enemy trenches to the STATION Road, where they will be organised for the attack on the second objective. On capturing the second objective, "Strong Points" will be consolidated in the most suitable positions on the BEAUCOURT RIDGE.

(b). At 1.30 strong patrols will be sent out, by these Brigades to cut the wire running North and South from R.7.a.5.2 to R.1.c.25.50, and bombing parties will be pushed along the communication trenches leading East. None of our artillery fire will be West of this wire after 1.35, but the artillery will continue to fire on the Area East of this wire until 2.30, when they will commence to creep towards the PUISIEUX Road.

ATTACK ON 3RD OBJECTIVE.

17. (a). As soon as the hostile second line has been captured, the 88th Brigade (with two Battalions abreast, each on a front of two Companies) will move forward with their right clear of the Northern edge of BEAUCOURT VILLAGE, to the PUISIEUX Road. They should be so timed as not to cross the line of wire (R.7.a.5.2. to R.1.c.25.50) before 2.30. They will re-form on the PUISIEUX Road and at 3.10 will advance to the enemy's third line trenches on the GRANDCOURT RIDGE.

(b). The boundary on the PUISIEUX Road between the 88th Brigade and the 4th Division on our left will be the road junction of the PUISIEUX Road with point 69.

(c). As soon as the 3rd Line has been captured, "Strong Points" will be consolidated along it, and patrols will be pushed forward to BAILLESCOURT, and to the SUNKEN Road running North from it. If the SUNKEN Road can be taken without undue loss, this line will also be occupied and consolidated.

FLANKS.

18. All troops in the advance will make arrangements to protect their flanks. The 86th Brigade will send parties of Grenadiers to bomb up any trenches on their left flank which have not been taken by the 4th Division, and will endeavour to join hands with this Division.
Similarly the 87th Brigade will send bombing parties towards and will join hands with the 36th Division on their right flank. The 87th Brigade will be responsible for the crossings over the RIVER ANCRE from the MILL (R.13.a.2.7) exclusive to the Railway Bridge at R.8.c.45.60 inclusive, and the 88th Brigade for the crossings East of the latter place.

UNDERGROUND GALLERIES.	19. Four underground galleries have been constructed leaving MARY REDAN (Q.17.a.4.3., 1ST AVENUE (Q.10.d.0,75), HAWTHORNE RIDGE (Q.10.b.0.7) and SAP 7 (Q.4.d.3.7) The 252nd Tunnelling Coy. have arranged to break through these tunnels on the morning of Z day. The tunnels will only be used for runners and for getting telephone wires and water pipes forward. They will not be used as communication trenches. The forward Brigades will be responsible for policing the entrances and exits of the tunnels in their Sub-sections.
COMMUNICATION TRENCHES.	20. As soon as the enemy's first line system of trenches has been captured, parties will be told off from the 1/2nd Monmouth Regt. to dig communication trenches across "No Mans" Land from the Eastern ends of the tunnels at MARY REDAN, 1ST AVENUE and HAWTHORNE RIDGE. These trenches will connect with the enemy's main communication trenches.
INSTRUCTIONS TO INFANTRY.	21. Arrangements will be made by Brigades to ensure that every man knows exactly what he has to do and to which party he belongs, whether assaulting, supporting or consolidating. The assaulting troops must be allotted definite objectives, and should be formed up as far as possible parallel to their objective prior to their advance. Machine and Lewis guns, and Stokes Mortars should be directed to their objectives by diverse routes, so as to reduce the chances of casualties.
TRENCH STEPS &c.	22. Brigades will arrange that steps leading from the bottom of the trench to the parapet are cut in every bay of the front, support or reserve trenches in their forming-up Areas. They will also ensure that the bulk of the traverses in their areas are covered over, so as to provide bridges over our own trenches.
BRIGADE RESERVE TROOPS.	23. Only 22 Officers per Battalion will accompany the advancing troops. The remainder, together with 10% of the strengths of the Battalions, will form Brigade reserves and will not accompany the attack. After the advance they will occupy the front line lightly with a view to guarding against counter-attack and to rallying stragglers. They will also furnish guards for prisoners, who will be handed over to them by the fighting troops at our present front line parapet. These reserves will eventually be used by Brigades to replace casualties after the day's engagement.
MACHINE GUNS.	24. Machine guns will fire 'bursts' throughout the bombardment, and especially at night to prevent the enemy mending his wire. The 88th Brigade Machine gun Company will take over all the gun positions in the YELLOW LINE on the night previous to the commencement of the bombardment. Immediately prior to the assault all machine guns

(7).

will open a heavy fire, direct and indirect, on to the German front and support trenches, and at the moment of the assault they will lift to the second objective and communication trenches leading to it, and will continue firing as long as the situation permits.

After the capture of the second objective, the 86th and 87th Brigades will move forward as many guns as possible to cover the advance of the 88th Brigade against the third objective.

STOKES T. MORTARS. 25. Six batteries of Stokes T. Mortars will be stationed in emplacements dug in the two tunnels and the SUNKEN Road as shown on the attached map. These emplacements will only be opened on Y/Z night. Prior to the assault, these batteries will open a hurricane bombardment on the enemy trenches, orders regarding which will be issued later. These batteries together with three additional batteries expected shortly, will be under the orders of their Brigade Commanders, who will issue to them the necessary instructions for the forward move, and will provide the necessary extra personnel for carrying ammunition, etc. 300 rounds per mortar will be stored in the forward emplacements, and 100 rounds should accompany every mortar which advances.

FORWARD BATTERIES. 26. As soon as the second objective has been captured, as well as the ridge North of THIEPVAL, two batteries of 48th Division, attached to the 29th Division, will move forward under orders from the Corps to a position in "No mans" Land South of the BEAUMONT Road, in order to support more closely the attack on the third objective.

Two F.A. Batteries also, to be detailed by the C.R.A. will move forward subsequently for the same purpose to a position North of STATION Road.

ROUTES FORWARD. 27. The routes forward for wheeled transport and guns are shown in Brown on the attached map. The C.R.E. will be responsible for ensuring that within our lines the barricades on these routes are removed, and the bridges are in repair on the day of the assault. He will also erect notice-boards on the routes, with arrows indicating the direction of the traffic.

PIONEER BATTALION. 28. The Pioneer Battalion (1/2nd Monmouths) will detail two Companies to prepare roads over the enemy's trenches by filling them in, and to dig the communication trenches mentioned in para. 20. Two platoons of the Pioneer Battalion will be allotted to each of the 86th and 87th Brigades, and one Company to the 88th Brigade as carrying parties.

ARTILLERY LIAISON OFFICER. 29. The C.R.A. WILL arrange for an artillery officer to accompany each Battalion during the forward move.

(8).

ROYAL ENGINEERS. 30. One Field Company R.E., to be detailed by the C.R.E., will be affiliated to each Infantry Brigade, and will be utilized for maintaining the roads over our lines, for arranging the water supply forward as well as in our lines, for demolitions and for consolidation of "Strong Points" at night. Searching for and cutting wires, which may be leading to hostile mines, and the destruction of any mines found will be carried out by the 252nd Tunnelling Coy.

DIVISIONAL OBSERVATION POSTS. 31. Northern and Southern Divisional Observation Posts have been made at Q.2.b.6.9. and Q.23.a.2.4. respectively. They will be in telephonic communication with Divisional and with the Advanced Brigade Headquarters. Each post will be manned continuously during the bombardment and attack by a Divisional Staff Officer. These Officers will report direct to Divisional Headquarters, and will not issue orders to Brigades, though they may be consulted by the latter as to the progress of the action visible from their posts. The Divisional Cyclist O.P. at Q.9.d.1.9. will also be manned by its normal complement of Cyclists.

REPORT CENTRES. 32. The Main Divisional Report Centre will be at Q.8.d.45.05. Subsidiary posts will also be established at Q.19.b.1.3. and Q.14.d.95.25. The O.C. Divisional Signals will arrange for communication back to Divisional Headquarters from these posts.

SIGNAL COMMUNICATIONS. 33. Brigades will establish Advanced Visual Signal Stations as early as possible in the enemy's lines. These Stations will communicate back with the visual signallers, stationed in the Divisional Observation Posts, who can receive messages but cannot acknowledge them.
Sending Stations will therefore call up with 20 Vs, and repeat the message slowly four times.
Every Battalion will take forward with it at least two light telephone wires in order to connect with Brigade Headquarters. They will also take forward one ground signalling sheet for communicating with aeroplanes.
The O.C. Divisional Signals will arrange for telephone wires to be run through the forward tunnels in "No mans" Land to connect with the Battalions. In addition, Battalion Commanders will arrange a system of runners to keep up communication with Brigade Headquarters and with their Companies.
The O.C. Divisional Signals will issue to each Brigade five baskets of pigeons.

EMPLOYMENT OF AIRCRAFT. 34. During the attack and subsequent operations two aeroplanes will be employed continuously as contact patrols. Signals to them by means of flares should be made by the troops in front, in accordance with the arrangements practised, vide "Instructions Regarding Liaison Between Infantry and Aircraft" i issued under C.G.S. 44 dated 1st June 1916.

(9).

DISTINGUISHING MARKS.	35. (a). Every infantryman taking part in the attack (Pioneer Bn. excluded) will wear a triangular piece of tin, 7" side, fastened to his back, between the shoulders.
	(b). Diamond shaped screens, one per platoon, will be carried of the following colours.
	    29th Division. Vertical Division - red one half
	                                          yellow one half.
	    4th Division. Horizontal Division - Red
	                                            above, yellow below.
	(c). The 29th Division will wear, in addition to regimental patches, the Divisional Red triangular badge on both arms.

TRENCH BRIDGES.	36. Trench bridges will be allotted as follows :-
	    86th Brigade 96
	    87th " 96
	    88th " 32
	These bridges will be drawn by Brigades from the C.R.E. dump at ENGLEBELMER as they become available, and will be dumped in convenient places in the trenches.

BATTLE POLICE.	37. Battle Police Posts, each consisting of one officer and three men, will be established at the following places in our communication trenches.
	Junction of Knightsbridge & GABION AVENUE) To be
	    " " UXBRIDGE RD. and WITHINGTON) found by
	                                       AVENUE) 88th Bde.
	THURLES DUMP.)
	
	Junction of BROADWAY and 88th TRENCH.) To be
	    " " 88th TRENCH and 2ND AVENUE) found by
	    " " 86th TRENCH and 3RD AVENUE) 86th Bde.
	
	Their duties will be to control traffic, to prevent straggling and to direct wounded men to Dressing Stations. Dug-outs have been prepared at these posts.
	Divisional Posts will also be established by the A.P.M. along the line ENGLEBELMER - MAILLY, and the Stragglers Collecting Station will be situated on the ENGLEBELMER - HEDAUVILLE Road, just West of ENGLEBELMER.

TRENCH TRAFFIC.	38. Trenches will be reserved as follows :-
	For "UP" traffic only towards the front line
	    WITHINGTON - TIPPERARY and 2ND AVENUE.
	For "DOWN" traffic only
	    GABION AVENUE, BROADWAY and 3RD AVENUES.
	The Brigades in occupation of these trenches will be responsible for policing them.
	Staff Officers and linesmen repairing wires will be allowed to use communication trenches in either direction.
	The trenches for "DOWN" traffic may be used for up traffic on Y/Z night, and for the advance of the 88th Brigade on the morning of Z day.

CAPTURED GUNS.	39. Any guns or machine guns, which are in danger of being lost, will be rendered useless by damaging the sights and breech mechanisms. As there is a

(10).

probability of some of the enemy guns falling into our hands, the C.R.A. will arrange to have teams placed so that they can be brought up to remove the guns during the first night of the battle.

MISCELLANEOUS ARRANGEMENTS.

40. Equipment to be carried.
(a). Infantrymen will carry : Rifle and equipment (less pack) 170 rounds S.A.A., one iron ration and the rations for the day of the assault, two sandbags in belt, two Mills Grenades, steel helmet, smoke helmet in satchel, water bottle and haversack on the back, also first Field Dressing and identity disc. A waterproof sheet should also be taken. The troops of the first and second waves will only carry 120 rounds S.A.A. The Pioneer Battalion will be equipped as above, except that they will only carry 120 rounds S.A.A.
At least 40% of the Infantry will carry shovels and 10% will carry picks.
The following Stores will be issued to each Brigade for the operations.

  128 French wire coils.
  64 Diamond shaped signalling screens. *and 5 Signalling Shutters*
  1600 flares for aeroplane signalling (4 for each officer and N.C.O)
  2 ~~5~~ large signal lamps (1 per Battalion and 1 per Brigade Headquarters).
  64 bundles of 5' wooden pickets.
  ~~48~~ 64 mauls.
  16 sledge hammers.
  640 wire cutters, and lanyards.
  640 hedging gloves.
  96 web braces or rifle slings)
  16 old haversacks.   )) Machine
  16 petrol cans for water   ) gunners.
  512 haversacks. (To carry Lewis magazines)
  33 Bangalore torpedoes.

Brigades will arrange to draw these Stores, and the picks and shovels from the C.R.E. as follows :-
86th Brigade on 14th, 87th on 15th and 88th on 16th inst.
The picks and shovels carried on the men will not be taken from the Battalion or Brigade reserve tools, which will be loaded up on vehicles ready to move forward. The remainder of the stores can be drawn on application to D.A.D.O.S.
Packs and greatcoats will not be taken to the Forming-Up Areas on the night preceding the assault, but will be labelled and stored under Brigade arrangements under guard in selected dumps in the billeting areas and front trenches, whence they will be salvaged by the Divisional Reserve Coy.
All bayonets will be sharpened.
All men carrying wire cutters will have a white label to that effect fastened on their backs.
The regulation amount of baggage to be carried forward in the baggage wagons of the train must be similarly collected, dumped, and labelled distinctly.
Grenadiers will carry equipment, less packs, rifle slung and 50 rounds S.A.A.. waistcoat with 10 grenades.

(11).

Carriers each carry two buckets, holding 10 grenades each.
Lewis and Machine gunners. 25% only carry rifles and 50 rounds S.A.A.
Light T.M. Gunners. 25% only carry rifles slung with 120 rounds S.A.A.
Signallers carry 120 rounds S.A.A. only and will not wear a tin disc.
Runners wear shorts (if available), runners badge and no tin disc, rifles slungs and 50 rounds S.A.A. only.
(b). Grenades.
Five reserve dumps each of 960 grenades are being formed in the forward line as shown on the attached map.
Grenades required for the attack will be drawn by Brigades from the grenades now being sent up to the Brigade dumps and from the Battalion and Brigade Reserves. The full establishment of equipment grenades will be kept by Battalions and the D.A.C. on wheels.
(c). S.A.Ammunition.
Cotton bandoliers with 50 rounds S.A.A. to complete up to 170 rounds per man will be drawn by Brigades from the ammunition placed in the Brigade Dumps for this purpose.
Five S.A.A. dumps will be formed under Divisional arrangements at the places indicated by notice boards in the forward trenches (vide map). Each dump will consist of 100 Boxes (100,000 rounds) A reserve of 250 boxes (250,000 rounds) will also be stored in the Divisional Dump at Q.9.c.5.2.)
The S.A.A. dumped in the trenches will be drawn on to replace ammunition used during the bombardment. The balance of the S.A.A. in the trenches will be transferred to the above five dumps just prior to the bombardment.
The existing Brigade Reserve stores in MAILLY WOOD and ENGLEBELMER will be kept intact to be drawn on if required. The S.A.A. in regimental reserve for rifles, Lewis and Machine guns will be kept intact on wheels at ACHEUX.
The S.A.A. and grenades on wheels in the D.A.C. will similarly be loaded up, and kept ready to move forward.
(d). Stokes Mortar Ammunition.
Two dumps of Stokes Trench Mortar Ammunition, each containing 1200 rounds, will be formed at the places shown on the attached map. 8400 rounds also will be stored in the Divisional Dump.
(e). R.E.Stores.
Three advanced Depots of R.E. Stores will be formed by the C.R.E. at the places shown on the attached map.
Each of these Stores will contain :-
Sandbags, picks, shovels, crowbars, wire-cutters, coils of plain and barbed wire, iron and wooden pickets, tracing tapes and axes.
A large central store will be established at the R.E. Depot at ENGLEBELMER.

(12).

(f). Water.
Five water dumps have been formed in the forward trenches (vide map). Each consists of 320 tins (640 gallons). These dumps must not be drawn on before the advance. In addition water storage of 1200 gallons in tanks connected with the pipe line from the SUCERIE has been arranged at ~~eight~~ five places in the support trenches for use during the bombardment, vide map. Brigades holding the line will place sentries over all water dumps in their areas.

(g). Rations.
A reserve of two days rations has been established at the Divisional Dump. Three advanced ration dumps have also been formed as shown on map, containing a total of 10,000 iron rations. These will not normally be drawn on till the advance takes place. Sandbags have been stored in the dumps in which the rations will be carried forward, but these bags will not be filled until the rations are actually required.

MEDICAL. 41. Advanced Dressing Stations will be established in the Left Sub-sector in the TENDERLOIN, AUCHONVILLERS (Q.9.a.1.1.) and MAILLY-MAILLET (Q.7.c.6.7. billet 87) and in the Right Sub-sector at KNIGHTSBRIDGE and near VITERMONT Church (Q.19.d.5.9)
The Divisional Collecting Stations will be at MAILLY and VITERMONT Church, alongside the Advanced Dressing Stations. The Main Dressing Station will be at LOUVENCOURT, and the Corps Collecting Station will be at ACHEUX.
All troops are reminded that the care of wounded is the duty of the Regimental Stretcher Bearers and Field Ambulances. Fighting troops are forbidden to accompany wounded men to the Dressing Stations.

PRISONERS. 42. Brigades will detail special prisoner escorts to take prisoners back to our front line, where the prisoners will be handed over to the parties allotted for the purpose, vide para 23. These latter parties will escort prisoners back to the Prisoners Enclosure at P.22.b., where they will be handed over to the A.P.M.

REFILLING POINT. 43. The Refilling Point will remain on the ACHEUX-LEALVILLERS Road as at present, but in the event of the third objective being attained, it will be moved to the HEDAUVILLE - MAILLY Road just West of MAILLY WOOD.

x **1ST LINE TRANSPORT.** 44. Should the 1st Line Transport be required application should be made to Divisional Head Quarters.
Cookers should be prepared to join the troops at dusk on Z day.
One Officer and six M.M.P. will be detailed by the A.P.M. to control the traffic in BEAUMONT HAMEL and BEAUCOURT sur ANCRE, with their Headquarters near Q.5.c.7.0.

Raid on Y.1/Y.2 night (29'inst)

Programme of Heavy Artillery Bombardment

Calibre of Gun	Point	No. of Rds	Time
6"	89	40	12 – 1.30 AM.
6"	54	17	12 – 12.25 AM.
6"	Q.11.c.45.75	23	12.25 – 1.30 AM.
6"	85	40	12 – 1.30 A.M.
8"	60	25	12 – 12.25 AM
8"	Q.17.b.27.95	15	12 – 12.25 A.M.
8"	Q.17.b.30.58	20	12.25 – 1.30 AM
		180	

C.J.S.
29/6/16.

APPENDIX 2.

Comprises the following :-

(a) 29th Division Order No. 34 re relief of 88th Brigade by 86th Brigade on night 7th/8th June.

(b) 29th Division Order No. 35 re 4th Division taking over from 29th Division portion of the line.

(c) 29th Division Order No. 37 re relief of 87th Brigade by 88th Brigade on night 15th/16th June.

(d) 29th Division Order No. 36. Preliminary instructions re forthcoming offensive.
Amendment to above dated 30th June.

(e) VIIIth Corps Operation Order No. 3. Preliminary instructions re forthcoming offensive.

(f) 29th Division Order No. 38 re 87th Brigade taking over Right Sector of the line from the 88th Brigade on the night prior to the commencement of the bombardment. March Tables "A" and "B" attached.

(g) 29th Division Order No. 39 with programme and details of attack. Appendices "A", "B" and "C" attached.
Amended Appendix "B" to above order issued 19th June is also attached. Amended Appendix "C" also attached, together with map showing lifts etc of Divisional Artillery.

(h) 29th Division Order No. 40. Tactical Exercise with Time Table and Map of training area attached. Also personal note from Corps Commander to G.O.C.
~~Copy of above order as issued by Corps for information of other Divisions.~~

(i) 29th Division Order No. 41 re postponement of Zero and alterations and re-arrangements of programme.

(j) 29th Divisional Artillery Operation Order No.1 re artillery action in forthcoming offensive, also correspondence relating thereto.

SECRET

HEADQUARTERS,
29th DIVISION,
GENERAL STAFF.

No. O.G.S. 5
Date.

86th Brigade.
~~87th Brigade.~~
~~88th Brigade.~~
C.R.E.
C.R.A.
A.A. & Q.M.G.

The programme for the reliefs of the Infantry Brigades for June will be as follows:-

	May – June. 28/29. - 7/8	June. 7/8 - 17/18.	June. 17/18 - 27/28.
RIGHT SECTOR.	87	87	88
LEFT SECTOR.	88	86	86
CORPS RESERVE.	86	88	87

It may not be possible to adhere strictly to this table.

W. M. Armstrong Capt.
for

1st June 1916.

Lieut Colonel, G.S.
29th Division.

Appendix 2 (a).

SECRET.   Copy No. 3

29th DIVISION ORDER NO. 34

Reference
Map 57.D. 1/10,000.   4th June 1916.

1.   The 86th Brigade will relieve the 88th Brigade in the Left Sector of the Line on the night of 7/8th June, and will report to these Headquarters when the relief is complete.

2.   The 88th Brigade on relief will be billeted at LOUVENCOURT, and will be in Corps Reserve.

3.   Brigades will report their respective dispositions to these Headquarters by 12 noon 8th inst.

4.   The reliefs may be carried out during daylight, provided that the troops are marched to and from the forward area in small parties.

C.G. Fuller
Lieut Colonel G.S.
29th Division.

Issued at 9 p.m.

Copy 1 - 3   General Staff.   15 A.P.M.
      4   86th Brigade.   16 O.C. Div. Train.
      5   87th Brigade.   17 A.D.V.S.
      6   88th Brigade.   18 A.D.M.S.
    7 -11   H.Q., R.A.   19 D.A.D.O.S.
     12   C.R.E.   20 VIII Corps.   ) for
     13   Off. i/c Signals.   21 31st Division) information
     14   A.A. & Q.M.G.   22 36th Division.)

Appendix 2 (b)

SECRET.   Copy No. 3

29th DIVISION ORDER NO. 35.

Reference.   10th June 1916.
Map 57.D.1/40000

1.   The 4th Division will relieve the 29th Division in that portion of the line between Q.4.d.2.9. and Q.4.b.5.4., our present Northern Boundary, on the night of the 14/15th inst.

2.   Arrangements for the relief will be made by the Brigadier of the 10th Infantry Brigade direct with the Brigadier of the 86th Infantry Brigade.

3.   Artillery of the 4th Division will go into the line on the nights of the 15/16th and 16/17th, under arrangements to be made direct by the Brigadier of the 29th Divisional Artillery with the Brigadier of the 4th Divisional Artillery.

4.   On completion of the Infantry relief as above, the boundary between the 29th and 4th Division will be as follows :-
Q.4.d.2.9. thence through Q.4.c.5.8., South of Third Avenue to the junction of the tracks at Q.2.d.5.2½ - thence to Railway, Q.2.c.80 - thence to road junction at Q.13.b.2.2. - thence to Q.11.c.0.7.) thence North of LOUVENCOURT, South of VAUCHELLES to the road junction midway on the direct road between MARIEUX and PUCHVILLERS.

5.   The 86th Brigade will vacate their present billets in MAILLY-MAILLET for the huts in MAILLY WOOD by the night of the 13/14th, by which time also the 86th Brigade Headquarters will have moved to the CAFE JOURDAIN, on the main road just West of MAILLY-MAILLET.

6.   The completion of the Infantry relief will be reported to these Headquarters.

                                           C.G. Fuller.

Issued at 3.45 p.m.   Lieut.Colonel.G.S.
                                           29th Division.

Copy 1 - 3 General Staff.   15 A.P.M.
     4   86th Brigade   16 O.C.. Div.Train.
     5   87th Brigade   17 A.D.V.S.
     6   88th Brigade   18 A.D.M.S.
     7 -11 H.Q., R.A.   19 D.A.D.O.S.
     12   C.R.E.   20 VIII Corps   )
     13   Off. i/c Signals   21 31st Division   )
     14   A.A.& Q.M.G.   22 36th Division.) FOR
                                23 4th Division.   ) INFOR-
                                                      MATION.

(13).

WATER.

45. The 86th Brigade will be responsible for policing the water supply in BEAUMONT HAMEL, and the 87th Brigade similarly for the water supply in BEAUCOURT, and along the ANCRE as far East as BEAUCOURT. Water carts will move up to the troops at dusk on Z day, and will refill at the water supply West of MAILLY WOOD on the HEDAUVILLE - MAILLY Road.

MAPS.

46. The only maps to be referred to in all messages, and to be carried in the attack, are the 1/10,000 BEAUMONT TRENCH Map sheet 57 D S.E. and 1/20,000 Sheet 57 D S.E., both of which show the German trenches, but not our own. These have been issued to all concerned. No Other maps will be carried by officers or men. Officers and N.C.Os. will carry notebooks, but no other papers will be taken.

SYNCHRONISING WATCHES.

47. Watches will be synchronised by the General Staff at 9.0 am. and 7.0 pm. on X and Y days.

DIVISIONAL HEADQUARTERS.

48. Divisional Headquarters will remain in its present position at ACHEUX.

C.G. Fuller

H.Q. 29th Division.

Lieut.Colonel, G.S.
29th Division.

Issued at 10 A.M

Through Signals to

86th Brigade	A.A.&.Q.M.G.
87th "	8th Corps.
88th "	4th Division.
Divisional Artillery	36th Division.
C.R.E.	48th Division.
O.C. Pioneer Battalion	General Staff
A.D.M.S.	Off i/c Signals.

S E C R E T.

86th Brigade.	A.A. & Q.M.G.
87th Brigade.	VIIIth Corps.
88th Brigade.	4th Division.
C.R.A.	36th Division.
C.R.E.	48th Division.
O.C. 1/2nd Monmouth Regt.	General Staff.
A.D.M.S.	Off. i/c Signals.

AMENDMENT TO DIVISION ORDER NO. 36.

With reference to paras. 31 and 33 of 29th Division Order No. 36, the Northern Divisional Observation Post at Q.2.b.6.9. has been closed. The Divisional Cyclist Observation Post at AUCHONVILLERS (Q.9.d.1.9.) is now manned by a Staff Officer, and visual signallers, who can receive messages, but cannot acknowledge them, will be stationed at this Post.

C.G. Fuller

Lieut-Colonel, G.S.,
29th Division.

30th June, 1916.

S E C R E T.

> HEADQUARTERS,
> 29th DIVISION.
> GENERAL STAFF.
> No. 21.6.16.
> Date

86th Brigade.
~~87th Brigade.~~
~~88th Brigade.~~
~~G.R.A.~~
~~Off. i/c Signals.~~

Herewith particulars of Divisional Signal Communications for the forthcoming operations.

[signature]

Lieut-Colonel, G.S.
29th Division.

21st June, 1916.

S E C R E T.

Headquarters,
    86th Brigade.

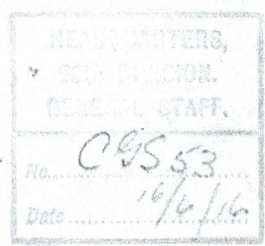

        The following is an extract of a letter received from 4th Division for your information :-

    "THIRD AVENUE will be at your disposal for evacuation purposes from 1.30 dating from zero onwards on "Z" day.

    "As regards the use of THIRD AVENUE for the 29th Division to march to assembly positions the Avenue must be clear of your troops by 10.15 p.m. on "Y/Z" night.

                                                Lieut-Colonel, G.S.,
16th June, 1916.   29th Division.

DIVISIONAL SIGNAL COMMUNICATIONS.

During the forthcoming operations the following systems of communications will be employed.

(a) Telephone.
(b) Telegraph.
(c) Visual.
(d) Despatch Riders.
(e) Pigeons.
(f) Wireless.
(g) Contact Patrol Aeroplanes.
(h) Kite Balloons.

General arrangements in detail.

(a) Telephone circuits.

(1) Each Infantry Brigade in its forward battle headquarters will be connected to an advanced exchange in MAILLY WOOD. In addition the 86th Brigade will be in direct touch with a Divisional O.P. at Q.2.b.6.9 and the 88th Brigade in direct touch with another Divisional O.P. at Q.23.a.2.4. Further each of the above named Brigades will have direct lines to the Brigades of 4th and 36th Divisions respectively. The 86th and 87th Brigades will be in direct communication.

(2) Observation posts at Q.2.b.6.9 and Q.23.a.2.4 are both connected direct to the MAILLY WOOD Exchange as well as to the Left and Right Artillery Group Exchanges (C.R.A. communications) communication also exists as per (1).
    The Cyclist O.P. at Q.9.d.1.9 will be connected direct to MAILLY WOOD Exchange.

(3) Divisional Dump situated at Q.9.c.5.4 will be connected to MAILLY WOOD Exchange.

(4) Telephone exchanges are established at MAILLY WOOD, ACHEUX Signal Office and ACHEUX Chateau. There are three trunk lines between the first two named exchanges; one of these trunks is for the exclusive use of the C.R.A. A direct trunk runs from MAILLY WOOD Exchange to ACHEUX Chateau. The Chateau Exchange is for emergency only, and independant of the ACHEUX Exchange. From both ACHEUX and the Chateau Exchanges the following calls may be effected - 4th Division, 36th Division, VIIIth Corps, Fourth Army and BELLE EGLISE.

(5) The Main Divisional Report Centre will be at Q.8.d.45.05. Subsidiary Report Centres will be at Q.19.b.1.3 and Q.14.d.95.2. From these report centres it will be possible to send written messages only.

(b) Telegraph Circuits.

In addition to the telephone line, each Infantry Brigade will be connected direct by telegraph from its battle headquarters to Divisional Headquarters. A telegraph circuit will also work direct to VIIIth Corps from Divisional Headquarters. There will be no other telegraphic communications.

(c) Visual reading stations will be established at the Northern (Q.2.b.6.9.) and Southern (Q.23.a.2.4.) Divisional O.P.'s. These stations can receive, but cannot send or acknowledge. Battalion and Company signallers, also F.O.O.'s can send back messages to these stations, which when received will be sent by wire to their destination. Sending and receiving stations will be established at the Main Divisional Report Centre (Q.8.d.45.05) and near the Cafe Jourdain, MAILLY (P.12.d.2.7.) Both these stations will work to a sending and receiving station at ACHEUX WOOD (P.15.a.1.1)

- 2 -

(d) Dispatch Riders.

Motor Cyclist Dispatch Rider posts will be established at AUCHONVILLERS Station (Q.8.b.5.9) and at the Subsidiary Report Centre (Q.19.b.1.3) These Motor Cyclists will convey messages back to the ACHEUX Signal Office.

(e) Pigeons.

Each Brigade will be issued with six baskets of pigeons, each basket containing two birds. Baskets will be issued to Battalions by Brigades as required.
Each Brigade will detail ten men to work the Pigeon Service. Pigeons must be used sparingly and not liberated except in daylight. Empty baskets should be returned immediately to AUCHONVILLERS Railway Station (Q.8.b.5.9), where they will be refilled, and the full baskets returned by bearers to their units.

(f) Wireless.

A Parent Trench Wireless Set with a range of 2½ miles will be installed in the trenches about 87th Brigade Battle Headquarters (Q.16.a.9.9). This set will work to the Corps Directing Set at COLINCAMPS. Attention is drawn to "Notes on employment of wireless" and to "Code for short range wireless during operations". A spare Trench Set will be stationed at Q.16.a.9.9 and will accompany 88th Brigade Headquarters when they advance. This set will work to the Corps Directing Set, and to the Parent Set at Q.16.a.9.9.

(g) Contact Patrol Aeroplanes.

Two aeroplanes will be employed continuously as Contact Patrols. Signals to them by means of lamp and flares will be made in accordance with the arrangements practised.

(h) Kite Balloons.

Signals to Kite Balloons will be made by lamp, but this method of communication should only be resorted to when other means fail.

(j) Stores.

A certain amount of Signal Stores will be dumped close to MAILLY Exchange. These stores will consist of cable, telephones and hop poles. The quantity of stores however is very limited and demands will only be met for pressing requirements.

(k) Burying Cables.

All lines both telephone and telegraph have been buried in trenches about six feet deep. Test dug-outs have been made at certain points. Information just received from YPRES shows that cable buried six feet deep has given good results.

ARTILLERY COMMUNICATIONS.

C.R.A. C.R.A. has communication with :-

    (1) ACHEUX Exchange.
    (2) G.S. direct.
    (3) MAILLY Exchange (direct) - for Group Headquarters.

GROUP HEADQUARTERS. Normal Headquarters are connected direct to MAILLY Exchange.

(a) Left Group - Left Group battle headquarters exchange is alongside the Main Divisional Report Centre (Q.8.d.45.05). To this exchange are connected :-

1. Left Group Battle Headquarters.
2. Left Group Normal Headquarters.
3. C.R.A. via MAILLY Exchange.
4. Batteries of the Group.
5. Group O.P.'s at K.33.d.20.80 and Q.15.a.80.20.
6. 86th Infantry Brigade Battle Headquarters (Advanced)
7. All battery O.P.'s.
8. 4th Division Right Group Exchange.
9. Right Group Exchange (4 lines)
10. Two lines forward to advanced Left Brigade Headquarters (86th Brigade Battle Headquarters) to be used by the four batteries advancing into "No Man's Land" and STATION Road. These lines connect back to Group Commanders.
11. Visual O.P. in Cemetry, AUCHONVILLERS.
12. Divisional O.P. at Q.2.b.6.9.

(b) Right Group forward exchange is at Q.22.c.50.70. To it are connected :-

1. C.R.A. via MAILLY Exchange.
2. Batteries of the group including two 48th Division Batteries.
3. Group Headquarters.
4. Group O.P. at Q.22.d.90.50.
5. Right Infantry Brigade Headquarters (87th Brigade Battle Headquarters.)
6. 36th Division "Centre" Group Exchange.
7. Left Group Exchange.
8. Battery O.P.'s.
9. Divisional O.P.' at Q.23.a.20.40.

    All lines forward from MAILLY Exchange are buried in trenches six feet deep.
    Divisional visual station back to ACHEUX is within a few yards of the Main Divisional Report Centre and of the Left Group Exchange.
    The Dispatch Rider assembly point is at AUCHONVILLERS Station some 500 yards North of the Divisional Report Centre.

Visual in Groups.
    Whenever it is possible to get visual between Batteries and Group Exchanges without a transmitting station, this has been done.
    All batteries have visual between O.P. and battery.
    Visual messages from F.O.O.'s will be picked up and transmitted not only by the Left Group Observation Post, but also by the Divisional Visual Stations at the Northern (Q.2.b.6.9.) and Southern (Q.23.a.2.4.) Divisional O.P.'s.

Appendix 2 (e)

SECRET

Copy No. 2.

VIII CORPS OPERATION ORDER NO: 3.

15th June, 1916.

Reference the maps issued with VIII Corps Scheme for Offensive and 1/20,000 SHEETS 57^D N.E. and S.E.

1. (a). In accordance with orders received from the Fourth Army, the VIII Corps will attack the enemy's position between Q.17.b.14 and K.23.d.81, both inclusive.

    The object of the VIII Corps attack is:-

    i. To capture the enemy's trenches running along the GRANDCOURT - SERRE RIDGE from R.8.b.57 inclusive to the CROSS ROADS at L.26.c.56 inclusive.

    ii. To form a defensive flank facing North-North-East from the above CROSS ROADS to our own trenches at JOHN COPSE.

    (b). Simultaneously with the attack of the VIII Corps strong attacks will be made :-

    i. By the remaining Corps of the Fourth Army to gain the line GRANDCOURT - POZIERES - CONTALMAISON - MONTAUBON.

    ii. By the French Sixth Army on the Right of our Fourth Army.

    iii. By the VII Corps on our Left against the GOMMECOURT SALIENT.

    iv. By the remainder of the Third British Army and by the First and Second British Armies.

    (c). After a pause of sufficient duration to enable the Heavy Artillery to be got up the Fourth Army will make a further advance.

    During this advance the VIII Corps will continue to form the defensive flank of the Fourth Army, pushing forward its right to seize, hold and consolidate a position on the SUNKEN ROAD from BAILLESCOURT FARM inclusive to L.32.b.25.20 inclusive, and to assist the X Corps in their capture of GRANDCOURT.

2. The Infantry assault will be preceded by a five days bombardment

- 2 -

bombardment. The date on which the bombardment will commence and the hour of "zero", i.e. the hour at which the Infantry attack will take place on the 6th day, will be notified later.

3. (a). The artillery bombardment will be carried out in accordance with the programme issued with VIII Corps Scheme for Offensive, pages 23 to 27, and supplementary artillery orders No.R.A.395/13 dated 14-6-1916, issued to artillery only.

(b). The 6 batteries, detailed on page 28 of Corps Offensive Scheme to take up positions in NO MAN'S LAND, will commence to move forward at the same time as the Infantry Brigades detailed for the attack on the 3rd Objective, i.e. the GRANDCOURT - SERRE RIDGE. These batteries must take care not to block the move of the infantry.

(c). In addition to the above 6 batteries, Divisional Commanders may, if the situation requires it, order two more batteries to move forward. Not more than 4 batteries in all, per Division, may be moved forward without reference to Corps Headquarters.

(d). It may occasionally be necessary for the Corps Commander to issue orders direct to Divisional Artillery. In this case, it will be the duty of the C.R.A. of the Division at once, to inform the Divisional Commander of the orders received.

4. (a). The infantry attack will be carried out in accordance with the instructions laid down in VIII Corps Scheme for Offensive, pages 3 to 12: the guiding principle being that all ground gained is to be consolidated at once and held at all costs. At "zero" the leading infantry must be formed up in NO MAN's LAND parallel to their objective.

(b). Where, as in the case of MUNICH and PUISIEUX TRENCHES a second line of German trenches has recently been dug, the

infantry

- 3 -

infantry will make this second line their objective, and not the original line.

(c). Commencing at 10 minutes before "zero" all 3" Stokes Mortars that can bear on the enemy's front line trenches will commence a bombardment which will continue until the infantry moves forward to the assault.

(d). The mine under the HAWTHORN REDOUBT will be fired at 10 minutes before "zero".

5. In view of the intention expressed in para: 1, (c) above, as soon as the trenches on the GRANDCOURT - SERRE RIDGE have been captured, the 29th and 4th Divisions will establish small posts well dug in and provided with Lewis Guns, on the line of the SUNKEN ROAD from BAILLESCOURT FARM inclusive to where this road enters our line about L.32.b.25.20, to deny this position to the enemy and to act as a covering line to our main position on the GRANDCOURT - SERRE RIDGE.

6. S.O.S. - Divisional arrangements must be made to send forward a supply of Rod Rockets with the troops detailed for the attack on the PUISIEUX TRENCH and the FLANK TRENCH. These will be used to give the S.O.S. signal in the event of a counter-attack either by day or night. The signal will be 5 Red Rockets in quick succession. In accordance with the place from which these Rockets are sent up the artillery will at once put a barrage in front of either (a) the 2nd line of trenches on the GRANDCOURT - SERRE RIDGE, or, (b), the defensive flank from the CROSS ROADS at L.26.c.56 to JOHN COPSE.

7. The attention of Divisional Commanders is specially drawn to pages 31 and 32 of VIII Corps Scheme for Offensive: "FURTHER NOTES ON ARTILLERY LIFTS". All ranks must thoroughly
understand

- 4 -

understand the system on which the Divisional Artillery lifts are carried out. The 18-prs will lengthen their range by 100 yards every 2 minutes.

8. Special instructions regarding Gas and Smoke have been issued under VIII Corps Nos. G.1368 dated 13th, G.1383 dated 13th, and G.1414 dated 15th instants.

9. Divisional Commanders will make arrangements to ensure that the watches of all officers in their Division are carefully synchronised with Corps time. In addition to the usual daily "clear the line time signal" at 9 a.m., a special "clear the line time signal" will be sent out from Corps Headquarters Signal Office at 12 noon on the day preceding the assault.

10. (a). Corps Headquarters will remain at MARIEUX whither all reports should be sent.
(b). Corps Observation Posts have been established at Q.22.b.75.15; Q.2.b.90; and K.21.b.20.45.
Each of these Observation Posts will be manned on and after the first day of the bombardment by a Staff Officer from Corps Headquarters. If urgently required, direct communication to Corps Headquarters can be obtained through these Observation Posts.

11. Acknowledge.

H.Q. VIII Corps.
15th June, 1916.

W. Ruttures
B.G., G.S
VIII Corps.

- 5 -

Issued to Signals at _9.15 pm 15-6-16._

Copy No.	1	-	4th Division.
"	"	2	-	29th Division.
"	"	3	-	31st Division.
"	"	4	-	48th Division.
"	"	5	-	Corps Commander.
"	"	6	-	"Q"
"	"	7	-	G.O.C., R.A.
"	"	8	-	B.G., R.A., C.H.A.
"	"	9	-	C.E.
"	"	10	-	A.P.M.
"	"	11	-	D.D.M.S.
"	"	12	-	A.D.A.S.
"	"	13	-	Corps Cavalry Regiment.
"	"	14	-	Corps Cyclist Battalion.
"	"	15	-	No.13 M.M.G. Battery.
"	"	16	-	No.15 Squadron, R.F.C.
"	"	17	-	War Diary.
"	"	18	-	War Diary.
"	"	19	-	File.
"	"	20	-	Fourth Army.)
"	"	21	-	VII Corps.) For Information.
"	"	22	-	X Corps.)

War Diary Appendix 2(f)

S E C R E T.   Copy No. 24

29TH DIVISION ORDER NO. 38.

Reference Map
Sheet 57 D. 1/40000.   18th June, 1916.

1.   With reference to para. 9, Divisional Order No. 36, the 87th Brigade will take over the Right Sector of the line from the 88th Brigade on the night prior to the commencement of the bombardment, leaving two Battalions in reserve in the huts in ACHEUX WOOD, and will report completion of the relief to these Headquarters. The moves of Brigades, Pioneer Battalion (1/2nd Monmouth Regiment) and transport will take place in accordance with the attached March Table "A".

2.   With reference to para. 10 of 29th Division Order No. 36, troops at ACHEUX and LOUVENCOURT will move forward to their forming up places on Y/Z night in accordance with the attached March Table "B".

3.   The detachments of the Pioneer Battalion allotted to the three Brigades will be under the orders of the respective Brigadiers who will give them instructions regarding their exact positions in the order of march, and in the forming-up areas.

4.   Each Brigade will detail a Senior Officer to take charge of their Brigade Reserves as noted in para. 23 of Operation Order No. 36. These Reserves will be accommodated in the forming-up area if space is available, or in ENGLEBELMER (87th Brigade) and MAILLY WOOD (86th and 88th Brigades). They will move forward immediately the assaulting troops commence to leave our lines and will occupy the trenches vacated. The 87th Brigade Reserve will not advance, until the 88th Brigade has commenced to vacate our lines. They will be followed by the 88th Brigade Reserve.

                                                G. Fuller
                                                Lieut-Colonel, G.S.,
Issued at 9 A.M.   29th Division.

Copies 1 - 3 G.S.   16 O.C. Div. Train.
        4 86th Bde.   17 A.D.V.S.
        5 87th Bde.   18 A.D.M.S.
        6 88th Bde.   19 D.A.D.O.S.
      7 - 11 C.R.A.   20 1/2nd Monmouth Regt.
       12 C.R.E.   21 VIIIth Corps.) For
       13 Off. i/c Sigs.   22 36th Division.) infor-
       14 A.A.&Q.M.G.   23 4th Division.) mation.
       15 A.P.M.

March Table "A"

Unit.	From	TO	To be clear of X roads at P.18.c.9.0 by.-	Route.
2 Battns. 87th Bde.	LOUVENCOURT	ENGLEBELMER and Trenches.	6 p.m.	ACHEUX - ROTTEN ROW - ENGLEBELMER.
2 Battns. 87th Bde.	LOUVENCOURT	Huts in ACHEUX WOOD		
2 Battns. 86th Bde.	MAILLY WOOD	(Tents in ACHEUX WOOD (1 Bn.) (ACHEUX VILLAGE (½ Bn.) (Huts in ACHEUX WOOD (½ Bn.)	8 p.m.	ROTTEN ROW - ACHEUX WOOD.
1/2nd Monmouth Regt.	MAILLY WOOD	Tents in ACHEUX WOOD	8.30	-"-
80th Brigade.	TRENCHES	LOUVENCOURT	11 p.m.	ENGLEBELMER - ROTTEN ROW - ACHEUX - LOUVENCOURT.

All transport vehicles must be clear of P.17.t. l2.9 by 1 p.m. If fine they will march by ROTTEN ROW to ACHEUX, if wet by BEAUSSART - BERTRANCOURT - LOUVENCOURT - ACHEUX.

R.E. transport horses must be clear of P.18.t.2.9 before 1 p.m. or they may pass that point after 11 p.m. as most convenient.

MARCH TABLE "B"

Units in order of march.	From.	To.	Route.	To be clear of point where ROTTEN ROW leaves eastern edge of ACHEUX WOOD by:-
(2 Battns. 87th Bde. (2 Platoons 1/2nd Monmouth Regt.	Huts in ACHEUX WOOD Tents in ACHEUX WOOD.	Forming up area.	ROTTEN ROW - ENGLEBELMER	8.p.m.
(2 Battns. 86th Bde. ((2 Platoons 1/2nd Monmouth Regt.	1 Bn. tents ACHEUX WOOD. ½ Bn. ACHEUX VILLAGE. ½ Bn. huts in ACHEUX WOOD. " tents in ACHEUX WOOD.	" " "	ROTTEN ROW-MAILLY WOOD P.18.c.9.0.	8.45 p.m.
(88th Brigade. (1 Coy. 1/2nd Monmouth Regt.	LOUVENCOURT tents in ACHEUX WOOD.		ACHEUX - ROTTEN ROW-ENGLEBELMER.	10.30 p.m.
2 Companies Monmouth Regt.	tents in ACHEUX WOOD.	"	ROTTEN ROW MAILLY WOOD	10.40 p.m.

The above troops will all be marched in small parties.

War diary Copy   Appendix 2 (9)

S E C R E T.   Copy No....................

29TH DIVISION ORDER NO.39.

18th June, 1916.

BOUNDARY ON RIGHT FLANK. 1. The dividing line between the 29th and 36th Divisions will be as follows, instead of as detailed in para. 3 (b) of Division Order No. 36, paras. 14 (b) and 18 of which order should be amended accordingly. A line from the point of MARY REDAN (Q.17.a.60.30) to houses at R.7.c.20.05, thence to railway and along railway to R.8.d.30.85. The houses and the railway line are inclusive to the 36th Division.

BOMBARDMENT. 2. The bombardment will last for 5 days, which are denoted by the letters U, V, W, X and Y.

GAS. 3. A discharge of gas will take place on V/W night should the wind be favourable, or on the first subsequent night, when the weather conditions are favourable. Detailed instructions are attached, vide Appendix "A".

SMOKE. 4. A discharge of smoke along our front will take place at intervals during the preliminary bombardment, but it will not be commenced until after the gas has been discharged. Consequently "W" is the first day, on which smoke will be used. Detailed instructions are attached, vide Appendix "B".

RECONNOITRING FIRE. 5.(a) In order to enable infantry officers to reconnoitre the enemy's wire, there will be no artillery fire on the front between the hours named below :-

```
V/W   11 p.m. to 12 midnight.
W/X   10.30 p.m. to 11.30 p.m.
X/Y   12 midnight to 1 a.m.
Y/Z   11.30 p.m. to 12.30 a.m.
```

Rifle, Lewis and Machine gun fire on the enemy's front (vide paras. 11 and 24 of Division Order No. 36) will cease during the above named hours. During the remainder of these nights, the enemy's wire will be kept under fire.

(b) The officers from the leading Battalions of the 86th and 87th Brigades detailed to reconnoitre the enemy's wire at night will be present all day at the Observation Posts of the wire-cutting batteries.

(c) The C.R.A. will inform the Brigadiers of the Sectors concerned and the Artillery Group Commander will notify the Battalion Commander of the date and time appointed for the wire cutting, together with the positions of the O.P.'s to be used.

PROGRAMME OF ATTACK. 6. With reference to para. 12 of Division Order No.36, a detailed programme of the Infantry advance and artillery lifts is attached, vide Appendix "C".

(2)

ATTACK ON 2ND OBJECTIVE. 7. With reference to para. 16 (b) of Division Order No. 36, the 87th Brigade, in addition to sending strong patrols forward to cut the wire, will at 1.30 assault BEAUCOURT VILLAGE, which the will immediately consolidate after capture, forming a defensive flank facing North and East along the northern and eastern edges of the village.

STOKES MORTARS. 8. The Stokes Trench Mortars in the tunnel emplacements and in the Sunken Road will open a hurricane bombardment at a rate not exceeding 25 rounds per minute, on the targets already notified to the Officers Commanding at precisely ten minutes before the hour fixed for the assault (i.e. - 10). The mortars will cease fire at the hour of the assault (i.e. 0.0), except those mortars specially furnished with red cartridges which will continue to fire for another two minutes (i.e. from 0.0 - 0.2) using these cartridges, at the enemy's support trenches.

S.O.S. SIGNAL. 9. A supply of red rockets will be taken forward by the 88th Brigade, which will be used to give the S.O.S. Signal in the event of a counter-attack either by day or night. The signal will be 5 Red Rockets in quick succession. On these rockets being sent up the Artillery will at once put a barrage beyond either the third objective (point 09 - point 20) or the Sunken Road (R.3.c.65.25 & R.3.a.3.0) according as to which of these lines has been captured by our troops. Red rockets will also be taken forward by the 86th and 87th Brigades to be used in a similar manner, in the event of the third objective not being attained.

SIGNALS. 10. In addition to the signals to the aeroplanes, detailed in para. 34 of Division Order No. 36, signals should be made to the VIIIth Corps Kite balloon, details regarding which were issued under C.G.S.44 of 17th inst.

BOMBERS' FLAGS. 11. One man in each Grenadier squad will carry a flag one foot square, with a vertical division red one half and yellow the other half, on a 6 ft. stick. These flags will be carried and must never be planted in the ground. 64 flags will be issued to each Brigade on application to D...D.O.S.

MISCELLANEOUS. 12. With reference to para. 40 of Division Order No. 36, following amendments should be made :-

    line 20 for "5" read "2" large signal lamps.
    line 22 for "64" read "48" mauls.
    line 19, after "1600 flares" add the words "and 5 signalling shutters".

Issued at 10.0 p.m.

C.G. Fuller.
Lieut-Colonel, G.S.
29th Division.

Copies 1-3 G.S.
    4 86th Bde.
    5 87th Bde.
    6 88th Bde.
    7-11 C.R.A.
    12 C.R.E.
    13 Off i/c Sigs.
    14 A...
    15 A.P.M.
16. O.C. Div. Train.
17. A.D.V.S.
18. A.D.M.S.
19. D.A.D.O.S.
20 1/2nd Monmouth Regt.
21 VIIIth Corps.)
22 36th Division.) for
23 4th Division.) information.

APPENDIX "A".

Arrangements for Gas Discharge.

1. 400 cylinders of White Star Gas will be installed prior to the bombardment in 20 emplacements on the 29th Division front between C.10/2 and Q.10/12. Each emplacement will hold 20 cylinders.

2. The programme of discharge will be as under on V/W or subsequent nights :-

   (a) Hour fixed - 0.4 ..... 4 cylinders simultaneously per bay.

   (b) From 0.4 - 1.24 ..... 8 cylinders per bay discharged one at a time every ten minutes.

   (c) At 1.24 .... 8 cylinders per bay simultaneously.

3. The "hour fixed" will be notified shortly after 5 p.m. on the evening before the discharge, and no discharge will take place without the direct authority of the Corps.

4. Just before and during the discharge at the "hour fixed" and 1.24, Brigades holding the front line will arrange for rifle and machine gun fire to be maintained to drown the noise of the discharging gas.

5. The following code will be used in connection with the gas discharge :-

   (1) Wind is favourable for discharge of gas .... BERLIN.

   (2) Wind is not favourable for discharge of gas ... HANOVER.

   (3) Is wind favourable for discharge of gas .... COLOGNE.

   (4) Discharge gas at --------------   .... DRESDEN.

APPENDIX "B".

Arrangements for Smoke Discharge.

1. Stations for the discharge of smoke will be placed along the whole of the Division front at intervals of approximately 25 yards; two men will be allotted to each Station. There will be approximately 40 stations in each Sector. The Special Brigade R.E. will supply 30 men to assist in each Sector and Brigades will make up the balance to the total number required for the operation.

2. The men selected by Brigades for throwing the smoke bombs need not be specially skilled, as all instruction that is needful will be given by the Special Brigade.

3. The following numbers of candles and smoke bombs will be discharged on each day should the weather permit :-

```
"W" day             3000 Candles    400 P. Bombs.
"X" day morning     3000    "       400      "
"X" day evening     3000    "       400      "
"Y" day morning     3000    "       400      "
"Y" day evening     3000    "       400      "
```

4. The discharge will last for 15 minutes and will take place at the following times :-

```
"W" day          from 10.10 a.m. - 10.25 a.m.
"X" day morning  from 5.40 a.m. - 5.55 a.m., and again
"X" day evening  from 6.50 p.m. - 7.5 p.m.
"Y" day morning  from 7.10 a.m. - 7.25 a.m., and again
"Y" day evening  from 5.10 p.m. - 5.25 p.m.
```

These times have been arranged to coincide with the special Artillery bombardments which will take place each day.

5. The discharge will be carried out under the direction of the officers of the Special Brigade attached to this Division, namely 2/Lieut. STEVENS, R.E., in left Sector and 2/Lieut. PHEASEY, R.E., in the Right Sector.

6. The decision as to whether smoke is to be discharged will be sent from these Headquarters. In the event of the wind changing or becoming unfavourable after the decision has been made, the officers mentioned in para. 5 are authorised to countermand the smoke discharge. They should report their action to these Headquarters.

7. The store of Candles and P. Bombs will arrive at AUCHONVILLERS at 10 p.m. on the 20th instant, and Brigades will arrange to have parties ready so that there may be no delay in unloading the lorries. The number of men required and the detail of parties will be notified later by these Headquarters. Each lorry will carry in addition to the Candles, an equal number of Vesuvian matches.

APPENDIX "C".

PROGRAMME OF INFANTRY ADVANCE AND ARTILLERY BOMBARDMENT.

Time.	Moves of Infantry.	Trench Mortars.	Divl. Artillery.	Heavy Arty.
- 10		Stokes Mortars open hurricane bombardment.		
- 5				Lift on to line Q.12.d.45.1 - Q.12.c.7.1 - Q.12.c.1.4 - Q.11.b.1.5 - Q.5.c.85.05 - Q.5.d.4.4.
0.0	87th and 86th Bdes. assault first objective and advance at rate not exceeding 50 yards a minute.	All Trench Mortars cease fire. Stokes Mortars, if red cartridges received, lift to support line.		Lift to enemy Support Trench or minimum of 100 yards beyond front line.
0.2		Stokes Mortars cease fire.		Lift another 100 yards.
0.4				Lift another 100 yards and continue lifting at rate of 100 yards every 2 minutes until they reach the Station and Wagon Roads.
0.15				Lift on to second objective.
0.20	87th and 86th Bdes. reach Station and Wagon Roads.			Lift 150 yards East of Station and Wagon Roads, and remain there till 1.00
1.00	87th and 86th Bdes. advance from Station and Wagon Roads against second objective at rate not exceeding 50 yards a minute.			Lift 100 yards.
1.2				Lift another 100 yards and continue lifting at this rate until they reach BEAUCOURT RIDGE trenches, where they remain till 1.20.

Time.	Moves of Infantry.	Trench Mortars.	Divl. Artillery.	Heavy Arty.
1.15				Lift on to BEAUCOURT VILLAGE.
1.20	87th and 86th Bdes. assault Second Objective.			Lift on to line of wire R.7.a.5.2. to R.1.c.25.50., (where they remain until 1.35) and also on to BEAUCOURT VILLAGE.
1.25				Lift to Third Objective.
1.30	87th and 86th Bdes. send out patrols to cut line of wire R.7.a.5.2. to R.1.c.25.50. 87th Bde. assault BEAUCOURT VILLAGE.			Lift off BEAUCOURT VILLAGE.
1.35	87th and 86th Bdes. cut wire.			Lift off line of wire to East of Artillery Lane and maintain barrage until 2.30
2.30	88th Bde. advance through wire to PUISIEUX Road at rate not exceeding 50 yards a minute.			Lift to the PUISIEUX Road.
2.40	88th Brigade reach PUISIEUX Road.			Lift 100 yards and continue lifting at rate of 100 yards every 2 minutes, until they reach line of wire R.2.d.1.15. to R.2.a.6.0. and BOIS D'HOLLANDE (R.8.a.) where they remain till 3.00.
3.00				Lift on to Third Objective and remain there until 3.30.
3.10	88th Bde. advance from PUISIEUX Road towards Third Objective.			

G.S.
86th Brigade.
87th Brigade.
88th Brigade.
C.R.A.
C.R.E.
Off. i/c Signals.
A.A. & Q.M.G.
A.P.M.

O.C. Div. Train.
A.D.V.S.
A.D.M.S.
D.A.D.O.S.
1/2nd Monmouth Regiment.
VIIIth Corps.
36th Division.
4th Division.

Appendix "B" 29th Division Order No. 39 is cancelled and the attached is substituted.

C.G. Fuller

Lieut-Colonel, G.S.,
29th Division.

19th June, 1916.

Time.	Moves of Infantry.	Trench Mortars.	Divisional Artillery.	Heavy Artillery.
3.25				Lift on to BAILLESCOURT and gun positions.
3.30	??th Brigade assault Third Objective.		Lift 300 yards beyond enemy's support line and barrage until 4.30.	
4.30			Barrage ceases.	

N.B. The timing of Artillery Lifts has been altered to 100 yards every 2 minutes, instead of 50 yards a minute, as noted in para. 12 of Division Order No. 36.

SECRET.

APPENDIX "B".

Arrangements for Smoke Discharge.

1. Stations for the discharge of smoke will be placed along the whole of the Division front at intervals of approximately 25 yards; two men will be allotted to each Station. There will be approximately 40 Stations in each Sector. The Special Brigade R.E. will supply 30 men to assist in each Sector and Brigades will make up the balance to the total number required for the operation.

2. The men selected by Brigades for throwing the smoke bombs need not be specially skilled, as all instruction that is needful will be given by the Special Brigade.

3. It has been decided that there will be no discharge of smoke, until the gas has been discharged. Consequently the first day on which smoke can be discharged will be "W" day.

4. The following numbers of candles will be discharged on each day should the weather permit.

       "W" day 2400
       "X" day morning 2400
       "X" day evening 2400
       "Y" day morning 2400
       "Y" day evening 2400

                                    12000

5. On "W", "X" and "Y" days each discharge will last for 10 minutes and 3 candles will be let off every minute for every 25 yards of front.

6. The times of discharge on "W" "X" and "Y" days are as under :-
These have been arranged to synchronise with the special Artillery bombardments that "W" day 10.15 a.m. to 10.25 a.m.
will take place   "X" day 5.45 a.m. to 5.55 a.m. and again
on those days.   6.55 p.m. to 7.5 p.m.
                    "Y" day 7.15 a.m. to 7.25 a.m. and again
                             5.15 p.m. to 5.25 p.m.

7. The discharge will be carried out under the direction of the Officers of the Special Brigade attached to this Division namely 2nd Lieut. STEVENS, R.E., in the Left Sector, and 2nd Lieut. PHEASEY, R.E. in the Right Sector.

8. The decision as to whether smoke is to be discharged will be sent from these Headquarters. In the event of the wind changing or becoming unfavourable after the decision has been made, the Officers mentioned in para. 7 are authorised to countermand the smoke discharge.
   They should report their action to these Headquarters.

9. The store of candles will arrive at the road junction Q.7.c.0.8 at 10 p.m. on the night of the 23rd instant. Each lorry will carry in addition to the candles an equal number of Vesuvian matches.

10. Three lorries containing 6000 candles for the Left Sector will proceed to AUCHONVILLERS Station Q.8.c.5.0 where they will be off loaded.
Three lorries containing 6000 candles for the Right Sector will proceed to ENGLEBELMER.

11. The Officers of the Special Brigade R.E. will be responsible for providing guides to meet the lorries and subsequently to direct the carrying parties to the dumps in the front line.

12. Each Brigade in the front line will detail a carrying party of 3 Officers and 150 men. The party for the Left Sector should report to Lieut. STEVENS at AUCHONVILLERS Station Q.8.c.5.0 at 10.30 p.m. and the party for the Right Sector should report to Lieut. PHEASEY at the cross roads Q.19.c.8.99 in ENGLEBELMER at 10 p.m.
Each party will have to do two trips.

SECRET.

86th Brigade.	O.C., Div. Train.
87th Brigade.	A.D.V.S.
88th Brigade.	A.D.M.S.
C.R.A.	D.A.D.O.S.
C.R.E	1/2nd Monmouth Regt.
Off. 1/c Signals.	VIIIth Corps.
A.A. & Q.M.G.	36th Division.
A.P.M.	4th Division.

2/Lieut Stevens, Special Brigade. R.E.
2/Lieut. Pheasey.   "   "   "

With reference to revised Appendix "B", 29th Division Order No.38 issued under this office O.G.S.53 of the 19th inst.

Para 9, line 2.

For 24th inst read 23rd inst.

21st June 1916.

W. M. Armstrong Capt
/or
Lieut Colonel, G.S.
29th Division.

APPENDIX "C".

PROGRAMME OF INFANTRY ADVANCE AND ARTILLERY BOMBARDMENT.

Time.	Moves of Infantry.	Trench Mortars.	Divl. Artillery.	Heavy Artillery.
-10		Stokes Mortars open hurricane bombardment.		
-5				Lift on to new trench in Q.11.d. and Q.12.c.
0.0	87th and 86th Bdes. assault first objective and advance at rate not exceeding 50 yards a minute.	All Trench Mortars cease fire. Stokes Mortars, if red cartridges received, lift to support line.	Lift to enemy support trench or minimum of 100 yards beyond front line.	
0.2		Stokes Mortars cease fire.	Lift another 100 yards.	
0.4			Lift another 100 yards and continue lifting at rate of 100 yards every 2 minutes until they reach a line 400 yards East of STATION and WAGON ROADS, where they remain till 1.5. Howitzers remain on new trench in Q.12.c.	
0.15				Lift on to second objective.
0.20	87th and 86th Bdes. reach STATION and WAGON ROADS.		Howitzers lift off new trench.	
1.00	87th and 86th Bdes. advance from STATION and WAGON ROADS against second objective at rate not exceeding 50 yards a minute.			
1.5				Lift 100 yards and continue lifting at rate of 100 yards every 2 minutes until they reach BEAUCOURT RIDGE trenches where they remain till 1.20.

Time.	Moves of Infantry.	Trench Mortars.	Divl. Artillery.	Heavy Arty.
1.15				Lift on to BEAUCOURT VILLAGE.
1.20	87th and 86th Bdes. assault Second Objective.		Lift on to line of wire R.7.a.5.2 to R.1.c.25.50 (where they remain until 1.35) and also on to BEAUCOURT VILLAGE.	
1.25				Lift to Third Objective.
1.30	87th and 86th Bdes. send out patrols to cut line of wire R.7.a.5.2 to R.1.c.25.50. 87th Bde. assault BEAUCOURT VILLAGE.		Lift off BEAUCOURT VILLAGE.	
1.35	87th and 86th Bdes. cut wire.		Lift off line of wire to East of ARTILLERY LANE and maintain barrage until 2.30.	
2.30	88th Bde. advance through wire to PUISIEUX ROAD at rate not exceeding 50 yards a minute.		Lift to the PUISIEUX ROAD.	
2.40	88th Bde. reach PUISIEUX ROAD.		Lift to a line 300 yards East of the PUISIEUX ROAD and remain there till 3.10.	
3.10	88th Bde. advance from PUISIEUX ROAD towards Third Objective.		Lift 100 yards, and continue lifting at rate of 100 yards every 2 minutes, until they reach front trench of Third Objective, where they remain till 3.27.	
3.22				Lift on to BAILLESCOURT and ground S.W. of it.
3.27	88th Bde. assault front trench of Third Objective.		Lift to Support Trench of Third Objective.	
3.30	88th Bde. assault support line of Third Objective.		Lift to SUNKEN ROAD.	

Time.	Moves of Infantry.	Trench Mortars.	Divl. Artillery.	Heavy Artillery.
4.25				Cease fire.
4.30	88th Bde. push forward small parties to establish themselves as an outpost line in SUNKEN ROAD and at BAILLESCOURT.		Lift 400 yards East of SUNKEN ROAD.	
4.40			Cease fire.	

N.B. The timing of Artillery Lifts has been altered to 100 yards every 2 minutes, instead of 50 yards a minute, as noted in para. 12 of Division Order No. 36.

SMOKE DISCHARGE.

The following numbers of candles will be discharged on each day should the weather permit.

"W" Day 4000
"X" Day 4000
"Y" Day 4000

The duration of each discharge will be 10 minutes.

The times of discharge on "W", "X" and "Y" Days are as under :-

"W" Day .... 10.15 a.m. to 10.25 a.m.
"X" Day .... 5.45 a.m. to 5.55 a.m.
"Y" Day .... 7.15 a.m. to 7.25 a.m.

These times have been arranged to synchronise with the special Artillery bombardments that will take place on those Days.

"C" Form (Duplicate).
MESSAGES AND SIGNALS.

Service Instructions.	

Handed in at VB1 .... Office 9.20 m. Received 9.30 m.

TO: 86 Bde — Gas file

Sender's Number	Day of Month	In reply to Number	AAA
GA415	22		

Ref appendix b 29th Div order on 30 camping party for tomorrow night should report to LIEUT STEVENS at junction of Road and BROADWAY point 77C80/60 and not as therein stated aaa added 86 Bde Repd Lieut STEVENS

FROM PLACE & TIME: 29 Div 10 pm

"C" Form (Duplicate).
Army Form C. 2123.
(In books of 50's in duplicate.)

MESSAGES AND SIGNALS. No. of Message

	Charges to Pay. £ s. d.	Office Stamp.
		ARMY AXO 20.VII.16 TELEGRAPHS

Service Instructions.

Handed in at .... Office .... m. Received .... m.

TO 86 Bde

Sender's Number	Day of Month	In reply to Number	A A A
QA295	20		

Ref OGS 52 Q 9/6/16
Erase 10 and 12 Q8C 5/0
Read Q8 5/0

FROM PLACE & TIME

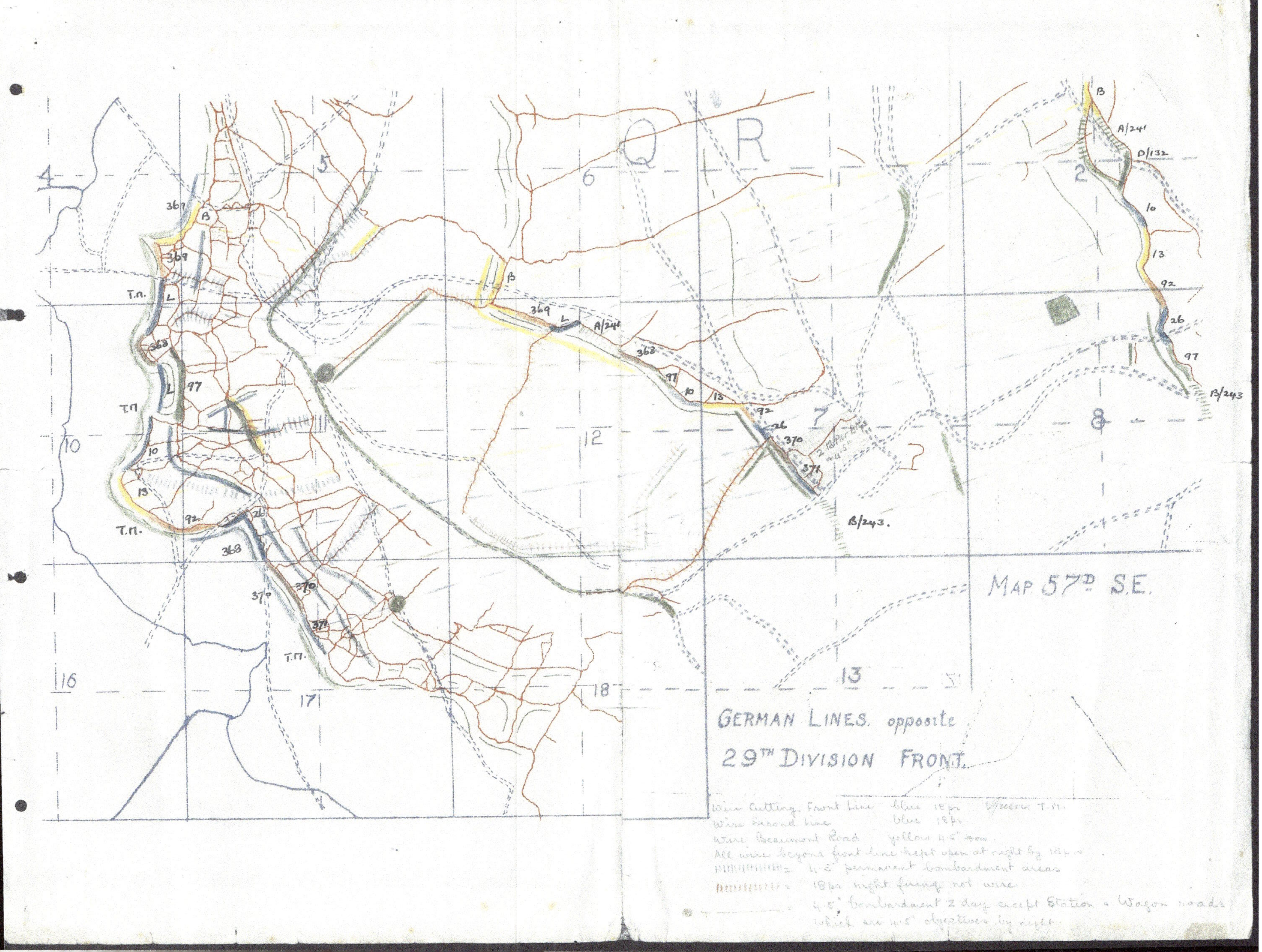
Q
R
MAP 57D S.E.
GERMAN LINES. opposite
29TH DIVISION FRONT.
Wire Cutting Front Line blue 18 pr Green T.M.
Wire Second Line blue 18 pr
Wire Beaumont Road yellow 4.5" how.
All wire beyond front line kept open at night by 18 pr's.
= 4.5" permanent bombardment areas
= 18 pr night firing not wire
= 4.5" bombardment 2 day except Station & Wagon roads which are 4.5" objectives by night.

SECRET.

86th Brigade.
87th Brigade. (for information)
88th Brigade. -"-
C.R.A. -"-
252nd Tunnelling Coy. -"-
C.R.E. -"-
1/2nd Monmouth Regt. -"-

HEADQUARTERS,
29th DIVISION.
GENERAL STAFF.
No. C.6.S.53
Date 24/6/16

1. The mine under HAWTHORN REDOUBT will be fired at 10 minutes before zero (-10) on "Z" day.

2. As soon as the falling debris from the mine has ceased, two platoons of the 86th Brigade will rush forward and seize the crater. They will be accompanied by a section of the Brigade Machine Gun Company, and a section of the Brigade Light Trench Mortar Battery.

3. In order to avoid damage from the falling debris, the number of troops in the front line opposite the HAWTHORN REDOUBT prior to the explosion will be reduced as much as possible.

4. The dug-outs in the support line opposite the HAWTHORN REDOUBT will be cleared of all troops before the time the mine is due to be fired.

5. The Divisional Artillery will arrange to lift from the HAWTHORN REDOUBT at -10 and to form a pocket there extending from point 16 via point 07 to Q.4.d.85.00.

6. After the explosion of the mine, the 252nd Tunnelling Company will break out to the surface from the tunnel leading to the crater, and the 1/2nd Monmouths will connect the place where the Tunnelling Company break out with the German trench by a communication trench.

Lieut-Colonel, G.S.
29th Division.

24.6.16.

SECRET

War Diary Copy App. 2 (h)

Copy No. 13

29TH TACTICAL EXERCISE.

OPERATION ORDER. No. 40

Reference 1/10000 Trench Map
BEAUMONT 57 D. S.E.
Edition 2 B.
and attached Training Area Map.

21st June, 1916.

1. The Division will attack the enemy's position on June 22nd and will be formed up in our trenches under instructions issued already, by 9.50 a.m.

2. At this hour the mine under ~~..........~~ will be exploded and an intense bombardment by all the Divisional Artillery and Trench Mortars will be carried on until 10 a.m. During this period the mine crater will be rushed by one Company 2nd Royal Fusiliers to which will be attached Stokes Mortars and Machine Guns.

3. The troops detailed to assault the first system will move out of the trenches and be formed up parallel to and about 100 yards from the enemy's first line ready to assault at 10 a.m. at which hour Guns and Mortars will lift to the second line. The forming up position for our leading troops will have been previously marked by lines of white tape (not continuous) as a guide.

4. During the assault each Company will be in line of platoon columns, two leading sections extended and two rear sections remaining in section columns as long as possible.

5. On approaching the front line bombing parties detailed to 'mop up' that line will double forward and jump into the trench followed by men carrying trench bridges. The assaulting troops will cross over the front line trenches in silence and move steadily against the support line where the mopping up parties for this line will act in a similar manner as those detailed in the front line. The leading troops will also pass over the support line and capture the reserve line without a check.

6. Battalion Headquarters will move with Battalion reserves and establish Headquarters in convenient places in or near the enemy's front line.

7. As soon as the first system of trenches has been captured strong points will be prepared with the utmost rapidity and the enemy's trenches connecting these points will be reversed ready to beat off any counter attack.

8. Prisoners will be collected and sent back to our front line during lulls of enemy Artillery and will there be handed over to the defenders who are left in the line.

9. As soon as Battalions detailed to attack the first system are clear of our front line, Battalions detailed for the second objective will move across "No Man's Land" passing through leading Battalions and reorganising for attack on the STATION ROAD.

- 2 -

10.   The advance from the STATION ROAD will commence at 11 a.m., but the assault will not be made until 11.20 a.m. at which hour the Artillery will lift from BEAUCOURT RIDGE. The line of march of the Battalions will depend on the success attained by the first attack. Should the Station buildings not have been captured by the 36th Division on our right it will not be possible to approach that place. In this case a battery of Machine Guns must be directed to keep down the enemy's fire from there.

11.   On gaining the BEAUCOURT RIDGE this line will be consolidated and patrols sent forward as far as our Artillery barrage will allow.

12.   At 11.35 a.m. the Artillery will lift on the line of wire 500 yards West of ARTILLERY LANE and wire cutting parties must reach the wire by this hour and cut lanes through to enable the 88th Brigade to advance against the third line.

13.   At 11.30 a.m. the Artillery will lift from BEAUCOURT VILLAGE which will be attacked at this hour by the right Battalion 87th Brigade.

14.   Special parties must be told off to guard the flanks of each Battalion and in the case of the 87th Brigade one Company must be prepared to establish a defensive flank if necessary.

15.   Brigades will arrange for a reserve to be collected during the advance on BEAUCOURT RIDGE and when the 88th Brigade advances through them each Brigade will send forward a reserve of four Companies under one Command to the PUISIEUX ROAD to be at the disposal of the 88th Brigade if required.

Lieut-Colonel, G.S.,
29th Division.

June, 1916.

Issued at 7.45 a.m.

Copies No. 1 - 2   G.S.
         3 - 5   86th Brigade.
         6 - 10   87th Brigade.
         11   C.R.A.
         12   VIIIth Corps.

TIME TABLE.

29th Divisional Exercise June 22nd.

Time.	Moves of Infantry.	Divisional Artillery.
10 a.m.	The 87th and the 86th Brigades assault first objective and advance at rate not exceeding 50 yards a minute.	Lift to enemy's support trench or minimum of 100 yards beyond front line.
10.2 a.m.		Lift another 100 yards.
10.4 a.m.		Lift another 100 yards and continue lifting at rate of 100 yards every 2 minutes until they reach the STATION and WAGON Roads.
10.20 a.m.	87th and 86th Brigades reach STATION and WAGON Roads.	Lift 150 yards East of Station and Wagon Roads and remain there till 11.0 a.m.
11.0 a.m.	87th and 86th Brigades advance from STATION and WAGON Roads against second objective at rate not exceeding 50 yards a minute.	
11.2 a.m.		Lift another 100 yards and continue lifting at this rate until they reach BEAUCOURT RIDGE trenches where they remain till 11.20 a.m.
11.20 a.m.	87th and 86th Brigades assault second objective. 87th Brigade capture BEAUCOURT Chateau.	Lift on to line of wire R.7.a.5.2. to R.1.c.25.50 where they remain till 11.35 a.m. and also on to BEAUCOURT VILLAGE.
11.30 a.m.	87th and 86th Brigades send out patrols to cut wire of R.7.a.5.2 to R.1.c.25.50 87th Brigade assault BEAUCOURT VILLAGE.	Lift off BEAUCOURT VILLAGE.
11.35 a.m.	87th and 86th Brigades cut wire.	Lift off line of wire to East of ARTILLERY LANE and maintain barrage until 12.30 p.m.

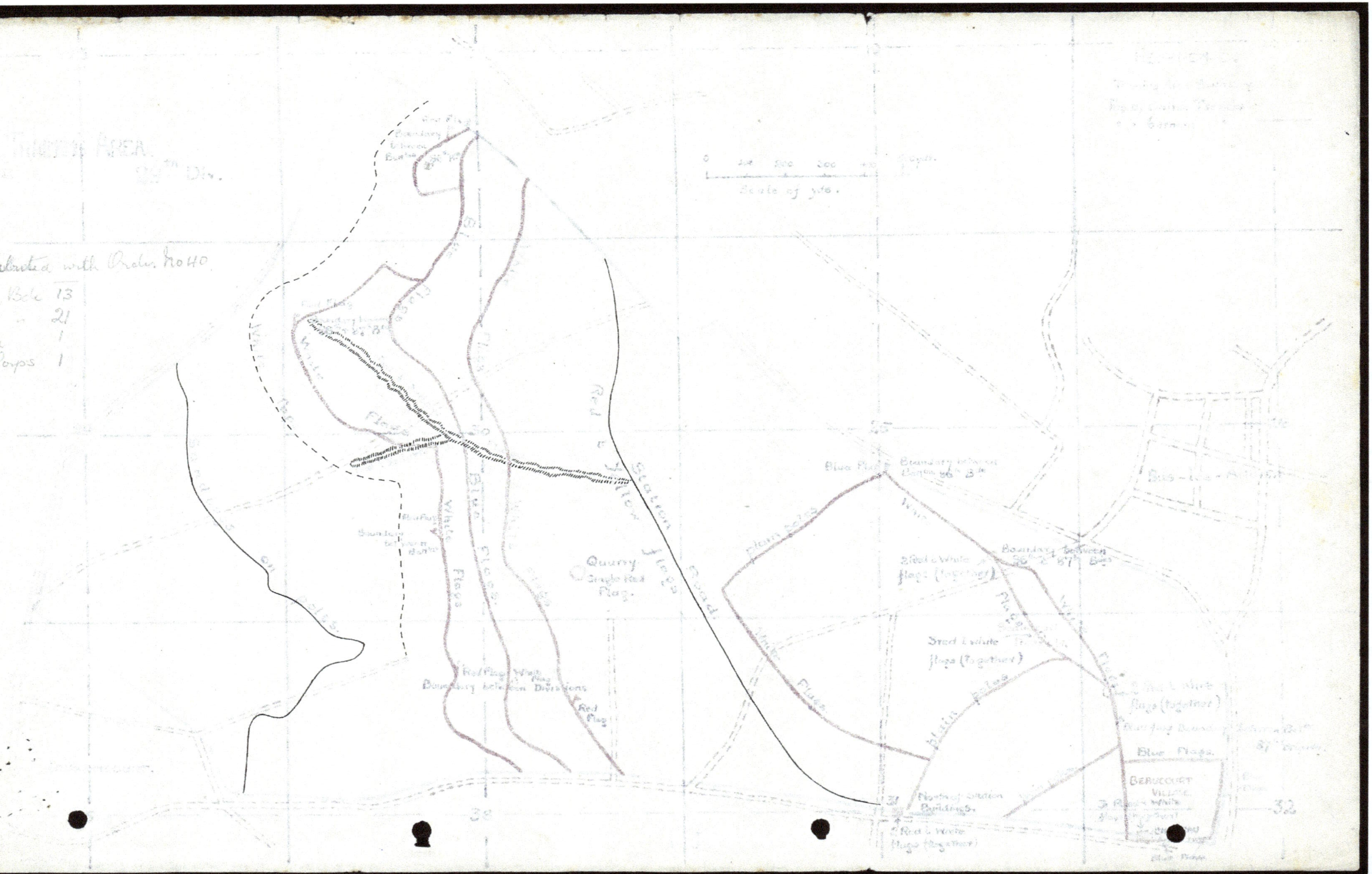

Headquarters, VIII Corps.
B.E.F. FRANCE.
June 21st, 1916.

My dear de Lisle,

I think your tactical exercise for the 87th and 86th Brigades is excellent, and I only wish that I could come and see it carried out. Unfortunately I have to be at a Conference at Army Headquarters tomorrow morning.

There are five points that strike me when reading the scheme, which call for comment.

(1) You should not put a whole Company into the crater. One Platoon, with machine guns, would be ample to hold it. To put more than two Platoons, with machine guns and Stokes Mortars, into the crater, would be to give the German Artillery a most magnificent target, and would in no way add to the strength of the defence, in fact it would weaken the defence by jamming the men up too tight.

(2) The new trench just beyond the Station road in X.12.c & d, must, I think, be taken in the first advance forward to the Station Road, unless you have some good reason to the contrary.

(3) As both you and Lucas seem to entertain very considerable doubts as to the determination and ability of the 36th Division to take Beaucourt Station, it is advisable that you should tell the Flank Battalion Commander to have half a Company from his Reserve ready to send forward to take the Station Buildings, under cover of heavy machine gun fire, if he finds that the 36th Division are slow in getting forward to take on this Station.

(4) I do not much like putting in orders that bit about sheering off from the Station Buildings. It might be told to the Battalion Commander separately but should not, I think, appear in orders. It would be very apt to lead to the right battalion sheering off if even the slightest rifle fire was to come from its right flank.

(5) I do not myself attach great importance to the danger of fire from the zig-zag communication trench on the south bank of the river against the right flank of your advance. I have been enquiring as to the trees in this valley, and find that they are very thick, and would prevent all view across the valley from any trench in the low ground, even if the wind were to prevent our putting on the smoke barrage I have arranged for.

Yours ever
Aylmer Hunter Weston

VIII CORPS
G.1583.

~~4th Division.~~
29th Division.
~~31st Division.~~
~~48th Division.~~

    The Corps Commander wishes me to forward the attached scheme for a tactical exercise, which is being carried out to-morrow by the 29th Division.

    He considers it to be an excellent example of the kind of training which he wishes carried out by all Divisions.

21/6/16.

                              B.G., G.S.,
                                  VIII Corps.

Appendix 2.(i)

SECRET.   Copy No............

29TH DIVISION ORDER NO. 41.

28th June, 1916.

1.   With reference to C.G.S. 53/3 of 27th instant, Zero will be postponed 48 hours.
   29th June will be called "Y.1" Day.
   30th June will be called "Y.2" Day.
   1st July will be "Z" Day.

2.   No alteration in the present dispositions of the Division will be made.

3. (a)   The Artillery programme will be carried out as for to-day, special attention being paid to the following :-

   (i)   The prevention of all hostile movements and work both by day and night; the night bombardments must therefore be fully maintained.

   (ii)   The completion of wirecutting.

   (iii) Counter-battery work, advantage being taken of all favourable weather to destroy hostile batteries.

   (b)   Concentrated bombardments will take place as follows :-

       "Y.1" Day .... 4-00 p.m. to 5-20 p.m.
       "Y.2" Day .... 8-00 a.m. to 9-20 a.m.

4.   With reference to para. 5 (a) of 29th Division Order No. 39, a reconnaissance of wire on the enemy's front will be carried out between the hours named below :-

       "Y" Night .... 11.30 a.m. to 12.30 p.m.
       "Y.1" Night .... 10.30 a.m. to 11.30 a.m.
       "Y.2" Night .... 11.00 a.m. to 12 midnight.

5.   The programme for "Z" Day will be as originally arranged.

6.   Watches will be synchronised by the General Staff at 9 a.m. and 7 p.m. on "Y.1" and "Y.2" Days.

7.   Please acknowledge.

                                        C.G. Fuller.
                                        Lieut-Colonel, G.S.,
                                        29th Division.

Issued at ..10.30 p.m.

         Copies 1 - 3 General Staff.
                    4   86th Brigade.
                    5   87th Brigade.
                    6   88th Brigade.
                    7   C.R.A.
                    8   C.R.E.
                    9   Officer i/c Signals.
                   10   A.A. & Q.M.G.
                   11   O.C. 252nd Tunnelling Coy.
                   12   O.C. 1/2nd Monmouth Regiment.

S E C R E T.   Copy No............

            CORRIGENDUM.

    With reference to 29th Division Order No. 41
dated 28th June, 1916, para. 4 after "below" read :-

    "Y" Night .... 11.30 p.m. to 12.30 a.m.
    "Y.1" Night .... 10.30 p.m. to 11.30 p.m.
    "Y.2" Night .... 11.00 p.m. to 12 midnight.

                                        [signature]
                                    for Lieut-Colonel, G.S.,
    29th June, 1916.   29th Division.

            Copies 1 - 3   General Staff.
                     4   86th Brigade.
                     5   87th Brigade.
                     6   88th Brigade.
                     7   C.R.A.
                     8   C.R.E.
                     9   Officer i/c Signals.
                    10   A.A. & Q.M.G.
                    11   O.C. 252nd Tunnelling Coy.
                    12   O.C. 1/2nd Monmouth Regiment.

SECRET.
R.A. VIII Corps
R.A. 595/49.

B.G.R.A., 29th Division.

1. Owing to definite instructions from Fourth Army, the following alterations are notified in the various instructions issued under R.A. 595/13, dated 14/6/16:-

   (a) Appendix (1) para: 5 (a) (b) (c) and (d) Programme of preliminary Bombardment.

   (i) "Y" day will be solely a repetition of "U" Day, but the amount of 4.5" How: ammunition to be expended on these days should be limited to 60 rounds per howitzer.

   (ii) "W" and the remaining days will rest as already arranged.

   (b) Supplementary Orders on special points.

   (i) Para: 3, Special Bombardments.

   The Special Bombardments ordered at the following times will not take place:-

   "X" day - from 6-30 pm to 7.pm.
   "Y" day - from 4.pm to 5.30 pm.

   NOTE.

   In these Bombardments, as far as 18prs: are concerned, the objective of H.E. shell will be, generally speaking, the most forward communication trenches, which are not being dealt with at other times by other natures of guns.

2. TRENCH MORTAR REGISTRATIONS.

   If it is thought necessary to carry out registration of heavy and medium Trench Mortars, this should not be done before 4.pm on "Y" day.

3. BARRAGES.

   (a) The barrage east of the final objective will now be kept up (with bursts of fire) from 3.30. to 4.30.; at this latter hour, a lift will be made to a line beyond any advanced posts thrown out on Divisional fronts; fire will cease at 4.40.

   (b) Special attention is to be paid to the observing Officer being able to locate the direction of the S.O.S. rockets, and to communicate this to their batteries.
   As soon as the point from which the rockets were sent up, is located, the barrage will only be maintained for 1000 yards on either side of this point.

   (c) The position of the S.O.S. barrage east of the final objective is to be well clear of any advanced posts thrown out on Divisional fronts.

22/6/16.
Sgd. R.H.MAINWRG, Major R.A.
Staff Officer R.A., VIIIth Corps

NOTE ATTACHED TO R.A. 595/49, dated 22/6/16.

1. It would seem highly desirable to have at least 450 rounds available for 18pr: guns at beginning of "Z" day.
2. Every endeavour should be made to limit the amount of 18pr: Shrapnel fired before active operations begin.
Whenever possible

Secret

Right Group, 29th Divl Artillery
26th June 1916.

In conjunction with Operation Order No 11 by Brigadier General D.E.Cayley C.M.G., Commanding 88th Brigade, circulated herewith, the 17th Brigade R.F.A. will fire as follows on night W/X.

From 2400 to 0015.
13th Battery from Q.10.d.55.70 to point 7347
92nd Battery from Point 7347 to Q.11.c.30.40
26th Battery from Q.11.c.30.40 to Q.11.c.60.30
Rate of fire - Battery Fire.20 seconds Percussion Shrap.

From 2400 to 0015.
460th Battery on Y RAVINE - Battery Fire.20 seconds.

From 0015 to 0025.
13th Battery from Point 89 to Q.10.b.80.50.
Time Shrapnel - Battery Fire 20 Seconds.
92nd Battery from Q.10.d.95.90 to Q.11.c.60.50
Percussion Shrapnel - Battery Fire.20 Seconds.
26th Battery from Point 54 to Q.11.c.60.00
Time Shrapnel - Battery Fire.20 Seconds.

From 0025 to 0030.
13th, 92nd and 26th Batteries concentrate on Line from point 7347 to Q.11.c.10.30.
Percussion Shrapnel - Battery Fire.15 Seconds.

At 0030. 13th and 26th Batteries same as objective for 0015.
Time Shrapnel - Battery Fire.15 Seconds.
92nd Battery - Fire on trench Q.11.c.10.95 to Q.11.c.60.75.
H.E. - Battery Fire.15 Seconds.

At 0105. 13th, 92nd and 26th Batteries shell from Point 89 to Point 60 in their own zones.
Battery Fire - 20 Seconds. Percussion Shrapnel.

At 0115. Cease firing unless otherwise ordered.
The 92nd Battery will detail an officer to be with the Brigade Major 88th Brigade for the raid.
This officer is responsible for communicating with Right Group during Raid.

Sd W.P.Monkhouse Lt Col.
Comdy Right Group

(This adds up to 795 Shrapnel and H.E. and 45 rounds for 460th Battery.)
~~Please telephone if approved.~~
25-6-16.   (Sd) W.P.M.

29th Division (GS)
For information

C.H.Clark Major RA for Comdr
29th DIVISIONAL ARTILLERY

25/6/16

App 2 (j) Copy No 2.

Secret

OPERATION ORDER NO. 1 by Brigadier General Malcolm Peake
C.M.G.,
Commanding 29th Divisional Artillery.

Ref: Trench Map BEAUMONT 57 D. S.E. 1 & 2 (parts of)1,10,000.

FRANCE   57 D. S.E.   1/20,000

1. On Z day at 0000 the 29th Division will attack the enemy's trenches from Q 17 b 15.40 to Q 5 c 20.80.
The 36th Division Xth Corps will attack on the right and the 4th Division VIIIth Corps on the left of the 29th Division.

2. The 29th Divisional Artillery will support the attack according to instructions previously issued.
The boundary on our right will be the line - point of MARY REDAN (Q 17 a 60.30) to houses at R 7 c 20.05 (inclusive to 36th Division) thence S.E. to the River at R 13 a 40.80, thence along the River Ancre to the point where it crosses the railway at R8c 45.60 thence along the Railway.
The boundary on the left will be the line Q5c 20.80 points 59 - 88 - 66 - 53 - 75 - 69 - 06 - R2b 80.99.
The 1st Objective will be the German front line system of trenches Q17b 15.40 to Q5c 20.80 including the village of BEAUMONT HAMEL.
The 2nd Objective will be the BEAUCOURT ROAD system of trenches, R 7 c 90.40 to Q 6 d 40.00.
The final objective will be the system of trenches from the River through points 67 - 38 to point 20 and support line through points 09 to point 20.

b   Posts will be thrown out on to the Sunken Road from BAILLESCOURT to R 2 a 80.99 and the final barrage will be formed about 400 yards east of this road.

3.   LIFTS OF THE 29TH DIVISIONAL ARTILLERY 'Z' DAY.
The fire of 18 pdr batteries will be turned at -20 on to the German front line.
0000.   LIFT from 1st line to support line or minimum of 100^X.
0002.   LIFT from Support line 100^X.lift.
Succeeding lifts of 100^X every two minutes until a line 400^X East of the Station & Wagon Roads is reached,(about 0020) where fire will be maintained at a rate of 3 rds per gun per minute, until 0030 when the rate will be reduced to 60 rds per battery per hour until the next lift.
At 0020 "B" R.H.A. will engage trench from Q5d 35.40 to point 66 and trench from point 41 to point 53 with one section.
At 0030 one section will lift from Q5d 35.40 - point 66 to point 41 - point 53 and both sections will engage that trench until 0045.
At 0045 both sections will concentrate on point 41 and no fire will be directed North of the BEAUCOURT ROAD.
0105.   Lift from the line 400^X East of the Station & Wagon Roads at 100^X per 2 minutes until reaching the BEAUCOURT RIDGE trenches, where fire will be maintained until 0120.
         Batteries firing North of point 50:-
0120.   LIFT to the line of wire R 7 a 50.20 to R 1 c 25.55.

0135.   LIFT to the ground East of ARTILLERY LANE.
0230.   LIFT to the PUISIEUX ROAD.
         Batteries firing South of point 50:-
0120.   LIFT 200^X.
0130.   LIFT 100^X every two minutes to the line R8c 15.20 - R7b 80.20 - R7b 20.50.
0240.   368, 369, 370, 371 & 'L' batteries cease firing and remain in observation.

0240. Remainder:-
LIFT to the line at R 8 d 45.95 through work at R8b 30.50 and wire R 2 d 10.15 - R 2 a 45.35 one battery per Group remaining on the line 300^X E. of the PUISIEUX ROAD.

0300. Fire to return to the line 300^X E. of the PUISIEUX ROAD.

0310 LIFT 100^X every two minutes to the 3rd Objective the PUISIEUX trench R 8 b 90.10 - R 2 b 00.60 through points 67 & 38.
0327. LIFT to the support line R9a 30.20 - point 09 - point 20 R2b 20.80.
0330. LIFT to SUNKEN ROAD R9b 10.40 - R2b 85.98.
0430. LIFT to line 400^X East of SUNKEN ROAD.
0440. Cease fire.

NOTE. During the lift from the Station Road to the Beaucourt Road the fire of the 370th Battery will be directed along the Railway Alley and that of the 368th Battery along the Station Alley.

~~4.5" Howitzers:-~~
~~4.5" Hows. batteries will engage objectives allotted to them in previous instructions.~~
~~D/132 will cease fire at 0325.~~

ACTION OF 4.5" HOWS. "Z" DAY.

460th Battery.

From -65 to zero ~~0000~~ 0020 The new trench in Q12c & d.
0020 - 0100 wire and trench R7c 95.45 to R7e 50.95. 0100 to 0125. Point 48 to
0125 ~~0000~~. To advance according to instructions issued separately. Point 02.

D/147:-

From -65 to zero ~~0000~~ -0000 2 Hows. Q11c 60.85 - Q11a 35.30
 -"- " " Q17b 55.65 -
0000-0015 " " BEAUMONT ALLEY Q11b 00.45.
0000-0020 " " RAILWAY ALLEY R7c 30.70 - R7c 50.95.
0020-0130 Battery BEAUCOURT SUR ANCRE
0130-0240 R7d 95.50 - R7d 95.90
0240 CEASE FIRE.

D/132.

From -65 to zero ~~0000~~ -0000 2 Hows. Point 50 to Point 23.
 -"- " " Q12d 00.05 - Q12d 80.90.
0000 ~~0015~~-0100 Battery BEAUMONT ALLEY from STATION ROAD to Q11b 70.98.
0015-0130. Point 02 to point 23. After 0020 fire must not be within 400 yards of the STATION ROAD. PUISIEUX ROAD R1d 45.00 to R1d 60.90. 2 Hows.
*0215-0230
0235-0300 2 Hows. R 8 b 30.55 to BOIS d' Hollande.
0310 Battery R 8 b 80.20 - R 8 b 55.90.
0325 LIFT 200^X.
0327 " 300^X.
0330 Cease Firing.

(5). The two batteries of the 48th D.A. under Lieut-Colonel F.C.B. WEST, detailed to advance will follow the instructions already issued.

'Y' R.H.A. & 460th How. Battery will remove their guns from the line at 0100 'Z' day, one hour after the commencement of the Infantry advance.
Their position of readiness will be the hollow in front of 'Y' R.H.A,-'s present position and each will detail an orderly to wait at Left Group H.Q. for orders.

Their advance will be through Auchonvillers and along the New Beaumont Road. They will come into action at some suitable position near the STATION ROAD.
4 Bridges will have been dumped near or laid over the near German trenches close to the road into Beaumont Hamel. Teams and wagons will return via Old Beaumont Road-Vitermont-Englebelmer-Rotten Row to wagon lines in MAILLY WOOD.
The four batteries above mentioned will support the attack on the final objective and will form a barrage to the East after the final objective has been captured. Ammunition from the 1st Line wagons should be dumped at the battery position when in action & empty wagon should return & refill & then rejoin battery. The procedure for supp

Page -3-.

The procedure for supply of ammunition and rations is dealt with in this Office No. 1632, dated 17th June 1916.

A.Clark
Major R.A.,
25th June 1916.   Brigade Major 29th Divisional Artillery.

Copy No 1 - Dand
     2   29° Div. ✓
     3   VIII Corps Ra
     4   Right Group
     5   Left Group.

SECRET

Headquarters,
29th Division.

No. BM.164/111

The following selected points have been told off to batteries of the Heavy Artillery for tomorrow morning:-

From 5 am to 6.5 am batteries will shell the 3rd and 4th lines of their bombardment areas; at -55 the ~~two~~ specially selected points will be engaged:-

SELECTED POINTS.

~~From 5.a.m. until -00.10 the Howitzers as detailed below will steadily shell the following points~~ - (see para. in letter.)

Point 03)		
Point 54)	77 Siege Battery.	(4 - 8")
Point 07)		
Q.5.c.28 72)		
Q.5.c.55 82)	79 Siege Battery.	(4 - 9.2")
Q.10.b.70 74)		
Q.10.d.95 85)		
Q.10.d.70 90)	23 Siege Battery.	(4 - 6")
Q.10.d.67 47)		
Point 00)	81 Siege Battery.	(4 - 6")
Q.17.a.88 76)		

30/6/16

Captain R.A., B.M.
for B.G.Comdg. VIIIth Corps H.A.

PROGRAMME OF HEAVY ARTILLERY.

Till 5	On front line system	2	15"
		4	9.2"
		4	8"
		4	6"
		1	6" on BEAUMONT ALLEY
		1	6" on Trench 41 - 53
		1	6" on Trench Q.5.d.12.35 to Q.5.d.75.65
		1	6" on House Q.11.a.75.25
At -5	Lift of line just East of Station and Wagon Roads.	4	9.2"
		4	8"
		4	6"
		2	15" on BEAUCOURT REDOUBT
		2	6" on Trench 41 - 98
		2	6" on BEAUMONT ALLEY
At 0.15	Lift to BEAUCOURT REDOUBT	2	15"
		4	9.2"
		4	8"
		6	6" on BEAUCOURT LINE North of REDOUBT
		2	6" on BEAUMONT ALLEY East end.
At 1.15	Lift to BEAUCOURT VILLAGE	2	15"
		4	9.2"
		4	8"
		8	6"
At 1.25	Lift to Third Objective GRANDCOURT RIDGE	4	9.2"
		4	8"
		8	6"
		1	15" at BAILLESCOURT
		1	15" North West exit of GRANDCOURT.
At 3.25	FIRE CEASES		

N.B. 15" fires one round in six minutes.

9.2" " " " " one minute.

8"   " " " " one minute and a half.

6"   " " " " one minute.

SECRET

Action of 29th D.A. Z day before Zero.

Rates:- 18 pdrs.
-65 to -10 1 rd per gun per minute H.E.
-10 to zero 3 rds per gun per minute H.E.

4.5" Hows.   6.5 am
5 am. to -65   60 rds per battery per hour.
-65 to -30   1 rd per gun per minute.
-30 to 00   2 rds per gun per minute.
(During this last 30 minutes the rate is doubled to allow fire on front line to be maintained at same intensity but from only two Hows. per battery while 2 Hows. per battery engage support line).

Objectives.
18 pdrs. open at -65 on front line and engage objectives according to instructions already issued.
4.5" Hows:-   (2 Hows 460th How battery C.B. work)
5 am. to -65 on objectives laid down in previous instructions for -65.
From -65 to -65. This period will be made use of to register if required.
-65 onwards as below:-

460th Battery:- (2 Hows. on C.B. work.)
-65 to 0000 2 Hows. Y Ravine point 89 to point 85.
0000 to 0008 2 Hows. Q11d 40.55 to Q11 central.
At 0008 Adhere to original programme.

D/147:-
-65 to -30 Front line point 03 to point 54
           (N.B. Heavy Hows. are on points 03, Q17a 90.80, and 54).
-30 to 0000   2 Hows. on front line as above.
               2 Hows. on support line in rear through points
               Q17b 15.70   Q17a 99.90   Q11c 72.30
0000 to 0008   Q18a 25.90 to Q17b 95.95
               At 0008 Adhere to original programme.

D/132:-
-65 to -30 2 Hows front line Q11c 50.50 to Q10d 70.50
            (N.B. Heavy How. on each of these points)
            2 Hows front line Q10d 70.90 to Q10b 85.50
            (N.B. Heavy How. on Q10d 70.90)
-30 to 0000 2 Hows on front line as above and 2 Hows. on support line
            in rear through points Q11c 60.55, 17, 01, and 16.
At 0000 Adhere to original programme.

HEADQUARTERS,
29th DIVISIONAL
ARTILLERY.
No. B.M/3001
Date. 30/6/16.

CH Carl
Major R.A.,
Brigade Major 29th Divl. Artillery.

29 Div G

SECRET

Headquarters 29th Divl. Artillery,
28th June 1916.

O.C., Right ⎫ Groups
      Left ⎭

In order to avoid a pause in the fire at 0000, at - 3 "Z" day, in each field battery, one section will lift on to the support line where it will remain until 0002.

The other section will lift on to the support line at 0000 and at 0002 both sections will lift according to instructions issued.

All trench mortars cease fire at 0000.

If a re-bombardment of any point is ordered, such bombardment will last for 30 minutes the last five minutes of which will be intense.

HEADQUARTERS,
29th DIVISIONAL
ARTILLERY.
No. B.M/2207
Date 29-6-16

C.N.Clark
Major R.A.,
Brigade Major,
29th Divisional Artillery.

29th Divn G.S.

For information

C.N.Clark Major RA for
Comdg 29th DIVISIONAL ARTILLERY.

28/6/16

SECRET

29th Div GS

"Y" Battery will not pull its guns out of the line until 0130 on Z day, i.e. 1½ hours after 0000.

His objectives are as follows:-

- 65 to 0010   Station Alley all its length. H.E.
                 Rate of fire 2 rounds per battery per minute.

0010 to 0100   Top part of Station Alley from Q.12.a.50.35
                 to wire in front of BEAUMONT Road.

0100 to 0130   H.E. on trench R.7 a.50.25 to R.7.a.30.30
                 specially on house in that line at R.7.a.55.25

Please report if O.C."Y" Battery anticipates any difficulty over this. The house and trench is invisible and he will have to shoot by the map.

For information

HEADQUARTERS,
29th DIVISIONAL
ARTILLERY.
No. B.M. 2702
Date. 27th June 1916.

Major R.A.
Brigade Major 29th Divisional Artillery

SECRET.   G.O.C., R.A. VIII Corps
                                           R.A.395/77.

B.G., R.A., 29th Division

1.   Owing to the amount of counter battery work that
is required by heavy howitzers and the number of new
trenches located, the 4.5" How: batteries will be required
tomorrow afternoon, from 3.0 pm onwards, to fire at first and
second line trenches in each area.

2.   The 4.5" Hows: will also probably have to fire on
three points from -65 to 00, on "Z" Day.

3.   During special bombardments on "Y" day the fire of
all natures of artillery will be INTENSE from 7.10 am to
7.20.am.

                                Signed R.H.HAINING, Major, R.A.
                                Staff Officer R.A., VIIIth Corps.
27/4/16

Right Group.
Left Group.

     Please see above and arrange fire of Hows: in your
area.

     Further instructions re Hows: "Z" day will be issued
if necessary.

     Please note para. 3 above.

                                C H Clark.
H.Q.29th D.A.
BM/2735.   Major R.A.
27/6/16.   Brigade Major 29th Div. Arty.

29 G.S.
             For information
                           C H Clark, Major RA for
                                              Comdg
27.6.16
                                    29th DIVISIONAL ARTILLERY.

SECRET   Copy No 53

Instructions for 29th Divisional Artillery

With reference to VIIIth Corps Artillery instructions attached.

1.   Reference paras 1 (a & c).
Points, trenches and areas have been detailed on sketch previously issued.

2.   Reference para 3.
Area for 4.5" Hows. detailed on Sketch XXX Phase III. One How. D/132 for which no task has been allotted will fire on the new trench in Q.12 c & d.

Group Commanders will detail the trenches selected on their own front for 18 pdrs and report the same to D.A.H.Q. as soon as possible. The Right Group Commander will select the new trench in Q.12.c & d as one point.

3.   Reference para 4.
(a) To ensure detachments having a proportion of rest during the night it is suggested that batteries employ sections in relief of each other for night firing.

(b) The times of firing will be:-

2100 - 2200	at	00	05	12	25	31	35	47	51	57
2200 - 2300	at	01	05	16	19	30	33	40	49	59
2300 - 2400	at	07	09	14	18	25	30	40	47	53
0000 - 0100	at	00	03	07	16	22	29	39	46	54
0100 - 0200		same	as	2100 - 2200						
0200 - 0300		same	as	2200 - 2300						
0300 - 0400		same	as	2300 - 2400						
0400 - 0500		same	as	0000 - 0100						

(c) At each time of firing, each gun of the section firing will fire one round, a total of 18 rounds per battery per hour, or 36 rounds per gun per night.

(d) Fire should be on the areas detailed on sketch for Phase II and should be so distributed as best to prevent parties repairing wire or moving along trenches.

(e) In addition, each gun of the section firing will fire two rounds on special points selected by Group Commanders - fire to be concentrated by Group Commanders at their discretion at the following times:-

2120 - 2210 - 2335 - 0034 - 0140 - 0245 - 0304 - 0411

This will make an additional 32 rounds per battery for the night.

(f) Attention is directed to para 8 of VIIIth Corps Artillery Instructions which prohibits firing by night on the enemy's front line at the following times:-

On V/W night 2300 - 2400
On W/X night 2230 - 2330
On X/Y night 0000 - 0100
On Y/Z night 2330 - 0030

No firing will take place during these periods on the enemy's front line.

4. Reference

(2)

4.   Reference para 5.
Only 18 pdr Batteries cutting wire will fire at the following times; all other guns will cease firing at these times:-

    V day   1745 - 1830
    W day   1400 - 1445
    X day   1500 - 1545
    Y day   1300 - 1345

5.   Reference para 7.
4.5" How. batteries will fire lachrymatory shell on BEAUMONT HAMEL, which will be divided into three sectors.

460th Bty will engage the Northern Sector Q5c 50.80 - Q5c 50.40
D/147 -:-   -:-   Centre Sector   Q5c.50.40 - Q5c 60.00
D/152 -:-   -:-   Southern Sector Q5c.60.00 - Q11.a.90.40

6.   Reference para 11.
When lifting off the front line at 0000 fire will be brought on to the support line, but in no case will the lift be less than 100 yards. Successive lifts will be made every two minutes i.e. at 0002 0004 0006 etc., 100 yards at each lift until the 0020 (Station and Wagon Roads) line is reached, where fire will be sustained until 0020 - when it will be lifted 150 yards beyond the station and Wagon Road excepting in the case of the batteries on the area Q.12.c. and d. in which the new fire trench has been made; these batteries will lift on to this trench where the trench is 150 yards or over from the road.

(Bursts of fire) The 368th Battery will, at 0020, switch its fire on to the South end of STATION ALLEY at least 150 yards from the Station road and lift its fire up that alley when the advance commences at 0100 until reaching the BEAUCOURT ROAD when its fire will be directed on to its allotted zone in the line. Similarly the 370th Battery will engage RAILWAY ALLEY and the new trench lying North of and parallel to it in Q.12.c. and d. with two guns on each.

When the infantry advance at 0100 from the Wagon and Station Roads batteries will lift 100 yards every two minutes until their fire reaches the BEAUCOURT ROAD position where it will remain until 0120 when it will be lifted, in one lift, to the wire R.7.a.50.20 to R.1.c.25.20 and the line in prolongation of that wire on either flank as far south as the River and as far north as the point R.1.c.25.55 fire being more concentrated on the wire R.7.a.50.20 to R.1.c.25.20 and rather less on the right flank.
Bursts of fire will be maintained on this line until 0135 when fire will be lifted in one lift to the ground just east of Artillery Lane, and bursts of fire will be kept on this area until 0230. At 0230 fire will be lifted, 100 yards every two minutes, to the PUISIEUX ROAD, and bursts maintained in that area from the river to R.1.d.60.90 until 0240 when the 368th, 369th, 370th, 371st and "L" Batteries will cease firing, and these batteries will remain in observation ready to place a barrage on this line if required.
The remaining batteries viz - "B", 10th, 97th, 92nd, 13th, 26th, A/241 and B/243 will lift from the PUISIEUX ROAD at 0240, 100 yards every two minutes, to the line of wire R.2.d.10.15 - R.2.c.60.100 with flanks extending to the river on the right and R.2.a.45.35 on the left, and fire will be maintained on this line from 0240 to 0300. At 0300 fire will be lifted to the double line of wire and trench R.8.b.50.70 to R.2.b.30.00 with flanks extending to the river on the right and R.2.a.100.60 on the left.
Fire will be maintained on this line until 0330 when it will be raised 300 yards to form a barrage behind this final objective with bursts of fire at intervals from the river on the right to
R.2.b.50.100

(3)

R2b 50.100 on the left. Unless orders are given to the contrary fire will cease at 0430.
~~* insert :- from 0240 to 0300. At 0300 fire will be lifted to the double line.~~

7. The two batteries 48th D.A. in Phase 1V will not open fire until 0020 when they will engage their objectives allotted on the sketch.
   These batteries will be under the Right Group Commander.

8. Rates of fire.
   For bombardments:-
   <u>Intense</u> 18 pdrs. 3 rds per gun per minute. 4.5" Hows. 2 rds per minute per gun.
   <u>Ordinary</u> 18 pdrs. 1½ rds per gun per minute. 4.5' Hows. 1 rd per minute per gun.
   <u>Supporting attacks.</u> 18 pdrs.
   During lifts of 100 yards - 3 rds per gun per minute.
   For bursts of fire, rounds of gun fire at a rate of 60 rounds per hour per battery.

9. The battery of the Right Group on the right flank will ensure that no fire is brought to bear within 300 yards of the buildings at the station in Q.18.b. or the two houses at R.7.c.20.00 as the Xth Corps will occupy these buildings.
   No fire should be directed on to the Railway Road, further west than the point R.7.c.80.40.

10. 4.5" Howitzers Rate 1 rd per minute per gun.
    In the support of the attack on Z day the 4.5" Hows. will be employed as follows :-

    460th Battery in readiness to advance.

    D/147th :-
    2 Hows. on trench Q.11.c.60.85 to Q.11.a.35.30 from -65 to zero till 0000.
    0000) BEAUMONT ALLEY at Q.11.b.00.45
    0015)
    2 Hows. on point Q.17.b.55.65 from -65 to zero till 0000.
    0000) RAILWAY ALLEY from R.7.c.30.70 to R.7.c.50.95
    0020)
    Whole battery
    0020) BEAUCOURT SUR ANCRE R.7.c.95.50 to R.7.c.55.95
    0115) searching village with bursts of fire.

    0115) Searching village from 250 yards N.E. of the trench
    0230) R.7.c.95.50 - R.7.c.55.95 to the rear with bursts of fire.
    (During this period there must be no fire within 200 yards of the trench named above).

    0230 Lift to a line 400 yards behind the trench R.7.c.95.50 - R.7.c.55.95 and fire three rounds gun fire and then lift to the point R.8.a.20.00 and the sunken road R.8.a.00.05 to R.8.a.50.25 and fire two rounds gun fire and then cease fire.

    D/132nd.
    Will fire lachrymatory shell from -40 to zero till 0000 on the batteries in the vicinity of R.7.b. searching this ground.
    0000 to 0115 one howitzer will continue with lachrymatory shell and at 0115 will cease firing lachrymatory shell.

    0000 Three howitzers will cease firing lachrymatory shell and will search with H.E. with bursts of fire up BEAUMONT ALLEY.

10 contd.

from its junction with STATION ROAD to Q11b 70.100 reaching that point at 0100 and then ceasing fire.
0215 the whole battery woll bombard with H.E. the PUISIEUX ROAD from R1d 45.00 to R1d 60.90 with bursts of fire until 0230.
0235 two howitzers will bombard the trench R8b 30.55 and two will bombard the BOIS d' HOLLANDE in R8a until 0300.
0310 the battery will bombard the trench R8b 80.20 to R8b 55.90
0325 lift 200 yards
0330 lift 300 yards.
0340 Cease fire.

11.

Each 18 pdr battery will detail a subaltern officer who will be attached, by the orders of the Group Commander, to a Battalion Commander.

A Field Officer (Lt Col T.M. Archdale D.S.O.) will be attached to the Left Infantry Brigade (86th) Lt Col J.R. COLVILLE D.S.O. to the Right Infantry Brigade (87th) and Lt Col H.W.R. Marriott Smith D.S.O. to the 88th Infantry Brigade as liaison officers.

An advanced Group will be formed later under Lt Col W.P. Monkhouse C.M.G. M.V.O., consisting of - 13th, 26th- 92nd, 10th, A/241 and B/243 from the Right Group and "B", 97th and D132nd from the Left Group.

In this case the 370th & 371st batteries will then come under the Left Group Commander 'Y' R.H.A. and the 460th Battery will be formed later into a moveable Group under Major J.H. Gibbon D.S.O.

12. COMMUNICATIONS.

At each Group exchange there will be stationed an orderly officer. All telephone wagons will be kept full with wire, ready for any eventuality. As far as possible batteries will ensure a line being laid to front line trench, so that communication can be established with the officers advancing with battalions.
All officers advancing as liaison officers should be accompanied by 1 N.C.O., 2 telephonists, 2 telephones, 2 small reels of D.1 cable, 2 periscopes, Visual signalling apparatus.

13. RATIONS & SUPPLIES.

Brigade Commanders must ensure that all O.Ps and Battery emplacements are properly supplied with water and reserve rations.
All telephonists must be supplied with box respirators.

14. STEEL HELMETS.

All ranks of batteries going forward must be provided with steel helemets. They must be indented for if not in possession.

15. **Batteries going forward.**

The two batteries of the 48th Division under Lt Col West detailed to advance to NO MANS LAND will spend the night of Y/Z in the hollow P.17.a.60.20 to P.11.c.30.00. At 0000 they will advance via ROTTEN ROW and road through Wood from P.18.c.80.00 to Q.7.d.50.40 into the hollow ground near Q.7.d.80.00 where they will wait for an order to advance.

They will detail an orderly to at Left Group Headquarters ready to receive any order that may come. They will take with them 4 trench bridges which they will unload near the German trenches alongside the New BEAUMONT HAMEL Road.

They will take Firing Battery and 1st line wagons with them, and will as soon as possible dump in some convenient place the ammunition of one wagon per gun which can at once return to the hollow near MAILLY MAILLET, where arrangements should be made with Divisional Ammunition Column to replenish their empty wagons.

16. "Y" R.H.A. and 460th Battery under Major Gibbon will at 0000 on Z morning move out their guns and proceed to a rendezvous to be appointed later. They will proceed, as soon as the two 48th batteries have got their guns into action, to cross the German lines and come into action in or near the Wagon & Station Roads. No detailed instructions can be given, but their object is to support the Infantry in the advance to the final objective.

Each of these batteries should take 2 trench bridges with them.

Should 2 guns 460th Battery be required for counter battery work they will remain behind and join the two forward guns later.

HEADQUARTERS,
29th DIVISIONAL
ARTILLERY.
No. B.M/1701
Date 18/6/16

CH Clark
Major R.A.,
Brigade Major 29th Dvl. Artillery.

Copy No 1 Band
2 VIII Corps RA
3 29 Div GS
4 HQ R Group
5 " L "
6 }
22 } Bdes & Batteries RA
23 Lt Col West
24 " Colville
25 86 Infy
26 87 "
27 88 "
28 36 Bde
29 4 Bde
30
31
32

29th Divisional Artillery - INSTRUCTIONS.

Appendix 'A'.

With reference to sketch issued.

Phase 1. 18 pdr. batteries:- wire cutting 0600 "U" day until -65 to 0000 "Z" day unless Group Commanders consider that the wire has been sufficiently cut, in which case special points may then be bombarded.

Phase 1. 4.5" Hows. Wire cutting BEAUCOURT ROAD and bombardment RAILWAY ALLEY and STATION ALLEY on "U" day 0500 "U" day - 2100 "U" day.

Phase 11. 18 pdr batteries:- Night fire on areas detailed.

Night U/V till night Y/Z both inclusive.

4.5" Hows. batteries fire on areas detailed.

Night U/V till night Y/Z both inclusive.

Phase 111. 18 pdrs & 4.5" Hows. on areas detailed, 0500 - 2100 -

"V", "W", "X" & "Y" days.

Phase 1V. 18 pdrs & 4.5" Hows. Support attack as detailed.

Phase V. Final barrage - special orders for 4.5" Hows.

Secret   Copy No 8

SUPPLEMENTARY INSTRUCTIONS - 29th Divisional Artillery.

Ref: paras. 1 & 2 D/132 will also include trench from Pt. 66
to Q5c 90.00 in their permanent bombardment area.

2. ~~Ref~~: para 5 is cancelled. No lachrymatory shell will be fired by the
29th Divl. Artillery.
    (the left flank battery)

3. ref: para 6. At 0020 Z day B R.H.A.(") will lift its fire ^to the trench from point Q5d 35 40 to point 66 and at 0030 lift^ to trench from point 53 to point 41 until 0045.
At 0045 this battery will concentrate its fire on
point 41 and no fire will be directed North of
the BEAUCOURT ROAD.
The 87th Brigade by 0120 will have taken the
fire trench in front of BEAUCOURT SUR ANCRE and
presumably the Chateau to the East of it.
  In consequence the lifts of the batteries firing
on the trench from point 50 to the road at R7c 90.45 and
from that point to the River will at 0120 place their
barrage fire 200 yards beyond that line and at 0130 when
the 87th Brigade attack BEAUCOURT SUR ANCRE they will lift
100 yards a 2 minutes to the line R7b 20.50 - R7b 80.20 -
R8c 15.20.
  They will fire bursts of fire on this line until
0240 when their original instructions will be adhered to.
  From -65 till 0000 A/241 and B/243 batteries of the
48th D.A. will bombard the line from point 50 to the River
along the trench and wire on the S.W. face of BEAUCOURT SUR ANCRE. At 0000 these batteries will cease firing and will
follow their original instructions.
The lift at 0230 will be one lift to the PUISIEUX ROAD &
not as stated previously.
  The final barrage at 0330 will be maintained only
long enough to ascertain that the barrage is correct & fire
will then cease. H.E. will be fired. Should a barrage be required
by the Infantry it will be called for by the "S.O.S." signal
of 5 red rockets in quick succession, whereupon the barrage
will at once be opened & maintained ~~in quick succession~~ for
15 minutes when it will cease and another "S.O.S." signal will
be sent if a further barrage is required whereupon it will
be opened for another 15 minutes.
Barrage "A" will be the barrage 200 yards behind the
BEAUCOURT ROAD LINE.   (PUISIEUX ROAD)
Barrage 'B' will be the barrage ~~500~~ 200 yards behind the ^line. Barrage C
300ᵗ behind line through points 09 20 06.

4 Ref. para 7 These batteries will now fire from -65 to 0000 as
detailed in para 3 of these supplementary instructions.

5 Ref. para 10:- D/147th Battery:-
At 0020 D/147 will turn their fire on to BEAUCOURT SUR ANCRE
and search the village with bursts of fire, 60 rounds per
battery per hour, until 0130 when it will lift in one lift to
the line R7d 95.50 - R7d 95.90 where it will maintain bursts
of fire until 0240, when it will cease fire.
The sub paras. of para. 10 relating to the fire of D/147 from
0020 to 0230 in the original instructions are cancelled.
D/132 Battery:- Cancel sub paras. relating to lachrymatory
shell & substitute:-
From -65 to 0000:- rate of fire one round per minute per gun.
Two Howitzers on road from Point 50 to Point 23 in Q7c and a.
Two Hows. on trench Q12d 00.05 to Q12d 80.90. 0015 to 0100 the
whole battery bursts of fire at 60 rds per hour per battery on
BEAUMONT ALLEY from its junction with STATION ROAD to Q11b 70.98
After 0020 fire must not be within 250 yards of STATION ROAD.
0215 Continue according to original instructions.

6. All trench mortars will cease firing at 0000 Z day.
7. All watches must be most carefully synchronized twice daily
from 'T' day inclusive, the time being obtained from D.A.H.Q.

HEADQUARTERS,
29th DIVISIONAL
ARTILLERY.

No. B. M/1721
Date. 20.6.16

29ᵗʰ Divn. Rs.   C H Clark Major RA

Copy No 8

Further Instructions for 29th Divisional Artillery.

All advances of the infantry in bodies will be preceded by a curtain of Artillery fire and in consequence, after the lift from the PUISIEUX ROAD at 0840 to the wire, fire will, at 0800, be brought back to a line 300 yards in advance of the PUISIEUX ROAD and at 0810 will be lifted 100 yards every two minutes up to the final objective.

During the fire at the wire one battery may be kept on a barrage with bursts of fire 300 yards in advance of the PUISIEUX ROAD in order to ensure that the infantry will not believe that the barrage has been permanently lifted to the wire.

At 0830 fire will be raised on to the final barrage which will be along the Sunken Road R.9.a.70.00 to R.2.b.80.99 and not as previously stated.

The fire curtain up to PUISIEUX ROAD will be by lifts as in original instructions.

With reference to supplementary instructions 29th Divl Artillery:-

The portion of para 3 referring to "B" R.H.A. will be cancelled and the following substituted:-

"B.R.H.A. 0082) One Sect on trench from point Q5.d.35 40
    0030) to point 66.
       One Sect on trench from point 41 to point 53.

    0030) Both Sections on trench from
    0045) point 41 to point 53.

    0045 Both sections concentrate on Point 41 and
      no fire will be directed North of the
      BEAUCOURT ROAD."

                Major R.A.
             Brigade Major 29th Divisional Artillery.,

29th Divn. G.S.

SECRET

Right Group.
Left Group.

Ref. my BM/2109 21-6-16

For "barrage to final objective" please read
"barrage beyond final objective"

McCall Major RA

BRIGADE-MAJOR 29th DIVL. ARTILLERY.

[Stamp: HEADQUARTERS, 29th DIVISIONAL ARTILLERY. No. B.M/2202 Date 22/6/16]

29th Division GS

For information

McCall Major RA

BRIGADE-MAJOR 29th DIVL. ARTILLERY.

Amendment made
26/6/16.

S E C R E T.

29th Divisional Artillery

Right Group.
Left Group.

The Barrage ~~on~~ beyond the final objective will now be kept up with bursts of fire until 4.30, when a lift of 300 yards beyond it will be made and fire will cease at 4.40.

The S.O.S. Call of 5 red rockets will be used if required after this, according to previous instructions.

CH Clark

H.Q. 29th Div.Arty.   Major R.A.
21st June 1916   Brigade Major R.A. 29th Division.

29th Division (GS.)

Copy for information

CH Clark Major RA

BRIGADE-MAJOR 29th DIVL. ARTILLERY.

HEADQUARTERS,
29th DIVISIONAL
ARTILLERY.
No. B.M./2107
Date 21-6-16

Right Group.

With reference to previous instructions -

From - 65 to 0000 "Z" day,

460th Battery will engage the new trench in Q.12.c and Q.12.d. with a steady rate of fire. Total expenditure this period - 200 rounds.

> HEADQUARTERS,
> 29th DIVISIONAL
> ARTILLERY.
> No. B.M./2205
> Date................

22-6-16.

C N Clark
Major R.A.
Brigade Major 29th Divisional Arty.,

29th Division G.S.
For information

C N Clark Major R.A.
BRIGADE-MAJOR 29th DIVL. ARTILLERY.

SECRET

Headquarters 29th Divisional Artillery,
23rd June 1916.

Officer commanding, Right ⎤
                    Left ⎦ Group

In the attack on the Station and Wagon Roads the Artillery Barrage will not halt in the road but will, continue lifting at 100' per 2' until 400 yards beyond it, where they will keep up their barrage until 0030.

At 0030 the artillery will continue their fire on this Barrage Line by bursts of fire at a rate of 60 rounds per battery per hour until the time of the lift from that line according to the original programme which will then be adhered to.

460⁺ Battery on Z day will continue on New trench Q.12 c & d from -65 to 0020 instead of till 0030.

HEADQUARTERS,
29th DIVISIONAL
ARTILLERY.
No. B.M/2302
Date 23/6/16

CH Clark
Major R.A.,
Brigade Major 29th Divisional Artillery.

29th Division GS.
Copy for information

CH Clark, Major RA for Comdg
29th DIVISIONAL ARTILLERY.

APPENDIX 3.

Comprises the following :-

Arrangements re installation of gas cylinders and discharge of gas during preliminary bombardment.
Correspondence relating thereto attached.
Arrangements re issue of "P" Bombs and Smoke Candles for Smoke discharges during preliminary bombardment.
Correspondence relating thereto attached.

SECRET

VIII Corps.
G.1365.

Gas!

App 3

4th Division.
29th   "
31st   "
48th   "
Capt. Slater.

The Corps Commander directs that all gas cylinders shall be installed in their emplacements by the early morning of the 20th.

Please inform the Corps as early as possible how many you will be able to instal.

                      (Signed)   W. RUTHVEN.

H.Q. VIII Corps.   B.G., G.S.
13th June 1916.   VIII Corps.

URGENT

HEADQUARTERS,
29th DIVISION.
GENERAL STAFF.
No. C.S.53
Date 13.6.16.

C.R.E.   (2).

Forwarded for your information and necessary action.

Please report to this office at the earliest possible moment the information required in para. marked "A".

                                       Lieut. Colonel, G.S.
13th June 1916.   29th Division.

S E C R E T.

Headquarters,
    VIIIth Corps.

No. C.G.S. 53
Date 15/6/16

      In reply to your G.1365, it is anticipated that 400 cylinders in 20 bays will be installed on the front between Q.10/2 and Q.10/12 by the evening of the 19th instant.

15th June, 1916.

Major General,
Commanding 29th Division.

SECRET

VIII Corps.
G. 1365

4th Division.
29th Division.
51st Division.
48th Division.
Capt. SLATER.

The Corps Commander directs that all gas cylinders shall be installed in their emplacements by the early morning of the 20th.

A

Please inform the Corps as early as possible how many you will be able to instal.

H.Q. VIII Corps.
13th June 1916.

B.G., G.S.
VIII Corps.

C.R.E. (2).

**HEADQUARTERS,
29th DIVISION.
GENERAL STAFF.**
No. C Gs.53
Date 13.6.16.

URGENT

Forwarded for your information and necessary action.

Please report to this office at the earliest possible moment the information required in para. marked "A".

Lieut.Colonel, G.S.
29th Division.

13th June 1916.

3

29 Div G.

At least 20 bays will be completed. It is hoped that every bay asked for by the local Special RE officers will be completed in the specified time. I do not know how many cylinders go to each bay.

15/6/16

SECRET

VIII Corps.
G. 1396.

4th Division.
29th Division.
31st Division.
48th Division.
Capt. Slater.
Major Monier-Williams.
Q.

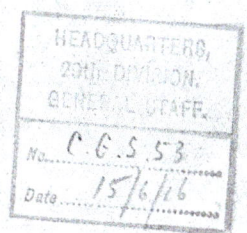

1. The following allotments of Gas cylinders are made to Divisions :-

	Cylinders.	Emplacements.
29th Division.	400	20
4th Division.	180	9
31st Division.	360	18
48th Division.	200	10

2. These cylinders will be sent by lorries from PUCHEVILLERS to such places as Divisions may arrange on the nights of the 17/18th and 18/19th instants. They will be installed in the line under Divisional arrangements.

3. Lorries are allotted to Divisions as under :-

(a). Night of 17/18th
29th Division.   5 lorries carrying 200 cylinders.
4th Division.   3 lorries carrying 90 cylinders.
31st Division.   4 lorries carrying 160 cylinders.

(b). Night of 18/19th.
29th Division.   5 lorries carrying 200 cylinders.
4th Division.   3 lorries carrying 90 cylinders.
31st Division.   5 lorries carrying 200 cylinders.
48th Division.   5 lorries carrying 200 cylinders.

4. The lorries will be loaded at PUCHEVILLERS under arrangements to be made by Major Monier-Williams.

5. Divisions will arrange to send guides to PUCHEVILLERS to guide their lorries to the dumping places they select.

6. The lorries will leave PUCHEVILLERS at 7 p.m. on both days, except the lorries of the 48th Division which will start at 6 p.m. on the evening of the 18th.

7. Divisions will report to Corps H.Q. each night when the cylinders have been installed.

B.G. G.S
VIII Corps.

14-6-16

S E C R E T.   C.G.S.53
                                 15/6/16.

O.C. Special Brigade VIII Corps.
Lieut. Stevens. Special Brigade.
Lieut. Pheasey.   "   "

       In continuation of my C.G.S. 53 15/6/16. Cylinders will be sent on 5 lorries each carrying 40 cylinders from PUCHEVILLERS on nights 17/18th and 18/19th leaving at 7.p.m.

2.   Lorries will be loaded under arrangements to be made by Major Monier-Williams.

3.   Two guides will be sent each night by Lieut. Stevens to PUCHEVILLERS to conduct the lorries to AUCHONVILLERS Station Q.8.b.4/0. There the lorries will halt and will be taken forward singly and off loaded at points stated in C.G.S. 53 dated 15/6/16.

4.   A report will be sent to this office each night by wire as soon as the cylinders have been installed.

                               W. M. Armstrong Cate

                                  for. Lieut. Colonel, G.S.

15th June, 1916.   29th Division.

SECRET.   C.G.S. 53
          15/6/16.

86th Brigade.
87th   "
88th   "
C.R.E.
O.C., Special Brigade, VIIIth Corps.
Special Brigade Officer attd. 86th Brigade.
   "   "   "   "   88th   "

----

1. 400 gas cylinders are to be installed in the front line trenches between Q.10.1. and Q.10.15. on night June 17/18 and 18/19.
100 per night will be installed in the right sector Q.10.1 to Q.10.7.
100   "   "   "   "   "   "   left   "   Q.10.7 to Q.10.15.

2.(a) The 86th Brigade will detail 5 carrying parties of 1 officer and 80 other ranks to report to Lieut. STEVENS at junction of Old Beaumont Road and western end of 2nd Avenue Q.29.b.10.20 on each of the above nights. The first party to report at 10 p.m. the remainder at half hour intervals.
Cylinders will be carried to the front line up 2nd Avenue. Parties returning down Broadway.

(b) The 88th Brigade will detail 5 carrying parties of 1 officer and 80 other ranks to report to Lieut. PHEASEY at the junction of Tipperary Avenue and AUCHONVILLERS - ENGLEBELMER Road Q.9.c.5.3. on each of the above nights. The first party will report at 10 p.m. the remainder at half hour intervals.
Cylinders will be carried to the front line via Tipperary Avenue - Thurles Dump - 1st Avenue. Parties returning via Praed Street - Fethard Street - Uxbridge Road and Withington Avenue.

3. Twenty cylinders each weighing 150 lbs are to be installed in each bay. Four men will be detailed to each cylinder. Two men carrying and two men as relief.

4. Each cylinder is provided with a pair of slings and a pole. On completion of work poles will be taken to the Brigade Dump by the carrying parties and stored there for future use.

5. Carrying parties and officers in charge should as far as possible be the same every night.

6. Guides will be told off by the Special Brigade R.E. to each ~~pair of selected~~ Selected bays and must know the routes to them.

7. All other traffic in the trenches up which the cylinders are being carried, will stop while this work is in progress. Wounded men even will not be moved but will be attended to on the spot and medical arrangements made accordingly.

8. (in the vicinity when work is in progress) All men in the trenches or handling stores will carry P.H. Helmets rolled up on their heads ready for instant use. Vermoral Sprayers will be ready for spraying the trenches in the event of any damage being done to the cylinders by either shrapnel or bullets.

9. On no account is smoking to be allowed.

10. It is important that silence should be maintained.

11. No.1 Battalion R.E. will detail one sapper to attend to each group of 6 selected bays as soon as the cylinders are in place. Troops in the trenches will assist them in any repairs to bays that may be required.

                                                G. Fuller
                                        Lieut-Colonel, G.S.
15th June, 1916.   29th Division.

VIII Corps
G.
14/54

~~4th Division.~~
29th Division.
31st Division.
48th Division.
Captain Slater.
VII Corps.
X Corps.

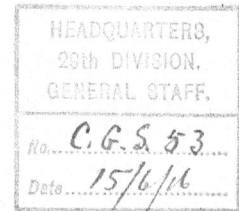
HEADQUARTERS,
29th DIVISION.
GENERAL STAFF.
No. C.G.S. 53
Date 15/6/16

1. A discharge of gas from the VIII Corps front will take place on the "V"/"W" night should the wind be favourable, or on the first subsequent night when the weather conditions are favourable.

2. The cylinders are being installed in bays of 20 cylinders each.

3. The programme of discharge will be as under :-

    (a) Zero to 0-4 ..... 4 cylinders simultaneously per bay.

    (b) From 0-4 to 1-24.... 8 cylinders per bay, discharged one at a time every ten minutes.

    (c) At 1-24 ..... 8 cylinders per bay simultaneously.

4. The hour of zero will be notified shortly after 5 p.m. on the evening before the discharge.

5. Gas will not be discharged except by orders of the Corps.

6. Just before and during the concentrated discharges at zero and 1-24, rifle and machine gun fire will be maintained in order to drown the noise of the discharging gas.

7. A code for use in connection with the discharge of gas is attached.

B.G., G.S.,
VIII Corps.

15/6/16.

S E C R E T.

COPY OF MINUTES 1 and 2.

> HEADQUARTERS,
> 29th DIVISION.
> GENERAL STAFF.
> No. C.6553
> Date 18/6/16

3.

Lieut. STEVENS, R.E., Special Brigade.
  "   PHEASEY,   "   "   "

Forwarded for your information.

W. M. Armstrong Capt.

for Lieut-Colonel, G.S.,
                29th Division.

18/6/16.

86th Brigade.
87th   "
88th   "
C.R.E.
O.C., Special Brigade, VIIIth Corps.
Special Brigade Officer attd. 86th Brigade.
   "   "   "   "   88th   "

C.G.S 53
16/6/16

      Reference our C.G.S. 53 dated 15/6/16.

Para. 8, line 1, should read :-

  "All men in the trenches in the vicinity where

  "work is in progress or handling stores will carry"

                  not
                   or
  "All men in the trenches/handling stores will carry."

                  W. M. Armstrong Capt.
                                Lieut-Colonel, G.S.
                    /or.
16th June, 1916.   29th Division.

CODE

1. Wind is favourable for discharge of Gas ... BERLIN

2. Wind is not favourable for discharge of Gas.. HANOVER

3. Is wind favourable for discharge of Gas ... COLOGNE

4. Discharge Gas at............ ... DRESDEN

SECRET

SECRET

VIII Corps.
G.1476

4th Division.
29th Division.
31st Division.
48th Division.
Capt. SLATER.
Major MONIER-WILLIAMS
"Q".

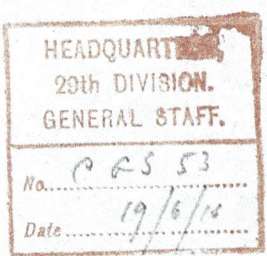

----

1.   Reference my G.1396 of the 14th instant, the dates should be altered as follows :-

for "17/18th and 18/19th" read "21/22nd and 22/23rd" respectively, and for "18th" in para 6 read "22nd".

2.   Acknowledge.

H.Q. VIII Corps.
18th June 1916.

W. Ruthven
B.G., G.S.
VIII Corps.

86th Brigade.
87th Brigade.
88th Brigade.
C.R.E.
Capt. Slater (attached VIIIth Corps).
Lieut Stevens. Special Brigade R.E.
Lieut Pheasey.   "   "   "

        Reference my C.G.S.53 of the 15th inst, the dated should be altered as follows:-

        For 17/18th and 18/19th please read 21/22nd and 22/23rd respectively.

W. M. Armstrong Capt.

for Lieut Colonel, G.S.

19th June 1916.   29th Division.

SECRET

<u>VIII Corps.</u>
G. 1683

4th Division.
29th Division.
~~31st Division.~~
48th Division.
VII Corps.   )
X   Corps.   ) For information.
Capt. SLATER.)

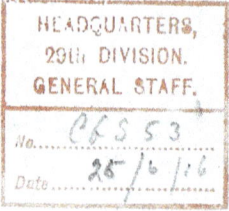

1. With reference to this office telegram G.641, the Corps Commander directs that gas shall be let off to-night or during the day to-morrow. Each Division will decide when the gas will be discharged, and will issue the necessary orders without any further reference to Corps Headquarters. Neighbouring Divisions should be informed direct.

2. The first favourable opportunity should be taken to let off the gas.

3. The whole of the cylinders will be discharged as rapidly as possible. The previous programme issued in this office No. G. 1414 is cancelled.

4. Should it not be possible to discharge the gas before 8-0pm to-morrow (26th) further orders will be issued from this Headquarters.

5. Divisions will report the hour fixed for the discharge, as soon as it is known.

6. Acknowledge.

H.Q., VIII Corps.
25th June 1916.

B.G., G.S.
VIII Corps.

SECRET.

Lieut. STEVENS, Special Brigade, R.E.
Lieut. PHEASEY, Special Brigade, R.E.

The Corps Commander directs that gas shall be let off to-night or during the day to-morrow, if the wind is favourable and that the decision for the discharge of gas will rest with these Headquarters.

2. In pursuance with the above, a telegram has been despatched to you, instructing you to let off gas at 12 midnight to-night, if the wind is favourable.

3. The whole of the cylinders will be discharged as rapidly as possible, and the programme laid down in Appendix "A" of Division Order No. 39, regarding rate of discharge from 00 - 1.24 will not be adhered to.

4. If it is not possible to discharge the gas to-night, you will keep these Headquarters informed of the condition of the wind, with a view of the gas being discharged during the day to-morrow.

25.6.16.

Lieut-Colonel, G.S.,
29th Division.

Note :- The 4th Division let off gas last night and found that all the pipes leaked. Please take all possible precautions.

(sd) D.O.

S E C R E T   4th Division GGG 766/14

2nd Lieut. Jones, R.E.
~~10th)~~
~~11th) Infantry Brigade~~
~~12th)~~
~~4th Division "Q".~~
~~A.D.M.S.~~
~~4th Divisional Engineers~~
~~4th Divisional Artillery~~
~~O.C. 4th Signal Coy.~~
29- Division (for information)

HEADQUARTERS,
29th DIVISION.
GENERAL STAFF.
No. CGS.53
Date 25/6/16

1.   The remaining gas will be discharged as soon as the wind is favourable between 10 p.m. tonight and 8 p.m. tomorrow.

   The hour of discharge will be the earliest possible, that is the gas should be discharged at 10 p.m. tonight if wind is favourable.

   State of wind to be reported by 2nd Lieut. Jones, through 10th Brigade, at intervals of one hour from 8.30 p.m. tonight onwards.

2.   The whole of the cylinders will be discharged as rapidly as possible.

25/6/16.

                                for Lieut.-Colonel,
                                General Staff, 4th Division.
                                for Maj. Gen. Cmdg 4th Div.

SECRET.

All Units.

C.G.S 35/3

The following report on Gas operations by the 4th Division on 24th - 25th instant is forwarded for information. All units supplied with the Tower Helmet must be warned to pay special attention to the points referred to.

"I have just returned from seeing 2/Lieut. Jones, attached 4th Division, who reports that at 10 p.m. on 24th instant, the wind being West and 3 m.p.h. he decided to discharge his cylinders. The discharge proceeded successfully until 11 p.m. when the wind failed completely and the gas hung over our trenches. It was at this point that the casualties from gas began among our men, 2/Lieut. Jones attributing them to three causes :-

(1) The gas came through the goggles of the Tower Helmet. He thinks that this was possibly partly the fault of his own men not fitting them on properly.

(2) During rapid movement the rubber tubes of the helmet got caught on projections in the trench, or on the men's own equipment, and pulled the mouthpiece out of the mouth.

(3) The mouthpiece is too short for some types of face, and it is difficult in such cases to keep it in the mouth. This is a point I have already reported on while we were still in training.

One officer who was wearing a P.H. Helmet experienced no inconvenience whatever."

C.G. Fuller.

Lieut-Colonel, G.S.,
29th Division.

26.6.16.

SECRET

VIII CORPS
G. 1693.

4th Division.
29th Division.
31st Division.
48th Division.
Captain Slater.
B.G.R.A., C.H.A.
G.O.C., R.A.
VII CORPS.
X CORPS.

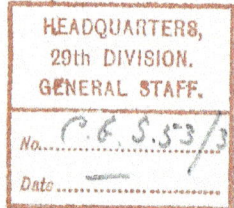
HEADQUARTERS,
29th DIVISION.
GENERAL STAFF.
No. C.6.S.53/3
Date

    If it is found impossible to let the Gas off to-night, it should, if the wind is favourable, be let off at the same time as the Smoke to-morrow morning,

    i.e., 10-15 a.m. to 10-25 a.m.

Should the wind not be favourable at this time, it may be let off at any time during the day, up to 8-0 p.m., but if it is let off during the day, it must be accompanied by an emission of Smoke.

    In order to provide for this Smoke 1,000 Candles per Division will be reserved from those allotted for the 10-15 Smoke Barrage to-morrow morning.

    These will be used whenever the Gas is let off by day.

Acknowledged by wire

W. Rintnver B.G., G.S.,
VIII CORPS.

25/6/16.

S E C R E T.

VIII Corps.
G.1693.

4th Division.
29th Division.
31st Division.
48th Division.
Captain Slater.
B.G. R.A., C.H.A.
G.O.C., R.A.
VII Corps.
X Corps.

If it is found impossible to let the Gas off to-night, it should, if the wind is favourable, be let off at the same time as the smoke to-morrow morning,

i.e. 10.15 a.m. to 10.25 a.m.

Should the wind not be favourable at this time, it may be let off at any time during the day, up to 8.0 p.m., but if it is let off during the day, it must be accompanied by an emission of ~~smke~~ smoke.

In order to provide for this Smoke 1,000 Candles per Division will be reserved from those allotted for the 10.15 Smoke Barrage to-morrow morning.

These will be used whenever the Gas is let off by day.

Sgd. W. Ruthven B.G., G.S.

25/6/16.

VIII Corps.

2/ Lieut. Stevens Special Brigade.
2/ Lieut. Pheasey Special Brigade.

For information.

Lieut. Colonel, G.S.

26th June, 1916.

29th Division.

Headquarters,
　　VIIIth Corps.

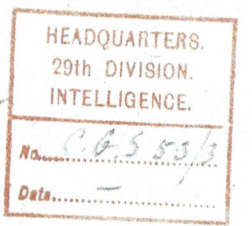

SECRET.

Report on Gas discharge on 29th Division front between Q.10.2 and Q.10.12.

A Gas discharge was ordered, on 26 inst at 10.15 a.m. in conjunction with a smoke discharge. The wind, however, at that hour was unfavourable and it was impossible to commence operations till 10.35 a.m. The gas was carried diagonally across to the enemy's lines and kept low and compact.

Two minutes after the first appearance of gas several rifle shots were fired but ceased almost immediately, there was no fire from machine guns. About 3 minutes later our front line was subjected to a heavy fire from well burst shrapnel, at the same time the communication trenches were shelled with H.E. This bombardment lasted for about an hour and blew a parapet pipe into the trench on two occasions; an atmosphere of almost pure gas was produced against which the box respirators of the crew were ineffective. Our casualties were 1 badly gassed and 4 slightly gassed. At 11.30 all cylinders were turned off and the parapet pipes were left for an hour to drain.

Eighteen cylinders were not discharged owing to the wind changing. One of these, however, was faulty and had been previously turned off. These eighteen cylinders were discharged at 2 a.m on the morning of the 27th, and all the rogers on this front are now empty

Smoke discharge.

A smoke discharge was ordered at 10.15 a.m. This however was not discharged till 10.35 a.m. owing to the wind being unfavourable. The smoke acted as a screen for the gas and was carried diagonally across to the enemy's lines.

(Signed) C E Suller

for. Major-General,
Commanding 29th Division.

27th June, 1916.

(about gas duty)

Smoke

SECRET

VIII Corps
G. 1368.

No.5 Bn. Special Brigade.

The following smoke barrages will be required to assist the attack of the VIII Corps :-

(a) RIGHT FLANK.

Guns to be moved forward to about Q.18.a immediately behind the attacking Infantry. The Infantry are due to arrive at the STATION ROAD at 0.20 and move on from there against the BEAUCOURT ROAD at 1.20. You will be required to screen the right flank of this attack (from the STATION ROAD against the BEAUCOURT ROAD) from the high ground on the opposite side of the valley of the ANCRE in R.19 and 20. This barrage to commence at 1.0 and continue to 1.20. The line of the BEAUCOURT ROAD trenches in Q.12 and R.7.a must not be obscured from our gun positions between AUCHONVILLERS and MESNIL.

(b) LEFT FLANK.

A barrage will be required to screen our defensive flank from the North. This flank will run from JOHN COPSE, North of SERRE to L.26.c,47, and no smoke must come South of this line.

This barrage will commence at "zero" and will be furnished by 4" Stokes Mortars situated in the 48th Division line. If necessary mortars will be moved forward to SERRE to prolong the barrage to L.26.c,47. The duration of the barrage will be as under :-

(a) From JOHN COPSE to the SERRE-PUISIEUX ROAD -
    from "zero" to 1.0.
(b) From the SERRE-PUISIEUX ROAD to L.26.c.47
    from 2.40 to 3.30.

B.G., G.S.,
VIII Corps.

13/6/16.

Copy to :   4th Division.   B.G., R.A., C.H.A.
            29th Division.   G.O.C., R.A.
            31st Division.   VII Corps.
            48th Division.   X Corps.
            No 15 Squadron, R.F.C.

SECRET

VIII Corps
G. 1383

Captain Slater.

~~4th Division.~~
29th Division.
~~51st Division.~~
~~48th Division.~~
G.O.C., R.A.
~~B.G., R.A., G.H.A.~~
} For information.

C.G.S. 53
14/6/16

~~VIII Corps~~
~~X Corps.~~ } for information

Please arrange for a discharge of smoke daily during the preliminary bombardment. The discharge will last for 15 minutes, and as far as possible be along the whole length of our front.

It will take place at the following times :-

"U"	Day	...	No discharge.
"V"	Day	...	~~From 4-10 p.m. to 4-25 p.m.~~ No discharge
"W"	Day	...	From ~~9~~ 10-10 a.m. to ~~9~~ 10-25 a.m.
"X"	Day	...	From ~~4~~ 5-40 a.m. to ~~4~~ 5-55 a.m., and again from ~~5~~ 6-50 p.m. to ~~6~~ 7- 5 p.m.
"Y"	Day	...	From ~~6~~ 7-10 a.m. to ~~6~~ 7-25 a.m., and again from ~~4~~ 5-10 p.m. to ~~4~~ 5-25 p.m.

These times have been arranged to coincide with the special artillery bombardments which will take place each day.

1. By whom is this carried out?
2. Who provides smoke bombs?
3. at what distance apart are the throwers?

[signature]

W. Ruthven
B.G., G.S.,
VIII Corps.

13/6/16.

VIII Corps.
G.1421.

~~4th Division.~~
29th Division.
~~31st Division.~~
~~48th Division.~~
~~"Q"~~
~~Capt. SLATER.~~

HEADQUARTERS,
29th DIVISION,
GENERAL STAFF
No. C.G.S.53
Date 15/6/16

1. With reference to this office No. G.1383 of the 13th, it has been decided that there will be no discharge of smoke until after the gas has been discharged. Consequently the first day on which smoke can be discharged is W day.

2. The following list shows the number of candles and P. bombs that will be drawn by divisions.

	Candles.	P.Bombs.
29th Division.	15,000	2,000
4th Division.	10,000	1,350
31st Division.	10,000	1,300
48th Division.	10,000	1,350
Total...	45,000	6,000

3. These will be drawn on the ~~26th~~ 24th instant. VIII Corps "Q" will arrange to send them up in lorries on that day to such places as Divisions may select. Divisions will inform VIII Corps "Q" by 6 p.m. on the 16th instant where they want the lorries sent and the time at which they should arrive.

4. Divisions will arrange to have unloading parties ready so that there may be no delay in unloading the lorries.

5. The following number of candles and smoke bombs will be discharged on each day should the weather permit. See this office No. G.1383 of the 13th instant as amended by G.1416 dated 15-6-16.

	29th Division.		4th Division.		31st Division.		48th Div.	
	Candles.	P.Bombs.	Candles.	P.Bombs.	Candles.	P.Bombs.	Candles.	P.Bmbs.
W. day.	3000	400	2000	300	2000	250	2000	250
X. Day. morning.	3000	400	2000	250	2000	250	2000	300
evening.	3000	400	2000	250	2000	300	2000	250
Y. Day. morning.	3000	400	2000	300	2000	250	2000	250
evening.	3000	400	2000	250	2000	250	2000	300

6. The

6. The discharge will be carried out under the direction of the officers of the Special Brigade attached to Divisions, and the candles and bombs will be operated by the men of the Special Brigade. Should the number of these prove insufficient, divisions will supplement them by infantry.

7. The Corps will decide whether the wind is suitable for the discharge of smoke, and telegraph the decision to divisions. In the event of the wind changing or becoming unfavourable after the decision has been made, the officers mentioned in para 6 are authorised to countermand the smoke discharge.

H.Q. VIII Corps.
15th June, 1916.

W. Ruthven B.G., G.S.
VIII Corps.

SECRET

VIII Corps.
G.1416.

Captain Slater.
4th Division.
29th Division.
31st Division.
48th Division.
G.O.C., R.A.
B.G., R.A., G.H.A.
VII Corps.
X Corps.

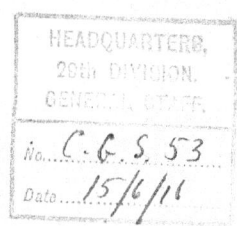
HEADQUARTERS,
29th DIVISION.
GENERAL STAFF.
No. C.G.S. 53
Date 15/6/16

Reference this Office No. G.1383 of the 13th inst., the following amendments will be made.

    V Day.   -   No discharge.

    Other days - one hour should be added to all the hours shown.   Thus 4.40 a.m. should now read 5.40. a.m.

H.Q., VIII Corps.   W. Ruttven   B.G., G.S.
15th June, 1916.   VIII Corps.

From Capt. SLATER, R.E.

To... G.S. 29th Div						17/6/16.

The size and weights of smoke candles and "P" bomb boxes are as follows :-

SMOKE CANDLES		Size about 24" x 10" x 18". Weight about 40 lbs.

"P" BOMBS.	(24 box) Size about 24" x 24" x 9". Weight about 56 lbs.
		(12 box) Size about 24" x 8" x 8". Weight about 18 lbs.

						E. v. Slater
						————————————— Capt. R.E.
						O.C. VIII Corps Unit.

S E C R E T.

Capt. SLATER, Special Brigade, VIIIth Corps.
Lieut. STEVENS,   -"-   attd. 86th Brigade.
Lieut. PHEASEY,   -"-   " 88th   "

---

1.   In accordance with VIIIth Corps G.1421 of the 15/6/16. smoke candles and P. bombs have been allotted to this Division as follows :-

   Candles 15,000   P. Bombs 2,000

2.   7,500 Candles and 1,000 P. Bombs are allotted to each Sector.

3.   These will be drawn on the night 20th instant. It is suggested to send lorries to the Station at AUCHONVILLERS Q.8.c.5.0 at 10 p.m. and have them off loaded there. The goods would then be taken forward on the Light Railway. Do you concur with this suggestion.

4.   Please state the number of men you can supply as an unloading party and the number of additional men you will require for this work.

W. M. Armstrong Capt.
/or Lieut-Colonel, G.S.,
29th Division.

16th June, 1916.

SECRET.

~~VIII Corps~~
~~G.S. 8th Division.~~
~~G.S. 7th Division.~~
~~G.S. 4th Division.~~
G.S. 29th Division.

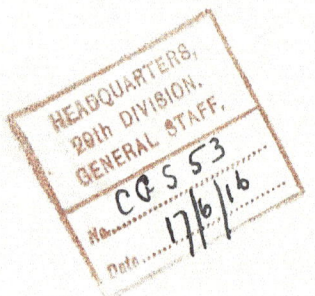

P bombs will come packed in boxes of 12 or 24, each box containing, in a separate tin, the necessary detonators. These are all ready for insertion and are cut to 9 sec lengths.

Fusee matches at the rate of one per candle, have been indented for, and it is to be hoped they will arrive in time. If not, there is a reserve store which can be drawn on, sufficient for the first 5 mins. on W.

H.Q. VIII Corps Mini.
7/6/16.

Q.V. Slater
Capt. R.E.

~~4th Division.~~
29th Division.
~~31st Division.~~
~~48th Division.~~
~~"Q".~~
Capt. Slater.

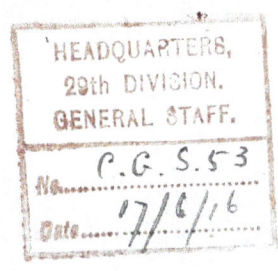

VIII Corps.
G.1465

With reference to this office No. G.1421 of the 15th instant. Arrangements have been made for the issue of an equal number of Matches Vesuvian as Candles.

Each lorry will carry in addition to the candles an equal number of Matches.

H.Q., VIII Corps.
17th June, 1916.

_____ B.G., G.S.
VIII Corps.

Gen: Staff

I forward attached to you, as I am informed all arrangements are being made to meet the lorries at the Rendezvous, and for the distribution of the Candles and P. Bombs, by G.S.O.3.

18.6.16

P. Fraser Major
DAA&QMG 29 Div

A.A.& Q.M.G.,
29th DIVISION.
No. A/06
Date 18 6 16

VIII Corps No. 976.Q.

~~4th Division.~~
29th Division.
~~31st Division.~~
~~42th Division.~~
~~Corps Ammunition Park.~~
~~Corps Siege Park.~~
~~G.S. (for Information.)~~
~~Capt. Slater (For Information.)~~

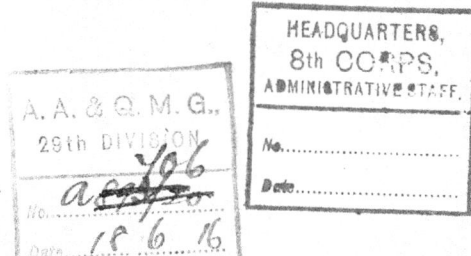

1. Candles and P. Bombs will be delivered by lorries to Divisions on June 20th as per attached Table.

2. Divisions will arrange unloading parties so that lorries are not delayed and also guides to meet the lorries at the rendezvous.

3. An equal number of matches Vesuvian to candles will be packed in each lorry.

P. Bombs do not require matches.

4. Candles and P. Bombs will not be mixed in the same lorries.

Approximately 2,000 candles can be carried in a lorry.

B.J. Lang

VIII Corps, H.Q.,
17th June, 1916.

Lieutenant Colonel,
A.Q.M.G.

TABLE SHEWING ARRANGEMENTS MADE FOR DELIVERING CANDLES AND P BOMBS TO DIVISIONS ON JUNE 20th. 1916.

1. Div.	2. No of Candles.	3. Lorries required.	4. P. Bombs	5. Lorries required.	6. Rendezvous where guides from Divisions will meet lorries.	7. Hour of arrival of lorries at rendezvous.	8. Place of ultimate delivery by lorry of Candles & Bombs.	9. Lorries to be supplied by.
29th	15,000	8	2,000	1	Road junction at Q.7.c.0.8.	10 p.m.	AUCHONVILLERS	(a) Siege Park.
4th	10,000	5	1,350	1	P.12.c.92.	8 p.m.	Level crossing at MAILLY MAILLET Station.	(b) Siege Park.
31st	10,000	5	1,300	1	X roads at J.30.d.97.	10 p.m.	COLINCAMPS.	(c) Corps Park.
48th	10,000	5	1,350	1	J.9.B.72.	11 a.m.	North side of COIGNEUX-SAILLY road at J.9.B.72.	(d) Corps Park.

NOTE:— (a) Lorries will start loading at PUCHEVILLERS railhead at 8 p.m.
(b) " " " " " " " " 6 p.m.
(c) " " " " " " " " 8 p.m.
(d) " " " " " " " " 9 a.m.

SECRET

VIII Corps.
G. 1478

4th Division.
29th Division.
31st Division.
48th Division.
"Q"
Capt. Slater.

[Stamp: HEADQUARTERS, 29th DIVISION. GENERAL STAFF. No. CGS 53 Date 18/6/16]

Reference this Office No. G. 1421 of the 15th June, in para. 3, line 1 for 20th read 24th.

Acknowledge

H.Q., VIII Corps.
18th June 1916.

W. Rutherford
B.G., G.S.
VIII Corps.

~~4th Division.~~
~~29th Division.~~
~~31st Division.~~
~~48th Division.~~
~~"Q"~~
~~Capt. SLATER~~
~~Major POLLITT~~
~~G.O.C., R.A.~~
~~VII Corps.~~
~~X Corps.~~
~~D.C., R.A., C.M.A.~~

VIII Corps
G. 1493.

1. This office Nos G.1383 of the 13th and G.1421 of the 15th instant are cancelled.

2. Divisions will draw Candles and P. Bombs as under:-

	Candles	P. Bombs
29th Division	12000	
4th Division	9000	
31st Division	9000	
48th Division	15000	6000
Total	45000	6000

3. These will be drawn on the 24th instant.
VIII Corps "Q" will arrange to send them up in lorries on that day to the places that Divisions have selected and at the times arranged. An equal number of Vesuvian Matches as Candles will be put into each lorry.
Divisions will arrange to unload the lorries without any delay.

4. It has been decided that there will be no discharge of smoke until the gas has been discharged. Consequently the first day on which smoke can be discharged will be W. day.

5. The following numbers of Candles and P. Bombs will be discharged on each day should the weather permit.

	29th Div.	4th Div.	51st Div.	48th Div.		Total	
	Candles	Candles	Candles	Candles	P.Bombs	Candles	P.Bombs
W. Day	2400	1800	1800	1800		7800	
X. Day							
Morning	2400	1800	1800	1800		7800	
Evening	2400	1800	1800	1800		7800	
Y. Day							
Morning	2400	1800	1800	1800		7800	
Evening	2400	1800	1800	1800		7800	
Z. Day				6000	6000	6000	6000
TOTAL	1200	9000	9000	15000	6000	45000	6000

6. On W. X and Y days each discharge will last for 10 minutes and 3 Candles will be let off every minute for every 25 yards of front.

-2-

7. The times of discharge on W. X and Y. days are as under :-
They have been arranged to synchronise with the special artillery bombardments that will take place on those days -

    W. Day   10.15 a.m. to 10.25 a.m.

    X. Day   5.45 a.m. to 5.55 a.m. and again
               6.55 p.m. to 7.5 p.m.

    Y. Day   7.15 a.m. to 7.25 a.m. and again
               5.15 p.m. to 5.25 p.m.

8. On Z day the 48th Division will carry out a special smoke programme details of which will be forwarded separately.

9. The discharges of smoke will be carried out by Divisions assisted by the personnel of the Special Brigade R.E. attached.

10. Divisions will decide whether the wind is suitable for the discharge of smoke on W. X or Y days. Any wind which does not blow the smoke directly back on our own lines should be considered suitable, i.e. any wind between N-N-W and S-S-W. The decision on Z day will be made by the Corps.

H.Q., VIII Corps.

18th June 1916.

W. Ruthven B.G., G.S.
VIII Corps.

[HEADQUARTERS, 8th CORPS. ADMINISTRATIVE STAFF.]
[A.A. & Q.M.G., 29th DIVISION.]

VIII Corps No. 976/Q.

4th Division.
29th Division.
31st Division.
48th Division.
Corps Ammunition Park.
Corps Siege Park.

SECRET

With reference to VIII Corps letters 976/Q. dated 17th June and June 18th, the Candles and P. Bombs will be drawn at PUCHEVILLERS and delivered tomorrow June 23rd and not on June 24th as previously arranged.

The Table forwarded with 976/Q. dated June 17th will be amended as under and in addition the rendezvous for the 48th Division will be the cross roads K.13.a.I.I. (eastern entrance to SAILLY) at 9 p.m.. Places of ultimate delivery (column 8) will in each be case be decided by the Divisional Staff Officers taking over the Candles and P. Bombs.

All other rendezvous and times will be as detailed in the Table sent out with this office 976/Q. dated June 17th.

1. Division.	2. No. of candles.	3. Lorries required.	4. P.Bombs.	5. Lorries required.
29th	12,000	6		
4th	9,000	5		
31st	9,000	5		
48th	15,000	8	6,000	3

VIII Corps, H.Q.,
22nd June, 1916.

B. J. Lang
Lieutenant Colonel,
A.Q.M.G.

~~4th Division.~~
29th Division.
31st Division.
48th Division.
"Q".
Capt. SLATER.
Major POLLITT.
G.O.C., R.A.
B.G., R.A., C.H.A.
VII Corps.
X Corps.

VIII Corps.
G. 1615

No. CGS 53
Date 23/6/16

1. Owing to the change in the Artillery programme, it is necessary to make some alterations in the programme for smoke candles referred to in this office No. G.1493 of the 18th instant.

2. The evening discharges on X and Y days are cancelled.

3. The number of candles discharged on each of W, X and Y days will be :-

           29th Division ... 4000
            4th Division ... 3000
           31st Division ... 3000
           48th Division ... 3000

The table in para.5 should be amended accordingly.

4. The duration of each discharge will remain unaltered - viz: 10 minutes.

H.Q., VIII Corps.
23rd June 1916.

M. Dobbie
Capt.
B.G., G.S.
VIII Corps.

APPENDIX 4.

Comprises the following :-

- (a) Notes on Divisional Conference on June 20th.
- (b) Table of Reserves of Ammunition, Grenades, etc.
- (c) Divisional Signal Communications for forthcoming offensive.
- (d) Table showing approximate expenditure of artillery ammunition from 12 Noon 23rd to 12 Noon 29th June.
- (e) Instructions re opening up tunnels on Y/Z night.
- (f) List of carrying and working parties from 13th to 19th June for 86th and 87th Brigades.
- (g) Orders for Northern and Southern Observation Posts for forthcoming offensive with complete programme of attack attached.

Appendix 4 (a)

NOTES FOR CONFERENCE ON 20/6/16.

(1) IDENTIFICATION MARKS.
How are wire-cutting and mopping-up parties identified?
Have lanyards been provided for the former, and torches and revolvers for the latter.
Employment of Stokes Mortar bombs as explosive charges.
86th Brigade apparently have not detailed special parties to seize the entrances to the caves in BEAUMONT HAMEL.

(2) MACHINE GUN COMPANY.
Each Machine Gun Company should have a scheme prepared, shewing the positions and lengths of enemy trenches they will fire on, as well as the ranges. These schemes will then be co-ordinated by the Divisional Staff to ensure that all the hostile trenches receive attention.

(3) RESERVES.
Presumably every Battalion attacking will have a Company in Reserve. This should be verified by checking Battalion Orders.
86th Brigade have not told off a Battalion to act as Brigade Reserve for the attack on the Second Objective, nor a Battalion to act as Reserve for the 88th Brigade attack on the Third Objective.
87th Brigade have told off the 1st Royal Inniskilling Fusiliers to act as Reserve for the attack on the Second Objective, but the
para 14) Inniskillings have been ordered to collect in the STATION ROAD
87 Bde.) after the 88th Brigade have passed through, i.e. at 2. This is
Orders.) too late.
The 87th Brigade have not told off a Battalion to act as Reserve for the attack on the Third Objective.

(4) The time the first assaulting troops leave our trenches should be carefully checked in Battalion Orders, to ensure that they are ready to rush into the enemy's first line at 0.0, when the Divisional Artillery lift.

(5) 87th Brigade have issued no orders regarding the cutting of wire in our front, support and reserve lines.

(6) 86th Brigade are firing on trench (66) with Machine guns up till 00.20. Presumably they have arranged this with the 11th Brigade.

(7) 88th Brigade are deploying into line 600 yards from the Third Objective. This seems unnecessarily far (page 4, 88th Brigade Orders)

(8) 88th Brigade have ordered even-numbered platoons to attack first line, and odd-numbered platoons to attack second line of Third Objective. This may lead to confusion, and to checking in the attack.

(9) 88th Brigade should get into touch with the 10th Brigade on our left.
87th Brigade are arranging to get into touch with 108th Brigade on our right.

(10) Warn 86th and 87th Brigades to clear their front line system, when gas and smoke are being discharged, so as to avoid enemy barrage.

(11) Diamond Screens are not to be planted. They must be carried in the hand.

(12) R.E. will send forward carrying parties behind the Brigades, and in front of the Brigade Reserve.

29TH DIVISION.
RESERVES OF AMMUNITION, GRENADES, &C.

App 4(6)

S.A.A.
5 dumps in forward system each of 100 boxes
                          (90 cub. ft. capacity) - 500,000
Already dumped in forward system   - 560,000
    "   "   "   Yellow Line   - 454,000
Divisional Ration Dump   - 250,000
Bde. Reserve Dumps at ENGLEBELMER and
                                  MAILLY WOOD - 168,000
                              Total dumped   1,932,000

On the man (13 Bns. at 120 rds. - 1,560,000)
            (10,000 men at 50 rds. - 500,000) - 2,060,000

At Divl. Gun Dump   - 578,000

On wheels.
Regtl. Reserve 13 x 88,000 - 1,144,000
Lewis Guns   13 x 3,600 -   468,000
Vickers Guns   13 x 4,500 -   216,000
Div. Amm. Col.   - 1,840,000
                              3,668,000   - 3,668,000

                              Total :-   8,238,000

MILLS GRENADES.
5 dumps (capacity 300 cub. ft.) in forward
       system of 920 grenades each - 4,600   - 4,600
On Grenadier Parties 13 x 16 x 150 - 31,200)
On the men at 2 grenades per man - 11,700) - 42,900
          (2 x 5,850)
On wheels.
Regtl. Reserve 13 x 768   - 9984)
D.A. Column   - 5,520)   - 15,500

                                              63,000

RIFLE GRENADES.
With 88th Brigade   - 1,200)
In Gun Dump (not required by Bdes.) - 3,800) - 5,000

STOKES T.M. AMMUNITION.
24 mortars for emplacements at 300 rounds)
            per mortar -   7,200)
12 mortars to move forward with 100 rounds) - 8,400
            per mortar -   1,200)

2 dumps (capacity 300 cub. ft.) in forward system
      each containing 1000 rounds   - 2,000
At Divisional Dump   - 7,600

                                            18,000

MEDIUM T.M. AMMUNITION.
24 mortars at 300 rounds per mortar
        dumped near emplacements   - 7,200

HEAVY T.M. AMMUNITION.
2 Guns with total of 200 rounds.   - 200

RESERVES OF WATER, RATIONS, &C.

WATER.   5 dumps containing a total of 1600 - 2 gallon tins
i.e. 3,200 galls.

400 tins in deep dug-outs in Right Sector and
400 tins in dug-outs in Left Sector.

60 tanks of 100 gallons, or total of 6,000 galls.
has been stored at six different places in
forward system.

An additional 1,000 water bottles per Brigade have
been issued.

There are 11 wells in BEAUMONT HAMEL
   "   " 6 "   " BEAUCOURT SUR ANCRE

RATIONS.   3 forward dumps (totalling 1400 cub. ft.) containing
a total of 10,000 rations

In Divisional Dump   20,000 rations

Total :- 30,000

NOTES.

Limber G.S. wagon will carry 90 complete rounds Stokes
or 25 complete rounds Medium Mortar Ammunition.

G.S. wagon will carry 201 complete rounds Stokes
or 50 complete rounds Medium Mortar Ammunition.

Box with 3 rounds Stokes Ammunition weighs 45 lbs.
 "   " 125 cartridges   " 22 lbs.
One round of Medium T.M. Ammunition   " 60 lbs.
Component parts for one round (in boxes of 5)
weighs 14 lbs. per box.

DIVISIONAL ARTILLERY.

Ammn. per gun 18 pdr. 760 rounds per gun (with gun)
    300 Divl. Dump 176 Batty. Wagons 103 Div. A.C.

Ammn. per gun 4.5" 450 rounds per gun (with gun)
    150 Divl. Dump 108 Batty. Wagons 114 Div. A.C.

SUB-PARK.

18 pdr.	75	Total	1414.
4.5"	40		862.

DIVISIONAL SIGNAL COMMUNICATIONS.

During the forthcoming operations the following systems of communications will be employed.

(a) Telephone.
(b) Telegraph.
(c) Visual.
(d) Dispatch Riders.
(e) Pigeons.
(f) Wireless.
(g) Contact Patrol Aeroplanes.
(h) Kite Balloons.

App. 4(c)

General arrangements in detail.

(a) <u>Telephone circuits.</u>

(1) Each Infantry Brigade in its forward battle headquarters will be connected to an advanced exchange in MAILLY WOOD. In addition the 86th Brigade will be in direct touch with a Divisional O.P. at Q.2.b.6.9. and the 88th Brigade in direct touch with another Divisional O.P. at Q.23.a.2.4. Further each of the above named Brigades will have direct lines to the flank Brigades of 4th and 36th Divisions respectively. The 86th and 87th Brigades will be in direct communication.

(2) Observation posts at Q.2.b.6.9. and Q.23.a.2.4. are both connected direct to the MAILLY WOOD Exchange as well as to the Left and Right Group Exchanges (C.R.A. communications) communication also exists as per (1).
The Cyclist O.P. at Q.9.d.1.9. will be connected direct to MAILLY WOOD Exchange.

(3) Divisional Dump situated at Q.9.d.5.4. will be connected to MAILLY WOOD Exchange.

(4) Telephone exchanges are established at MAILLY WOOD, ACHEUX Signal Office and ACHEUX Chateau. There are three trunk lines between the first two named exchanges; one of these trunks is for the exclusive use of the C.R.A. A direct trunk runs from MAILLY WOOD Exchange to ACHEUX Chateau. The Chateau Exchange is for emergency only, and independant of the ACHEUX Exchange. From both ACHEUX and the Chateau Exchanges the following calls may be effected - 4th Division, 36th Division, VIIIth Corps, Fourth Army and BELLE EGLISE.

(5) The Main Divisional Report Centre will be at Q.8.d.45.05. Subsidiary Report Centres will be at Q.19.b.1.3. and Q.14.d.95.25. From these report centres it will be possible to send written messages only.

(b) <u>Telegraph Circuits.</u>

In addition to the telephone line, each Infantry Brigade will be connected direct by telegraph from its battle headquarters to Divisional Headquarters. A telegraph circuit will also work direct to VIIIth Corps from Divisional Headquarters. There will be no other telegraphic communications.

(c) Visual reading stations will be established at the Northern (Q.9.d.1.9.) and Southern (Q.23.a.2.4.) Divisional O.P.'s. These stations can receive, but cannot send or acknowledge. Battalion and Company Signallers, also F.O.O.'s can send back messages to these stations, which when received will be sent by wire to their destination. Sending and receiving stations will be established at the Main Divisional Report Centre (Q.8.d.45.05) and near the Cafe Jourdain, MAILLY, (P.12.d.2.7.) Both these stations will work to a sending and receiving station at ACHEUX WOOD (P.15.a.1.1.)

\- 2 -

(d) <u>Dispatch Riders.</u>

Motor Cyclist Dispatch Rider posts will be established at AUCHONVILLERS Station (Q.8.b.5.0) and at the Subsidiary Report Centre (Q.19.b.1.3.) These Motor Cyclists will convey messages back to the ACHEUX Signal Office.

(e) <u>Pigeons.</u>

Each Brigade will be issued with Eight baskets of pigeons, each basket containing two birds. Baskets will be issued to Battalions by Brigades as required.
Each Brigade will detail ten men to work the Pigeon Service. Pigeons must be used sparingly and not liberated except in daylight. Empty baskets should be returned immediately to AUCHONVILLERS Railway Station (Q.8.b.5.0) where they will be refilled, and the full baskets returned by bearers to their units.

(f) <u>Wireless.</u>

A Parent Trench Wireless Set with a range of $2\frac{1}{2}$ miles will be installed in the trenches about 87th Brigade Battle Headquarters (Q.16.a.9.9.) This set will work to the Corps Directing Set at COLINCAMPS. Attention is drawn to "Notes on employment of wireless" and to "Code for short range wireless during operations". A spare Trench Set will be stationed at Q.16.a.9.9. and will accompany 88th Brigade Headquarters when they advance. This set will work to the Corps Directing Set, and to the Parent Set at Q.16.a.9.9.

(g) <u>Contact Patrol Aeroplanes.</u>

Two aeroplanes will be employed continuously as Contact Patrols. Signals to them by means of lamp and flares will be made in accordance with the arrangements practised.

(h) <u>Kite Balloons.</u>

Signals to Kite Balloons will be made by lamp, but this method of communication should only be resorted to when other means fail.

(j) <u>Stores.</u>

A certain amount of Signal Stores will be dumped close to MAILLY Exchange. These stores will consist of cable, telephones and hop poles. The quantity of stores however is very limited and demands will only be met for pressing requirements.

(k) <u>Burying Cables.</u>

All lines both telephone and telegraph have been buried in trenches about six feet deep. Test dug-outs have been made at certain points. Information just received from YPRES shows that cable buried six feet deep has given good results.

ARTILLERY COMMUNICATIONS.

C.R.A.　　C.R.A. has communication with :-

(1) ACHEUX Exchange.
(2) G.S. direct.
(3) MAILLY Exchange (direct) - for Group Headquarters.

GROUP HEADQUARTERS.　　Normal Headquarters are connected direct to MAILLY Exchange.

(a) Left Group - Left Group battle headquarters exchange is alongside the Main Divisional Report Centre (Q.3.d.45.05). To this exchange are connected :-

1. Left Group Battle Headquarters.
2. Left Group Normal Headquarters.
3. C.R.A. via MAILLY Exchange.
4. Batteries of the Group.
5. Group O.P.'s at K.33.d.20.80 and Q.10.a.80.20.
6. 86th Infantry Brigade Battle Headquarters (Advanced)
7. All battery O.P.'s.
8. 4th Division Right Group Exchange.
9. Right Group Exchange (4 lines)
10. Two lines forward to advanced Left Brigade Headquarters (86th Brigade Battle Headquarters) to be used by the four batteries advancing into "No Man's Land" and STATION Road. These lines connect back to Group Commanders.
11. Visual O.P. in Cemetry, AUCHONVILLERS.
12. Divisional O.P. at Q.2.b.6.9.

(b) Right Group forward exchange is at Q.22.c.50.70. To it are connected :-

1. C.R.A. via MAILLY Exchange.
2. Batteries of the Group including two 48th Division Batteries.
3. Group Headquarters.
4. Group O.P. at Q.22.d.90.50.
5. Right Infantry Brigade Headquarters (87th Brigade Battle Headquarters).
6. 36th Division "Centre" Group Exchange.
7. Left Group Exchange.
8. Battery O.P.'s.
9. Divisional O.P.' at Q.23.a.20.40.

　　All lines forward from MAILLY Exchange are buried in trenches six feet deep.
　　Divisional visual station back to ACHEUX is within a few yards of the Main Divisional Report Centre and of the Left Group Exchange.
　　The Dispatch Rider assembly point is at AUCHONVILLERS Station some 500 yards North of the Divisional Report Centre.

Visual in Groups.

　　Whenever it is possible to get x visual between Batteries and Group Exchanges without a transmitting Station, this has been done.
　　All batteries have visual between O.P. and battery.
　　Visual messages from F.O.O.'s will be picked up and transmitted not only by the Left Group Observation Post, but also by the Divisional Visual Stations at the Northern (Q.2.b.6.9.) and Southern (Q.23.a.2.4.) Divisional O.P.'s.

ARTILLERY AMMUNITION.
Approximate Expenditure.

App. 4 (d)

Day	Hours	18 pdr. Shrap. (A)	18 pdr. H.E. (AX)	4.5" How. (BX)	Trench Mortars 2"	Trench Mortars Heavy
U	12 noon 23rd to 12 noon 24th	1164	-	316	-	-
	Noon 24th to 8 p.m. 24th	3667	84	185	-	-
V	8 p.m. 24th to Noon 25th	5824	39	1006	-	-
	Noon 25th to 8 p.m. 25th	3390	7	612	-	-
W	8 p.m. 25th to Noon 26th	3656	1483	1166	-	-
	Noon 26th to 8 p.m. 26th	3099	132	1111	-	-
X	8 p.m. 26th to Noon 27th	3576	1621	1081	1090	76
	Noon 27th to 8 p.m. 27th	4641	396	725	-	-
Y	8 p.m. 27th to Noon 28th	3638	2608	1049	1005	107
	Noon 28th to 8 p.m. 28th	3177	405	975	-	-
Y.1	8 p.m. 28th to Noon 29th	2705	717	917	1115	55
		38537	7492	9143	3210	238

44 18-pdr. guns have fired 46,029 shells in 6 days or average of 162 rounds per gun per day.

12 4.5" Hows. " " 9,143 " " 6 " or average of 127 rounds per gun per day.

22 Medium Trench Mortars have fired 3210 rounds in 3 days or average of 48 rounds per mortar per day.

2 Heavy Trench Mortars have fired 238 rounds in 3 days or average of 39 rounds per mortar per day.

	18 pdrs.	4.5" Hows.
Expenditure allowed	160 by day 63 by night	160 for 24 hours.

"Z" DAY.

	18 pdrs.	4.5" Hows.
Allowed by Corps.	300	200
Actually available	450	300

War Diary

App. 4(e)

S E C R E T.

86th Brigade.
87th Brigade.
88th Brigade.
1/2nd Monmouth Regt.
252nd Tunnelling Co. R.E.
VIII Corps. (for information).

---

1.   The Stokes Mortar Emplacements in MARY and FIRST Avenue tunnels will be opened by the 252nd Tunnelling Co. by 2.a.m. on Y/Z night.

2.   The tunnel at the end of sap 7 will be opened by the 252nd Tunnelling Co. at 10.30.p.m. on Y/Z night, and the 1/2nd Monmouth Regt. will arrange to dig a communication trench from the opening to the SUNKEN ROAD during that night. The 86th Brigade will provide a covering party while this work is in progress.

(Signed) D.Ovey, Major, G.S.
for Lieut Colonel, G.S.
29th Division.

24.6.16.

CARRYING AND WORKING PARTIES.

86th Brigade.

(App.4(B)

	CARRYING							REMARKS
	13th	14th	15th	16th	17th	18th	19th	
2" and Heavy T. Mortars	470	490	200	430	250	280	280	
Rations)								
Stokes Mortars)								
Water)	300	300	300					
S.A.A.)								
Grenades)								
Gas cylinders					400	400		

	WORKING.							
Deep dug-outs	150	150	150	150	150	150	150	
A.P.M.'s and Runners Posts	50	50						
Advanced Dressing Station in WHITE CITY.		50	50	50				
R.E. working parties	100	100	100	100	100	100	100 (approximately)	
Total	1070	1140	800	730	900	930	530	

If work is to be continuous
the following working parties
will be required.

13/6/16.

CARRYING AND WORKING PARTIES.

87th Brigade.

	CARRYING							REMARKS
	13th	14th	15th	16th	17th	18th	19th	
2" and Heavy T.Mortars			400	120	120	120	120	
Rations		300						
Stokes Mortar Ammn.			100					
S.A.A.		already dumped.						
Water			150	150				
Grenades				80	xx			
Gas cyclinders					400	400	xxx	

	WORKING.							
Deep dug-outs	405	405	405	405	405	405	405	
Normal R.E. W.parties	190	190	190	190	190	190	190	
Special work	150	150	150	150	150			
Carrying bridges etc under R.E.	20	20	20	20	20	20	20	
Total	1065	915	1015 (1415)	965	1285	1135	635	

If work is to be continuous the following extra parties will be required :-

VIIIth Corps O.P.	12	12	12	12	12	12	12	(or till completion)
Installation of water tanks	24	24	24	24	24	24	24	-"-
Deep dug-outs	200	200	200	200	200	200	200	(of which 50 must be miners)

Grand Total	1301	1151	1251	1201	1521	1371	871	

13/6/16.

D.O. Major.

App 4 (9)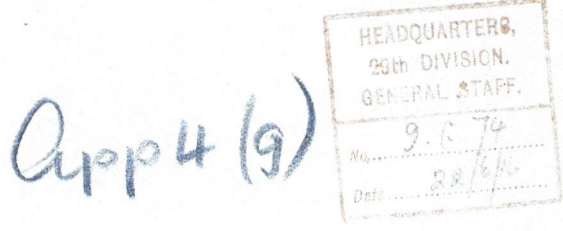

Major Hardress Lloyd.
Lieut C.T.Ball, Divisional Grenadier Officer.

        Please add the attached Appendix "A" to the orders for 29th Divisional Northern and Southern O.Ps.

                                                      Lieut Colonel, G.S.

22nd June 1916.   29th Division.

APPENDIX "A".

In order to enable Infantry Officers to reconnoitre the enemy's wire there will be no Artillery, Lewis Gun, or Rifle fire on the enemy's front between the following hours :-

        V/W Night   11 p.m. to 12 midnight.
        W/X Night   10.30 p.m. to 11.30 p.m.
        X/Y Night   12 midnight to 1 a.m.
        Y/Z Night   11.30 p.m. to 12.30 a.m.

During the remainder of these nights the enemy's wire will be kept under fire.

ORDERS FOR NORTHERN AND SOUTHERN OBSERVATION POSTS.

COMPOSITION OF O.P.
1. Each Observation Post will consist of 2 officers, and 2 linesmen and 3 visual signallers from the Signal Service. One officer's servant may be taken.

OCCUPATION OF
2. Posts will be occupied by 5 a.m. on "U" day. The 3 visual signallers will however only join on Y/Z night.

DUTIES.
3. The Officers in the posts will make themselves acquainted with the Divisional Orders for the operations, and the attached programmes of Artillery Lifts, smoke and gas discharges. The Officer on duty will keep Divisional Headquarters constantly informed whether this programme is being carried out according to the times laid down, and also the results visible from the O.P.

During the Artillery Bombardment, notes will be made of any places which do not appear to be receiving sufficient attention and the matter reported to Divisional Headquarters. Notes on the progress of events will be sent to Divisional Headquarters at the end of each day.

Reports will be made direct to Divisional Headquarters, and these officers will not issue orders to Brigades, though they may be consulted by the latter as to the progress of the action visible from their Posts.

REPORT CENTRES.
4. The Main Divisional Report Centre will be at Q.8.d.45.05. Subsidiary Posts will also be established at Q.19.b.1.3. and Q.14.d.95.25.

TELEPHONES.
5. There will be 3 telephones in each Post, 1 to Divisional Headquarters, and in Northern Post 1 to 86th Brigade Advanced Headquarters and 1 to Left Group Artillery; and in Southern Post 1 to 87th Brigade Advanced Headquarters and 1 to Right Group Artillery. These telephones will be tested.

WATCHES.
6. Watches will be synchronised every day at 9 a.m. and at 9 a.m. and 7 p.m. on "X" and "Y" days.

DIVISIONAL CYCLISTS.
7. The Divisional Cyclists at present manning the North and South Observation Posts will be sent to Divisional Headquarters.

SECRET APPENDIX "C".

PROGRAMME OF INFANTRY ADVANCE AND ARTILLERY BOMBARDMENT.

Time.	Moves of Infantry.	Trench Mortars.	Divl. Artillery.	Heavy Artillery.
-10		Stokes Mortars open hurricane bombardment.		
-5				Lift on to line Q.12.d.45.1 - Q.12.c.7.1 - Q.12.c.1.4 - Q.11.b.1.5 - Q.5.c.85.05 - Q.5.d.4.4.
0.0	87th and 86th Bdes. assault first objective and advance at rate not exceeding 50 yards a minute.	All Trench Mortars cease fire. Stokes Mortars, if red cartridges received, lift to support line.	Lift to enemy Support Trench or minimum of 100 yards beyond front line.	
0.2		Stokes Mortars cease fire.	Lift another 100 yards.	
0.4			Lift another 100 yards and continue lifting at rate of 100 yards every 2 minutes until they reach the Station and Wagon Roads.	
0.15				Lift on to second objective.
0.20	87th and 86th Bdes. reach Station and Wagon Roads.		Lift 150 yards East of Station and Wagon Roads and remain there till 1.00.	
1.00	87th and 86th Bdes. advance from Station and Wagon Roads against second objective at rate not exceeding 50 yards a minute.		Lift 100 yards.	
1.02			Lift another 100 yards and continue lifting at this rate until they reach BEAUCOURT RIDGE trenches, where they remain till 1.20.	
1.15				Lift on to BEAUCOURT VILLAGE.
1.20	87th and 86th Bdes. assault second objective.		Lift on to line of wire R.7.a.5.2. to R.1.c.25.50. (where they remain until 1.35) and also on to BEAUCOURT VILLAGE.	

Time	Moves of Infantry	Trench Mortars	Divl. Artillery	Heavy Artillery
1.25				Lift on to third objective.
1.30	87th and 86th Bdes. send out patrols to cut line of wire R.7.a.5.2. to R.1.c.25.50. 87th Bde. assault BEAUCOURT VILLAGE.		Lift off BEAUCOURT VILLAGE.	
1.35	87th and 86th Bdes. cut wire.		Lift off line of wire to East of ARTILLERY LANE and maintain barrage until 2.30.	
2.30	88th Bde. advance through wire to PUISIEUX ROAD at rate not exceeding 50 yards a minute.		Lift to the PUISIEUX ROAD.	
2.40	88th Bde. reach PUISIEUX ROAD.		Lift 100 yards and continue lifting at rate of 100 yards every 2 minutes until they reach line of wire R.2.d.1.15. to R.2.a.6.0. and BOIS D'HOLLANDE (R.8.a.) where they remain till 3.00.	
3.00			Lift on to third objective and remain there until 3.30.	
3.10	88th Bde. advance from PUISIEUX ROAD towards third objective.			
3.25				Lift on to BAILLESCOURT and gun positions.
3.30	88th Bde. assault third objective.		Lift 300 yards beyond enemy's support line and barrage until 4.30.	
4.30			Barrage ceases.	

N.B.   The timing of Artillery Lifts has been altered to 100 yards every 2 minutes, instead of 50 yards a minute, as noted in para. 12 of Division Order No. 36.

PROGRAMME OF PRELIMINARY BOMBARDMENT 29TH DIVISION.

DIVISIONAL ARTILLERY.

Nature of gun.   "U" Day.

18 pdrs.   Cut all wire West of line Q.6.c.5.4. to
                 R.7.a.3.2. inclusive. (except what can be
                 dealt with by Trench Mortars.)

4.5" Hows.   Assist in wire cutting on BEAUCOURT ROAD Line
                 and bombard BEAUMONT ALLEY and RAILWAY ALLEY.

2" T.M.'s.   NIL.

240 m.m. Mortars.   NIL.

                 "V", "W", "X", "Y" Days.

18 pdrs.   Same as "U" Day.

4.5" Hows.   Bombard selected points and trenches
                 RAILWAY ALLEY Q.11.a.00.95 - 50.90.

2" T.M.'s.   Wirecutting.

240 m.m. Mortars. On BEAUMONT HAMEL North of AUCHONVILLERS ROAD.

Note.   The day unless otherwise stated begins at 5 a.m.
         Wire cutting and Trench Mortars begin at 6 a.m.

Night.   (See Table for times for Night firing.)

18 pdr. Frequent bursts of fire at irregular intervals on all
         wire fired at previously that Machine Guns cannot keep
         under fire, and on communications and approaches on the
         line WAGON ROAD - BEAUMONT ALLEY - STATION ALLEY -
         RAILWAY ROAD - RAILWAY LINE and BEAUCOURT ROAD, especially
         at Q.5.d.85.20.

4.5" Hows. Frequent bursts at irregular intervals on
            WAGON ROAD - STATION ROAD - BEAUMONT ALLEY -
            STATION ALLEY.

PRELIMINARY DIVISIONAL ARTILLERY BOMBARDMENT.

Times for Night Firing.

2100 - 2200 at 00, 05, 12, 25, 31, 35, 47, 51, 57 minutes.

2200 - 2300 at 01, 05, 16, 19, 30, 33, 40, 49, 59 "

2300 - 2400 at 07, 09, 14, 18, 25, 30, 40, 47, 53 "

0000 - 0100 at 00, 03, 07, 16, 22, 29, 39, 46, 54 "

0100 - 0200 at same as 2100 - 2200

0200 - 0300 " " " 2200 - 2300

0300 - 0400 " " " 2300 - 2400

0400 - 0500 " " " 0000 - 0100

In addition bursts of fire at :-

2120 - 2210 - 2335 - 0034 - 0140 - 0245 - 0304 - 0411.

HEAVY ARTILLERY PRELIMINARY BOMBARDMENT.

"U" Day.

Wire Cutting. 6-60 pdr. Batteries and 2-4.7" Batteries will when not employed in Counter Battery work attempt to cut the wire at :-
Q.6.a.40.00 to Q.6.c.30.00.
Q.12.b.40.56 to R.7.a.30.20.

U/V Night. The 60 pdrs. will fire frequent bursts at irregular intervals on the line R.7.b.90.00 to R.8.c.40.60 paying particular attention to roads, trench tramways and communication trenches.

"V" Day.

5 a.m. to 5.15 a.m.
1-8" How. Battery - Q.6.c.5.3. to Q.6.c.4.0.
2-60 pdr. or 4.7" Batteries - BEAUCOURT ROAD.
2-15" Hows. and 1-9.2" How. Batteries
and 1-8" How. Battery - BEAUCOURT REDOUBT.

5.20 a.m. to 5.30 a.m.
1-8" How. Battery, 2-6" How. Batteries, and 2-60 pdr. or 4.7" Batteries - WAGON ROAD to BEAUMONT HAMEL CHURCH.
1-9.2" Battery, 1-8" How. Battery, 1-6" How. Battery, and 2-60 pdr. Batteries - CHURCH down STATION ROAD to Q.12.c.4.0.

2-15" Hows. BEAUCOURT REDOUBT.

5.35 a.m. to 5.45 a.m.
1-9.2" Battery, 1-8" How. Battery, 2-6" How. Batteries, 3-60 pdr. Batteries - BEAUCOURT REDOUBT.

6-60 pdr. Batteries will do all necessary Counter Battery work; the 4.7" and remaining 60 pdr. Batteries will shell O.P.'s, working parties, or any movement in addition to the set programme of the day.

V/W Night and succeeding Nights.
60 pdrs. and 4.7" Batteries same as U/V Night. Heavy Hows. will fire salvoes twelve times during the night (with a view to keeping the enemy awake) on their permanent area.

"W" Day and succeeding Days.
Same as "V" day except that all Heavy Hows. and Guns start permanent bombardment at 5 a.m.

"Z" Day.
Heavy Artillery will in all cases lift 5 minutes before times laid down for Divisional Artillery, except on the final objective when they will maintain their fire up to the moment of assault at 3.30.

S M O K E.

On "Z" day, it is intended to form a smoke barrage on the South Flank of the attack. It will be made by 4" Stokes Mortars pushed forward to O.18.a. immediately behind the two leading Battalions of the 87th Brigade.
This Barrage will commence about 0.55 and will be directed up the valley of the RIVER ANCRE a short distance North of the RAILWAY ROAD.

Smoke will be discharged along the whole Divisional Front on the following days and at the following times, if the wind is favourable.

"W" day. 10.15 a.m. to 10.25 a.m.
"X" day. 5.45 a.m. to 5.55 a.m. and
  again   6.55 p.m. to 7.5 p.m.
"Y" day. 7.15 a.m. to 7.25 a.m. and
  again   5.15 p.m. to 5.25 p.m.

G A S.

Gas will be discharged along our Front Line
Q.10.2. to Q.10.12. on V/W night if favourable. If not
on W/X night or X/Y night. It will commence from zero
and go on till 1.28.

Zero hour will be notified shortly after 5 p.m. on the
evening before the discharge.

Rifle fire and Machine Gun fire will cover the noise
of the escaping gas.

ORDERS FOR N.C.O. IN CHARGE OF 29TH DIVISIONAL O.P.
AUCHONVILLERS.

COMPOSITION OF O.P.
The observation Post will consist of 1 N.C.O. and 3 men from the Divisional Cyclists.

Occupation of Duties.
Posts will be occupied by 5 a.m. on "U" Day.
The N.C.O. in charge will have issued to him every evening before 8 p.m. a programme of the sequence of events for that night and the following day. His duty will be to keep Divisional Headquarters informed whether this programme is being carried out according to the times laid down, and also the results visible from the O.P.

Report Centres.
The Main Divisional Report Centre will be at Q.8.d.45.05. Subsidiary Posts will also be established at Q.19.b.1.3. and Q.14.d.95.25.

Telephone.
There will be one telephone in the post to the MAILLY EXCHANGE. This telephone must be tested.

Watches.
Watches will be synchronised every day at 9 a.m. and at 9 a.m. and 7 p.m. on "X" and "Y" days.

Reports.
Reports for Divisional Headquarters will be sent by Messenger to the Motor Cyclists Post, AUCHONVILLERS STATION.

22.6.16.

Lieut-Colonel, G.S.,
29th Division.

APPENDIX "A".

In order to enable Infantry Officers to reconnoitre the enemy's wire there will be no Artillery, Lewis Gun, or Rifle fire on the enemy's front between the following hours :-

        V/W Night   11 p.m. to 12 midnight.
        W/X Night   10.30 p.m. to 11.30 p.m.
        X/Y Night   12 midnight to 1 a.m.
        Y/Z Night   11.30 p.m. to 12.30 a.m.

During the remainder of these nights the enemy's wire will be kept under fire.

APPENDIX 5.

Comprises the following :-

29th Division Daily Intelligence Summaries for the month of June.

=============

29th DIVISION DAILY SUMMARY.
for
From 6.a.am 31/5/16 to 6.a.m. 1/6/16.

HEADQUARTERS,
29th DIVISION.
INTELLIGENCE.

No. DS 59
Date 1/6/16

Period

OPERATIONS.

Artillery. During the afternoon the enemy shelled 5th AVENUE, ST HELENS, JACOBS LADDER and front and support trenches left of JACOBS LADDER. 2nd AVENUE was registered on with H.E. at 9.a.m., AUCHONVILLERS was also fired on during the day. At 2.p.m. shells were dropped near POMPADOUR.

Nine out of 25 shells fired on the Right Sector yesterday were reported to be "blinds".

Between 5.p.m. and 6.p.m. a number of heavy shells were fired round about the RUINED MILL at Q.21.Centre.

The entrance to GABION AVENUE has been heavily shelled. An orderly had his rifle stock pierced by a fragment of shrapnel about 7.a.m. today.

Our aeroplanes were subjected to the usual shrapnel and machine gun fire. The latter seemed to come mostly from BEAUMONT HAMEL. During the afternoon our guns did some damage to the enemy trenches in Q.11.c. especially to the two front lines S. of Y RAVINE. Lewis Guns were then trained on the area and fire opened at midnight to catch any working parties there might be.

Trench Mortars. Two or three Trench Mortar bombs fell near our lines about Q.17.a.2.4. between 8-0 and 8-30.p.m.; no damage reported.

Patrols: (1) Officers' Patrols were out in front of the REDAN and in front of Q.16.2. respectively (the latter to reconnoitre dead ground). They had nothing to report

(2) An officers' Patrol went out from the lines of the Battalion in the left half sector and took up its position in the trees at Q.16.b.7.8. inorder to listen for sounds of work as well as to act as a covering party for one of our wiring parties. Nothing was heard or seen. The patrol was out from 9.0p.m. to 11.30.p.m.

INTELLIGENCE.

Enemy Movements. The usual movements were observed in BEAUMONT HAMEL.

Except for a few isolated groups of men on the WAGON ROAD no movements were observed.

Working parties could be observed in trench right and left of point Q.5.c.40.56. New earth has been thrown up from this point to rear of village.

A working party was observed in trench at point Q.6.a.20.85.

Men were seen carrying brush wood down the communication trench at Q.10.d.65.71. They seemed to go down steps as the brush wood disappeared from view in jerks

Trains and Transport. 2 horse transport wagons were observed coming from GREVILLERS on road at point G.22.d.6.7.

The following train movements were observed:-
10.50 To BAPAUME from ACHIET-LE-GRAND.
3.35 To ACHIET-LE-GRAND. from BAPAUME.
5.40 To BAPAUME from ACHIET-LE-GRAND.

MISCELLANEOUS.

(a) A pigeon was seen to fly from German Lines over AUCHONVILLERS. at 6.pm.
(b) A sniper fired on a man appearing in a gap in a wall and believes he hit him.
(c) An anti-aircraft gun is suspected at Q.11.d.40.85.
(d) A camouflage observation tree is suspected at Q.11.c.65.80.
(e) Lights were seen in BEAUMONT HAMEL about 11.45.p.m Bursts of Lewis Gun fire were opened on them.
(f) At 9.15 a succession of flares rose from the direction of GRANDCOURT, including blue, white, red and green flares. No action seemed to follow.

-2-

<u>NOTE</u>. Reference report of hostile mining in yesterday's summary, two officers listened with instruments but heard no sounds.

                                                                     Captain, G.S.

1st June 1916.   29th Division.

HEADQUARTERS.
29th DIVISION.
INTELLIGENCE.
D.S.60
No.
Date 2/6/16.

29th DIVISION DAILY SUMMARY.
for
Period   From 6.a.m. 1/6/16. to 6.a.m. 2/6/16.

OPERATIONS.

Artillery.   Enemy artillery was again active in the left Sector. At 6.a.m. a few light shells fell near CARDIFF STREET. At 2.15.p.m. 4th AVENUE and KING STREET were also shelled. At 8.30.p.m. 4 rounds shrapnel were fired on ESAUS WAY.
   Our own artillery fired on BEAUMONT ROAD at 10.10.p.m. and 11.15.p.m.
   Starting shortly before 5.a.m. yesterday the enemy bombarded the ENGLEBELMER end of GABION and WITHINGTON AVENUES and the Battery immediately South with 15.c.m. shells.
   Occasional rounds of shrapnel were fired over the MOULIN REDOUBT in the course of the day.
   Occasional rounds were also fired in the direction of working parties in WITHINGTON AVENUE. The same area was again shelled about 3.p.m.
   About 11.a.m. from Q.10.1. to Q.10.6., between the old firing line and the support trench, about 15 7.7. c.m. shells were dropped, otherwise the day was quiet on our front.

Machine Guns.   Enemy machine guns were especially active against our aircraft.
   Two independant observers locate an enemy machine gun as having fired on our aeroplanes from a position approximately Q.10.d.70.75. Our artillery fired at it but slightly to the right where some casualties are supposed to have been caused as several of the enemy were seen running to the spot.
   At 11.p.m. the enemy opened a burst of machine gun fire along the parapet of the front line trenches from Q.16.4. to Q.10.6. Similar bursts occurred at intervals during the night.

Patrols.   The front of the line west ans South of MARY REDAN were patrolled and nothing suspicious discovered.

Sniping.   Sniping was normal on both sides.

INTELLIGENCE.

Enemy Work.   A white chalky trench at Q.10.7.5. has been covered over with grass during the night.
   Fresh chalk has been observed at Q.17.b.2.2.
   A considerable amount of work is being done to the trench which runs North and South from Q.6.a.2. top to Q.6.c.60.35.
   Enemy are still working in trenches South of BEAUMONT HAMEL as several small working parties can be observed throughout the day.
   Hammering on iron was heard throughout the night near spot Q.10.b.9.7. Revetting material was also observed being carried along trench in HAWTHORN REDOUBT.
   New earth has been thrown up all along trench running from point Q.5.b.7.5. to point Q.6.a.28.85.

Enemy Movements.
   Six horse transport wagons were observed going towards PYS on road at point G.33.d.4.0.
   A party of troops about 100 strong were seen coming from direction of GREVILLERS on road at G.22.d.6.7.
WAGON ROAD

HEADQUARTERS.
29th DIVISION.
INTELLIGENCE.
No.
Date. 3/6/16.

29th DIVISION DAILY SUMMARY
for
Period From 6.a.m. 2/6/16 to 6.a.m. 3/6/16.

OPERATIONS.

Artillery. Between 8.a.m. and 9.a.m. the enemy fired H.E. at the front and support line trenches between our left Boundary and Q.16.4. blowing in a Bay in FETHARD STREET. South of Q.16.4. the enemy was fairly active in the morning ranging on the new communication trench at the point where it enters Q.17.21. and placing some H.E. in the neighbourhood of CHARING CROSS ROAD. Our artillery shelled the S. front of the Salient from Q.10.b.6.5. to Q.11.c.4.3.

A few shells were sent over near 5th Avenue, 88th Trench and 2nd Avenue.

About 3.30.p.m. some H.E. was fired into the northern outskirts of ENGLEBELMER.

Trench Mortars. Three bombs were fired into the REDAN at intervals of 20 minutes. The first arriving at 6.40.p.m. The second bomb did not explode.

One of our medium Trench Mortars South of JACOBS LADDER registered again on enemy wire.

Machine Guns. The enemy continued his practice of sweeping our front with Machine Gun fire during the night, some of it crossed our front line at a sufficient height to support the inference that it was indirect fire aimed at the road between THURLES' DUMP and AUCHONVILLERS, as the same bit of road had been spattered with M.G. fire on the preceding night as well. It may also have been intended for working parties out on the top behind the firing line.

Enemy machine guns were observed firing at Q.4.d.86.00. Artillery fire was opened on this and one shell was observed to hit the mark.

Patrols. A patrol consisting of 1 Officer and 8 other ranks left Sap in Q.17.19. at 9.30.p.m. and lay out in "NO MAN'S LAND" until 1.a.m.

A patrol of 1 Officer and 7 other ranks patrolled from No.2 Sap in Q.17.14. to enemy wire in front of SALIENT in Q.10.d. from 11.p.m. to 12.30.a.m.

At 9.30.p.m. a patrol of 2 officers and 15 men left Sap 3 (MARYLEBONE ROAD) for the trees at Q.10.d.8.8. the Fork at Q.16.B.95.95. in order to discover if the enemy had carried out a relief and if possible to secure an identification by capturing 1 or more prisoners. Nothing however was seen or heard nor were there any signs that the long grass on the road has ever been trodden or that the area is patrolled at all at that point.

Neither of the first two patrols found anything to report. All was quiet.

From that houri 1 Officer and 4 men wounded down the road to

Snipers. Sniping by enemy was as usual & not causing us any casualties. Our snipers claim two hits.

INTELLIGENCE.

Enemy Work. Enemy were working in small parties in several support trenches behind BEAUMONT HAMEL and other places behind their lines.

Listening Post reported hearing enemy driving in stakes opposite ROONEY'S SAP at point approximately Q.10.b.70.40.

WAGON ROAD is still frequented by small groups, especially between two trenches the exact position of which will be reported. Lewis Guns were trained on to it yesterday.

Train Activity.   The following train movements were observed:-

8.5.   To ACHIET-LE-GRAND FROM BAPAUME.
8.40.   " LE SARS   "   "
10.10.   " ACHIET-LE-GRAND   "   "
10.30.   " BAPAUME from ACHIET-LE-GRAND.
11.30.   "   "   "   "   "
4.2.   " ACHIET-LE-GRAND from BAPAUME.
4.40.   "   "   "   "   "
4.53.   " BAPAUME from ACHIET-LE-GRAND.
5.30.   " ACHIET-LE-GRAND from BAPAUME.
5.45.   " BAPAUME from ACHIET-LE-GRAND.

MISCELLANEOUS.

Reliefs.   A relief is suspected to have taken place opposite our lines recently, as there has been a cessation of work and noise and a change in fire tactics. During the last two days there has been hardly any sniping and machine guns have been considerably more active. The bursts of machine gun fire last night were similar to those reported on the night of 16th and 17th May. It is just possible therefore that the Battalion which was then opposite to us has now returned to the trenches.

Fires.   It has been observed that the enemy usually has a number of fires burning in his lines about 5.p.m. At 7.30.p.m. smoke was observed to rise from Q.10.d.90.80. and again about 10.p.m. smoke or steam was observed to come from approximately Q.11.a.01.30. under light of strong enemy flare.

Signals.   Immediately prior to the first burst of machine gun fire at 11.p.m. a faint white flash was seen about 50 yards in front of the enemy's line. This was also observed to precede the second burst.

General.   The front line opposite to us is believed to be held very lightly at night time, as any rifle fire comes from the 2nd or 3rd line.

Supplementary to yesterday's Report.   A succession of red, white and green flares is reported from the right sector. They went up in the following order:-
           1 Green, 3 White, 1 Red.
           1 Green, 3 White, 3 Red.
           2 Green, 1 White, 1 Red.
           1 Green, 1 White, 2 Red.
           2 Green, 1 White

Captain, G.S.
29th Division.

2nd June 1916.

-2-

A new trench has been dug, and is visible from point Q.6.c.70.65 to Q.6.d.38. where it passes through wire. More wire and stakes have been placed between points Q.6.d.5.2. and Q.6.b.1.3.

Enemy Movements. Four horse transport wagons were observed coming from PYS on road at point M.1.b.2.1.

Much horse transport could be observed passing to and from GREVILLERS on road at point G.22.d.6.7.

The part of WAGON ROAD on which the enemy exposes himself lies between Q.5.d.25.50 and Q.5.d.4.7. During the course of the 2nd inst 57 men were counted in all moving singly or in small groups.

At about 9.15.a.m. two Germans, one presumed to be an Artillery Observation Officer, were seen watching the effect of their fire, through glasses at Q.10.d.70.87. At 1030.a.m. a man was again seen, with head and shoulders above the parapet at the same place. He was fired on and is believed to have been hit. At 8.p.m. 5 men who appeared to wear white clothes or clothes covered with chalk were seen at Q.5.d.45.00.

Train Activity. The following train movements were observed
8.45. To BAPAUME from LE SARS.
9.55. " LE SARS from BAPAUME.
9.58. " ACHIET-LE-GRAND from BAPAUME.
10.35 " BAPAUME from ACHIET-LE-GRAND.
10.55 " " " " " "
10.59 " " " " " "
11.35 " ACHIET-LE-GRAND from BAPAUME.
1.30 " BAPAUME from ACHIET-LE-GRAND.
4.25 " ACHIET-LE-GRAND from BAPAUME.
5.45 " BAPAUME from ACHIET-LE-GRAND.

MISCELLANEOUS.

Balloons. Two enemy observation balloons were up for the greater part of the day.

A balloon was observed to rise over wood BOIS-DE-LOGEAST.

Observation Posts. An observation Post is believed to have been discovered at point approximately Q.5.c.20.70. Work has been noticed at this point before.

W. M. Armstrong.
Captain, G.S.
3rd June 1916.
29th Division.

> HEADQUARTERS.
> 29th DIVISION.
> INTELLIGENCE.
>
> No. D.S. 68
> Date 4/6/16.

29th DIVISION DAILY SUMMARY
for
Period From 6.a.m. 3/6/16 to 6.a.m. 4/6/16.

OPERATIONS.

Artillery. Quiet during the day. Intermittent shelling of support lines at one or two points only.

4 shells dropped near ST MARTINS and a few on 88TH TRENCH at 11a.m.

During the raid carried out by the 88th Brigade enemy's fire was vigourous and accurate.

Our front line received less attention than the supports and communication trenches.

TENDERLOIN STREET was very heavily shelled, also the vallet just beyond. Casualties occurred here in corrugated iron huts, just as these were being rapidly evacuated.

Damage to trenches was slight considering intensity of fire.

In the right sector the shell fire was supplemented by a certain amount of accurate rifle fire on to our front line parapet and also by machine gun fire.

At 3.p.m. our artillery put two shells into a trench at Q.11.b.00.11., where enemy were working, and also fired upon parties working at Q.11.c.77.00.

Machine Guns. Enemy machine guns were active and one is believed to have been located at Q.5.b.30.60.

On both sides they traversed opposite trenches during the raid.

Patrols. After last night's bombardment finished, two patrols went out from Q.17.19. and Q.17.14. respectively and found nothing special to report.

INTELLIGENCE.

Enemy Work. More fresh earth has been thrown up at point Q.4.d.9.5.

Enemy parties were seen at work on trenches during the day. One party at point 7747 were fired on with H.E. at 4.p.m. and 5.p.m. Men were also observed at Q.6.c.10.80.

Much new earth has been thrown up at point Q.12.a.50.95. A working party was observed here about 9.20.a.m.

About 12.45.a.m. a working party was observed in trench at point Q.6.a.83.90.

Enemy Movements. Small groups of three or four, apparently working parties, as they wore no equipment and had whiteish clothes on, were seen at various times during the day on the WAGON ROAD.

Horse transport wagons were observed going towards and coming from the direction of GRIVILLERS on road at point G.22.d.6.7.

Sound of transport were heard along the STATION ROAD at 9.30.p.m. and at 10.20.p.m.

Train Activity. The following train movements were observed:-

7.40	To	BAPAUME from LE SARS
10.30	"	ACHIET-LE-GRAND from BAPAUME
11.5.	"	BAPAUME from ACHIET-LE-GRAND
11.47	"	ACHIET-LE-GRAND from Bapaume.
11.5.	"	" " " "
1.45	"	BAPAUME from ACHIET-LE-GRAND.
3.35	"	" " " "
5.45	"	" " " "

MISCELLANEOUS.

Searchlights. A searchlight estimated as having 12" diameter and casting a fairly strong white light swept our lines several times between 10p.m. and 12 midnight. It appeared to be in S.E. corner of BEAUMONT HAMEL. On one occasion it stopped at a particular spot on our firing line upon which machine gun fire opened immediately. It also swept up and down 'No Man's Land'. A considerable number of flares, red, white and green in colour, were used during the bombardment, appearing to be put up from the 2nd or 3rd line trenches behind the nose of the Salient in Q.10.d. Some of them seemed scarcely to reach the enemy's front line.

Pigeons. One pigeon was observed to fly high from between MAILLY and AUCHONVILLERS over KNIGHTSBRIDGE BARRACKS in the direction of the German lines about 6.p.m. on the 29th ulto. On the 30th ulto. the same thing occurred about 7.p.m. On 1st inst. about another pigeon within gun shot range and on 2nd June about 7.p.m. yet another pigeon passed over KNIGHTSBRIDGE BARRACKS flying from the same place as the others and in the same direction. This bird also was within gun range.

Captain, G.S.

4th June 1916.   29th Division.

HEADQUARTERS.
29th DIVISION.
INTELLIGENCE.
D.S.63
No. ....
Date. 5/6/16.

29th DIVISION DAILY SUMMARY.
for
Period From 6.a.m. 4/6/16 to 6.a.m. 5/6/16.

OPERATIONS.

Artillery.   Quiet during the day. Between 7.15. p.m. and 8.p.m. about 14 shells were fired on KING STREET and MINDEN STREET, our 18 pdrs retaliated and enemy ceased almost at once. During the morning Sap 5 (Q.10.4.) was slightly shelled; about 4.p.m.the support trenches in the area between LIMERICK JUNCTION and Q.16.6. on our side and on the enemy's side the trenches between BEAUMONT HAMEL and Y RAVINE.

Machine Guns.   Enemy Machine Guns were normal, their fire being chiefly confined to shooting at our aeroplanes. Our machine guns fired at irregular intervals on the enemy wire and front line where these had been damaged during the previous night's operations. This was kept up during the night.

INTELLIGENCE.

Enemy Work.   Listening Posts in front of ROONEY'S SAP reported hearing digging in enemy front line near Q.10.b.8.7.

Signs of work in varoius enemy trenches were seen behind BEAUMONT HAMEL, chalk being thrown up occasionally.

Enemy Movements.   Parties some of whom appeared to be digging were observed on WAGGON ROAD.

Between 10.55.a.m. and 5.30.p.m. about eight horse transport wagons and two motor transport wagons were observed on road coming from GREVILLERS at point G.22.d.6.7.

At 11.30.a.m. 2 horse transport wagons were observed going towards PYS on road at point M.1.d.5.9. At 5.25.p.m. a party of about 10 men were observed at same point going towards PYS.

Train Activity.
10.20.	To ACHIET-LE-GRAND.	from BAPAUME.
11.4.	" BAPAUME	from ACHIET-LE-GRAND
11.12	" " "	" " "
11.40	" ACHIET-LE-Grand	from BAPAUME.
11.50	" BAPAUME	from LE SARS.
12.10	" ACHIET-LE-GRAND	from BAPAUME.
12.46	" BAPAUME	from ACHIET-LE-GRAND.
5.30	" " "	" " "

MISCELLANEOUS.

A large periscope about 5' high was observed on 3rd instant to be sticking up in a small sap running out from a point in the front line a few yards North of the nose of the salient in Q.10.d. Our snipers fired on it and it is believed to have been hit, but is still in the same position.

W. M. Armstrong
Captain, G.S.

5th June 1916.   29th Division

29th DIVISION DAILY SUMMARY
for

Period   From 6.a.m. 5/6/16 to 6.a.m. 6/6/16.

OPERATIONS.

Artillery.   About 6 rounds H.E. were fired at 86th TRENCH between 11.a.m. and 12.a.m.

"Whizz bangs" also interrupted work going on in KING STREET. There were three casualties in support trench behind Q.10.7.

The enemy registered at 5.a.m. with a few 7.7.c.m. along FETHARD STREET from 1st AVENUE to CLONMEL AVENUE, between 8.a.m. and 9.a.m. with about 20 H.E. probably 15.c.m. on SAP 6 close to Mine Head and Upper End of 1st Avenue; between 10.a.m. and 10.30.a.m. with about 20 7.7 c.m. and small H.E. om C STREET, FETHARD STREET, and CLONMEL AVENUE. He also registered on MARY REDAN.

The enemy's retaliation to our bombardment which began at 11.p.m. was not carried out on a large scale. Left of MARY REDAN only a few shells burst short of the firing line and a few in the neighbourhood of FETHARD STRET.
 Right of MARY REDAN a certain amount of damage was done to the new trench and the old firing line and four men were wounded.

Machine Guns.   Enemy machine Guns were not very active. Ours swept at intervals the enemy's wire while indirect fire was maintained on BEAUMONT HAMEL and its approaches.

A hostile machine gun is believed to have been located at point approx Q.5.c.17.76.

Trench Mortars. Our Trench Mortars fired on junction of BEAUMONT ROAD and SUNKEN ROAD at 9.15.p.m.

Snipers.   Enemy snipers rather quiet. Ours claim to have hit a man showing himself outside a house in BEAUMONT HAMEL.

Patrols.   Patrols left our lines at point Q.4.d.2.8. and examined ground to the left. Returned at point Q.4.b.4.1. All was quiet.

Listening Posts went out from 9.30.p.m. to 2.0 a.m. from Q.10.8., Q.10.11., ROONEY'S SAP, Q.10.13 and Q.10.15.   ROONEY'S SAP post reported hearing enemy digging hard during early part of the night.

Snipers.(contd)   At about 9.p.m. an enemy sniper was observed to be firing from the trees at point Q.16.b.70.80. A Lewis Gun opened fire on him but he continued firing until soon after 11.p.m.

INTELLIGENCE.

Enemy Work.   Enemy's wire has been renewed in several places along the front.

Near point Q.4.d.8.5. some sandbags were laid during the night. They appear to mark entrance to sap or mine as men were seen carrying timber in during the day. The men were in shirt sleeves.

A gap in the enemy's wire at Q.11.c.65.10. has been cut and is marked by pegs.

Enemy Movements.   At 1.45.p.m. at spot approx. Q.5.c.05.40. observerx saw enemy pass opening, wearing leather equipment, packs and what looked like blankets attached to packs. One or two of the men carried small parcels. At 6.30.p.m. an officer who wore an overcoat and a red band round hat, passed the same spot. He was accompanied by another officer who wore
no

-2-

no distinguishing mark. The uniforms looked to be quite new.

Number of parties were seen on WAGON ROAD was some what less than usual.

At about 6.p.m. six motor lorries with two men mounted and three men walking were seen leaving BEAUCOURT on the road to BAILLESCOURT and shortly afterward a convoy with seven men was seen moving in the same direction.

The usual horse transport movements were observed on the road to and from PYS.

Transport was also seen at various times during the day moving to and from GREVILLERS at point on road G.22.d.6.7.

A party of 200 troops were observed proceeding towards GREVILLERS in parties of about 50, at about 100 yards interval between each party at point G.22.d.6.7.

TRAIN ACTIVITY.

Trains were observed passing along STATION ROAD at 9.30.a.m., 3.15.p.m. and 6.30.p.m.

The following train movements were also observed;-

7.0	To	BAPAUME from LE SARS.
7.25	"	" " " "
10.35	"	ACHIET-LE-GRAND from BAPAUME.
11.15.	"	BAPAUME from ACHIET-LE-GRAND.
11.17.	"	" " " " " "
11.45.	"	" " " " " "
12.35	"	" " " " " "
3.40	"	" " " " " "
4.0	"	ACHIET-LE-GRAND from BAPAUME.
4.2.	"	LE SARS from BAPAUME.
4.45	"	ACHIET-LE-GRAND from BAPAUME.
5.11.	"	BAPAUME from LE SARS.

MISCELLANEOUS.

Signals. From about 6.45.p.m. to about 7.p.m. red, green and white lights were seen behind some trees at abou L.28.c.Centre. The enemy are thought to have been practising. A considerable number of flares were put up over the ROAD in Q.16.b. in "No Man's Land" as though the enemy were apprehensive of operations there on our part.

During the earlier stages of the bombardment which began at 11.p.m. numerous red flares were observed from FORT MOULIN to be sent up from either the 1st or 2nd enemy lines.

6th June 1916.

Captain, G.S.
29th Division.

D.S. 65.
8/6/16.

DAILY SUMMARY.

HEADQUARTERS.
29th DIVISION.
INTELLIGENCE.

No.
Date.

Period from 6.0 a.m. 7/6/16 to 6.0 a.m. 8/6/16.

OPERATIONS.

Artillery. Enemy's artillery shelled AUCHONVILLERS intermittently from 5.0 pm. to 8.0 pm. and about eight fell in the Right Sector. Our artillery retaliated and a heavy did some registering some about 3.30 pm.
The bombardment of GABION AVENUE and KNIGHTSBRIDGE reported yesterday stopped at 9.15 am; practically no damage was done. Soon after mid-day the enemy burst some shrapnel at intervals of from three to five minutes close to ENGLEBELMER on the South Eastern side. At 2.30 pm., three 15 cm. shells fell near KNIGHTSBRIDGE, at 3.25 pm. a few 7.7 cm. shells near PICCADILLY and at 3.45 pm. a few more 7.7 cm. in the direction of the battery right of the entrance to GABION AVENUE. The enemy finished his bombardment of this part of the line by shortening, later on, to the neighbourhood of the batteries near KNIGHTSBRIDGE with 15 cm. Only a few shots were fired.
At 4.0 pm. our artillery was observed to fire on the trenches on the South side of the Salient in Q.10.d. and South of the re-entrant in Q.11.c. doing considerable damage, especially at Q.17.a 85.85, where pieces of timber were seen blown into the air.

Trench Mortars. Enemy's trench mortar fired five rounds to North of WHITE CITY about 6.45 pm. Position located approximately Q.5.c.1.3., this is being watched and position will be confirmed. One casualty occurred.

Machine guns. Enemy machine guns were active from HAWTHORNE REDOUBT from 6.0 pm. to about 10.0 pm.

Patrols. A patrol was sent out at midnight to a point about 50 yards in front of the mine at Gap 6 on the extreme left of the Sector. It returned at 2.a.m. without having seen or heard anything suspicious. A listening patrol posted outside Q.16.7. from dark til dawn had also nothing to report.

INTELLIGENCE.

Enemy Work. Much earth has been thrown up between Q.6.b.35.20 and Q.6.b.2.9.
A working party of about 30 men were observed at point G.25.b.6.5.; they seemed to placing stakes and wire N. and S. of said point. They were engaged for some 3 hours.

Enemy Movements. Transport was below normal. Some was heard behind enemy lines at 2.45 am.
The usual horse transport was observed on the roads going to and from PYS and GREVILLERS

Train activity.

Usual train activity heard in BEAUMONT HAMEL last night between 8.30 and 8.45.
About 3.15 pm. a train passed along station road line from direction of BEAUMONT HAMEL towards the station Q.18.b.
The usual train movements between BAPAUME - LE SARS - ACHIET LE GRAND were observed.

MISCELLANEOUS.

Smoke. A considerable volume of smoke was seen to rise from a point about Q.11.b.46 at dawn. It is supposed to be

(2).

MISCELLANEOUS CONTD.

Notice Boards. The enemy has put up a notice board in front of their lines near the OLD BEAUMONT ROAD "Lord Kitchener and his Staff are drowned in the North Sea".

Signals. A number of red and green lights were seen but no results observed.

Search Light. A searchlight was seen about 8.30 pm. and 11.30 pm. to right front of "F" Street.

Aeroplanes. Our aeroplanes were very activy and drew a great deal of hostile machine gun and rifle fire. The position of an anti-aircraft gun has been noted, but further observation is required to locate it exactly.

Fuse found with flat top. marked as below :-

on the other end it is marked $\frac{I}{14}$

Major. G.S.
29th Division.

HEADQUARTERS.
29th DIVISION.
INTELLIGENCE.
D.S.66.
No.
Date. 9/6/16.

29th DIVISION DAILY SUMMARY.
for
Period   From 6.a.m. 8/6/16 to 6.a.m. 9/6/16.

OPERATIONS.

Artillery.   The enemy devoted his attention to the following areas:-
(i) The front line and supports round about PICADILLY and CONSTITUTION HILL with something over 30 rounds of 7.7.c.m. Three men were wounded but not seriously.
(ii) Round about ST JOHN'S ROAD near junction with CARLISLE STREET, also 1st AVENUE and POMPADOUR with small H.E. and Shrapnel. Two of the last named landed close to our front line trenches between Q.10.3. and Q.10.5. No damage was done. Between 4.0. and 5.0.p.m. several large H.E.s. fell near FETHARD STREET.
(iii) Attention was also given to MINDEN TERRACE, 4th AVENUE KING STREET. Shells also fell in LANWICK STREET? ST HELENS and WHITE CITY. Most of these appeared to be from a $5\frac{1}{2}$" how.
      At 6.30.a.m. a heavy gun was firing in the direction of MAILLY MAILLET, and from 2.0.p.m. to 4.0.p.m. and again at 6.20.p.m. a considerable number of H.E. and Shrapnel were fired at long range, apparently west of AUCHONVILLERS and N. of ENGLEBELMER.

Trench Mortars.   Front line right of MARY REDAN was registered at 6.15.a.m. with small Trench Mortar Bombs without damage beyond the splintering of two rifles, at 8.15.a.m. with six medium Minnenwerfer Bombs and at 5.30 this morning with twelve rifle grenades.

Machine Guns.   The usual activity against our aeroplanes, one of which was observed on one occasion to retaliate with its Lewis Gun.
      Enemy Machine Gun at Q.4.d.9.45. was heard and seen firing at our aeroplanes.

Trench Mortars.(contd)   Enemy Trench Mortar at Q.5.a.1.3. dropped a few shells round MINDEN TERRACE-(North end) of 4th Avenue.
Snipers. in right subsector claim two hits yesterday.

INTELLIGENCE.

Enemy Work.   Enemy were laying telephone wire from reel along 3rd line Q.5.a.9.1. at 11.30.
      The wire at the nose of the Salient in Q.10.d. has the appearance of having been strengthened.
      More wire and stakes have been placed from point Q.12.a.6.8. to point Q.12.b.5.5.
      Wire and stakes have been placed from Q.12.a.6.8. to Q.12.b.5.5.
Enemy Movements.
      Four transport wagons, one covered van, one ambulance and one water cart were observed entering or leaving BEAUCOURT during the course of the day. At 12.30.p.m. a gun of some size was seen to leave BEAUCOURT in the direction of GRANDCOURT.
      The usual small parties were seen on the S.E. flank of BEAUMONT HAMEL. They were moving about quite casually, not apparently on any definite errand.
      3 horse transport wagons and horseman in front were observed proceeding towards IRLES on road at point G.32.c.9.5.
      A party of about 20 strong were observed at work at point G.32.d.4.7., engaged for some $2\frac{1}{2}$ hours; 2 horse wagons came to said point from direction of PYS and returned towards PYS 20 minutes later.

Train Activity.

-2-

Train Activity. At 1.30. and at 3.30.p.m. respectively a train was observed in Station Road. The following train movements were observed:-
8.20 Achiet LE GRAND to BAPAUME.
9.50 " " " " "
10.45 BAPAUME from ACHIET LE GRAND.
11.0 " " " " "
12.50 " " LE SARS.
4.7. ACHIET LE GRAND from BAPAUME.
4.12. BAPAUME from LE SARS
4.17. " " " "
4.25. ACHIET LE GRAND from BAPAUME.
5.33. To BAPAUME from ACHIET LE GRAND.

MISCELLANEOUS.

Balloons. Three balloons were observed to rise over BOIS - de - LOGEAST, LE SARS and BUCQUOY respectively.

Signals. A series of flashes were noticed from Church Tower at SERRE.

Unusually large number of white, red and green flares were sent up far away on our left, no results could be observed to follow.

Mining. Sounds have been recently heard apparently below a deep dug-out in BUCKINGHAM PALACE ROAD which have given rise to a suspicion of enemy mining. The place has been and still is under careful observation, including that of expert listeners and the results so far do not confirm the suspicion.

Two men were seen at Q.4.d.90.48. and had what seemed to be a khaki cap with shiny black peak; it is reported from the Right Sector that some of the enemy appear to be black men.
A Man was seen by one of our snipers and was dressed like our soldiers with service cap and puttees.

Smoke. Smoke was observed rising from trench at Q.5.c.1.6. and also at Q.5.c.45.15.

W. M. Armstrong.

9th June 1816.

Captain.G.S.
29th Division.

HEADQUARTERS.
29th DIVISION.
INTELLIGENCE
No. 57.
10/6/16.

29th DIVISION DAILY SUMMARY.
for
Period From 6.a.m. 9/6/16 to 6.a.m. 10/6/16.

OPERATIONS.

Artillery. Enemy artillery was active yesterday. 28 H.E. shells fell in the area of KING STREET, LANWICK STREET and 5 in the area of ESAUS'WAY - TENDERLOIN. 44 H.E. fell in the sector from Q.4.d.20.95. to Q.4.b.40.80.

From 4.p.m. to 2.a.m. 71 shells fell in the area Q.4.d.30.85. to Q.4.c.90.65., 44 being howitzer, 22 field gun shells and 5 Trench Mortars.

10 H.E. fell in area of TENDERLOIN and WHITE CITY at about 3.p.m. and 10 more at 5.p.m.

Front line and MINDEN TERRACE was considerably damaged.

MARY REDAN, PICADILLY, CONSTITUTION HILL, FETHARD STREET, FIRST AVENUE and the Front Firing Line on the left of the Right Sector were briskly shelled with 7.7. c.m., 15.c.m. and "whizz bangs"; no damage being reported.

Machine Guns. Machine Gun activity was chiefly confined to firing on our aeroplanes. Infantry observers locate one of these anti-aircraft machine gun positions as at Q.11.a.45.90. in the top window of a house.

Trench Mortars. Commenced firing at 7.a.m. on the REDAN area. 12 large and 25 smaller bombs were counted. They seemed to come from Q.17.b.5.7., Q.17.b.3.7. and Q.17.a.99.99. (N.B. This may be the same position as the one already located, Q.17.a.99.96.) The mortars were silenced by our heavy artillery about 7.p.m.

Patrols. Listening patrols were out in "No Man's Land" between the end of FIRST AVENUE and the SUNK ROAD in Q.16.b. and found nothing to report.

A patrol under Lieut Davies, 1st R.Dublin Fusiliers and 3 men left ROONEY'S SAP at 9.45.p.m. and after they had been out about 7 minutes bombing and rifle fire were heard. Some of the bullets passed low immediately over our front line from two directions. Lieut Davies and party were armed with bombs and one revolver and it would appear that they were outflanked. A patrol went out from ROONEY'S SAP 15 to 20 minutes after the fight but could find nothing. A listening Post about 50 yards to the left of ROONEY'S SAP heard one of Lieut Davies patrol shouting, went out and brought him in. He had been hit with a bomb in the thigh. He states that his patrol had been surprised and the rest had been wounded and presumably captured. There is nothing to be seen this morning.

Snipers. A sergeant claims to have hit a hostile sniper in crater in front of BEAUMONT HAMEL, he had a peakless cap and appeared to be in his shirt sleeves.

INTELLIGENCE.

Enemy Work. A shell crater at Q.4.d.7.4. has been sapped out to and is being worked upon

Enemy heard working in BEAUMONT and was putting up stakes at Q.10.d.5.7., cleaning front line with scoop on poles.

Working Parties were seen in second line at Q.5.a.5.2. to Q.5.a.5.5. Six or eight men were observed filling sandbags at the foot of tower at Q.5.a.5.9.

A working party of about 50 strong was observed going from IRLES towards PYS.

A working party was seen at point M.3.c. repairing a cable wire.

ENEMY MOVEMENTS.

-3-

Enemy Movements. Constant passing to and from in communication trench at Q.5.a.9.5. was observed; this appears to be a busy thoroughfare.

Much transport was observed about 8.15. a.m. coming from PYS about R.6.a.

Somewhat less movement was observed in the ANCRE VALLEY on the railway and adjacent road than on 8/6/16. One limber, two covered vans, one ambulance, one wagon were observed entering BEAUCOURT.

Small parties of men were observed working on the railway.

Much horse transport and small parties of men could be observed at various times during the day passing to and from PYS on road at point R.1.b.2.1.

The usual transport was also observed moving to and from GREVILLERS at point on road G.22.d.6.7.

Train Activity. The following train movements were observed:-
6.45. To BAPAUME from LE SARS
7.15. To   "   "   "
7.35. To ACHIET LE GRAND from BAPAUME.
9.30.   "   "   "
10.15.   "   "   "
11.0. To BAPAUME from ACHIET LE GRAND
11.3. To   "   "   "
11.10. To BAPAUME from LE SARS.
3.10. To ACHIET LE GRAND from BAPAUME.
3.30. To BAPAUME from ACHIET LE GRAND
4.28. To ACHIET LE GRAND from BAPAUME.
5.38. To BAPAUME from ACHIET LE GRAND.
5.53. To   "   "   "

MISCELLANEOUS.
(a). There has been an increase in hostile artillery and especially trench mortar activity during the period under review, the night however passed off quietly.
(b). A machine gun emplacement or observation post (a very distinct structure in front of the parapet) is visible at G.17.b.40.12
(c). Two dogs, a fox terrier and a black retriever were seen in enemy's lines at Q.5.a.3.2.
(d). Enemy gun in pit a pit near Lime Tree at Q.5.b.8.9 was observed firing on our front line. It was observed to fire eight times.
(e). There appears to be a loophole plate at Q.5.c.05.85.
(f). White screen seen in enemy's front line at Q.5.a.3.1. seems to be removed at dusk and replaced at dawn.

D.W. ?? Major.
for Lieut.Colonel. G.S.
29th Division.

10th June 1916.

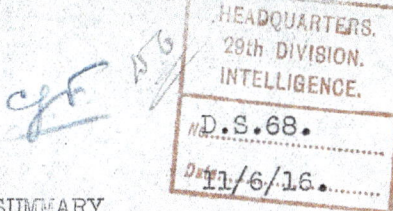

29th DIVISION DAILY SUMMARY
for
Period From 6.a.m. 10/6/16 to 6.a.m. 11/6/16.

OPERATIONS.

Artillery. At 6.30.a.m. some 50 shells fell in the region of MARY REDAN, the top of CONSTITUTION HILL, NEW TRENCH and PICADILLY, only doing slight damage to parapets. The enemy continued to register during the day on FETHARD STREET and 1st AVENUE with H.E. and Shrapnel. Between 2.p.m. and 3.p.m. some six shells burst over the road betweem FORT MOULIN and ENGLEBELMER. Shortly after 3.p.m. a fair amount of shrapnel burst over the MAILLY-AUCHONVILLERS ROAD and over the S.E. outskirts of ENGLEBELMER in the neighbourhood of the Battery there. Most of the bursts in the last named area were high.

At 11.30.p.m. hostile machine guns started traversing our front. Shortly afterwards a lively bombardment opened with shells of all calibres up to 15.c.m., and with Trench Mortar Bombs, concentrating chiefly on TENDERLOIN and MARY REDAN. The fire was directed on the front and support lines. Considerable damage was done. Our casualties were 16 killed and 44 wounded.

Our artillery replied vigorously throughout the bombardment which ceased at 1.15.a.m.

Trench Mortars. Trench Mortars continued their activities beginning at 9.a.m. on the wire in front of MARY REDAN and the Sap just to the right of it. Large cylinder bombs were seen in flight, coming approximately from Q.17.a.96.99. Some smaller bombs were fired from a point in Q.17.b. which could not be accurately determined, the bulk falling in the wire in front of the point in MARY REDAN. They were always fired three together.

Trench Mortar position at Q.4.c.4.3. was shelled yesterday by our artillery fire, there would appear to be 3 positions quite close together. This is being watched.

Machine Guns. Enemy fired very little except at our aeroplanes. During the bombardment all opened our machine guns opened fire.

Patrols. A listening patrol was out opposite the right sector from dusk till the bombardment began when it returned having nothing special to report.

INTELLIGENCE.

Enemy Work. A sap from which working parties come out is at Q.4.d.90.55.

At Q.5.c.3.8. observers were seen taking compass bearings and later a working party was seen on the parapet; 2 cylinders were brought into the trench. In the evening more working parties were seen and several men carrying or placing cylinders. The place seems to be a deep dug-out with a screen in front.

Working parties were seen at Q.5.a.9.3., Q.5.a.9.1. and Q.5.a.7.2.

The earthworks at points Q.12.a.37.100. and Q.12.a.85.80. have been enlarged.

Enemy work is still being carried on in the Salient at about Q.10.d.55.71. in a Sap. A sound resembling that of a muffled explosion or a bomb bursting was heard about mid-night. The mounds of earth round the Sap continue to grow.

Enemy Movements. Two covered vans, one light cart and one small motor car were noted entering and leaving BEAUCOURT
close

-2-

close to the railway.

Five motor transport wagons were observed coming from the direction of GREVILLERS on road at point G.22.d.6.7.

A party of men were observed passing in a trench at point Q.5.c.12.65. carrying objects on shoulder which seemed to be pipes.

TRAIN ACTIVITY. A train was observed East of GRANDCOURT moving South.

The following train movements were observed.

7.15.	To BAPAUME from ACHIET LE GRAND.	
8.15.	To ACHIET LE GRAND from BAPAUME.	
8.25.	To BAPAUME from LE SARS.	
9.55.	To ACHIET LE GRAND from BAPAUME.	
10.10.	To " " " " "	
10.40.	To BAPAUME from ACHIET LE GRAND.	
11.0.	To " " " " "	
11.5.	To ACHIET LE GRAND from BAPAUME.	
3.45.	To BAPAUME from ACHIET LE GRAND.	
5.30.	To " " " " "	

MISCELLANEOUS.

Aeroplanes. At 6.30.a.m. three enemy aeroplanes came over our lines. Our anti aircraft guns opened fire and they retired towards the S.E. within ten minutes. They were flying very high.

Signals. At the commencement of last night's bombardment one red and two green flares were sent up. One red flare sent up on our left preceded the stoppage of hostile fire.

A number of coloured lights went up during the bombardment but no definite results were observed.

Pigeons. A pigeon was seen to fly towards enemy lines about 7.45.a.m.

Steam. Steam in long puffs was seen issueing from enemy's support trench in Q.5.a.5.2. for ½ an hour.

W. M. Armstrong

11th June 1916.

Captain, G.S.
29th Division.

29th DIVISION DAILY SUMMARY
for
Period from 6.a.m. 11/6/16 to 6.a.m. 12/6/16

D.S.69
12/6/16.

OPERATIONS.

Artillery Enemy Artillery was quiet all day.

Machine Guns. A Machine Gun has been active against our aircraft from Q.11.c.42.49. A periscope has been seen there.

Trench Mortars. During the bombardment of the 10/11th June, a Trench Mortar appeared to be operating from a position near the re-entrance in Q.11.c. Q.11.c.42.49 is the approximate position given by the Infantry.

A sniper in the Right Sub-sector reports an enemy Trench Mortar about Q.10.d.6.7., this might be the old one at Q.10.d.85.65 moved or in its old place. A parculiarity noticed about this Mortar is its projectile which has a lighted tail and gives the appearance od a "dud" flare going through the air.

Patrols. A Patrol left Rooney's Sap at 9.45 p.m. and went half left. No sign of lost patrol and no enemy patrol met. Enemy appeared to be working on their trenches damaged by our artillery. Patrol returned same way at 12.midnight.

INTELLIGENCE.

Enemy Movements. A transport and small parties in front of BAILLESCOURT.

Observation was going on from the White Screen previously reported, observers were wearing blue uniforms with white piping. There is an opening in the screen which was opened and closed several times during the day.

Men carrying timber observed at Q.15.a.9.1.

Enemy movements near BEAUCOURT were below normal. 1 covered van, 1 motor wagon, 1 limber and 1 transport wagon were noticed as either entering or leaving the village. A working party was seen busily engaged all day on a road in rear of BEAUCOURT and North East of PYS.

A working party carrying timber were observed to enter trench from rear at point Q.6.a.25.93.

3 horse transport wagons and 2 horsemen were observed coming from the direction of GREVILLERS on road at point G.22.d.6.7.

Men were seen moving at point Q.4.d.95.50., headcover has been placed at this point.

Enemy Work. The earth work at point Q.12.b.35.85 has been enlarged.

Fresh chalk has been thrown up at the point of the salient Q.10.d.55.70. Frequently a fire is lit there at 3.30.a.m. as large volumes of smoke are seen for some time as long as 1 hour.

Train Activity. The following train movements were observed:-
7.50 to ACHIET-LE-GRAND from BAPAUME
8.10 " " " " "
8.55 " BAPAUME from ACHIET-LE-GRAND.
9.33 " ACHIET-LE-GRAND from BAPAUME.

-2-

Train Activity (contd.)

10.3 to BAPAUME from ACHIET-LE-GRAND.
10.15 " " " LE SARS.
10.55 " " " ACHIET-LE-GRAND.
11.9 " " " " "
11.40 " " " " "
2.47 " " " " "
3.24 " " " " "
3.35 " ACHIET-LE-GRAND from BAPAUME.
3.55 " " " "
4.26 " " " "
5.30 " BAPAUME from ACHIET-LE-GRAND.

MISCELLANEOUS.

Aeroplanes.

A hostile aeroplane flew over our lines at 4.0 a.m.

Projectiles.

The following numbers were noticed on fuses of shells fired in the bombardment of 1140 p.m. 10/6/16:-

DOPP Z92   DOPP Z92.   lg.
SP16.   Brig
15.c.m.   SP.16.M.
                  10.5 c.m.

A gun appeared to be firing from bank were there are two tall trees at Q.19.b.40.45.

Enemy Raid of 10/11th

Further to my report of 11th June the following is the latest information to hand.

A heavy bombardment took place on our line between 11.30 p.m. and 12 midnight along the front and support line from Q.4.b.4.1. to JACOBS LADDER. During the bombardment our front line was evacuated with the exception of a small party in Sap 7, who awaited the attack but were unmolested. It is not certain whether the enemy attempted a raid or not. Our Vickers Maxims swept our front both during the bombardment and after it, and the Divisional Artillery put a barrage on the enemy's line. A considerable amount of damage was done to the support trenches between Q.4/7 and Q.4./14. Our casualties were 14 killed and 21 wounded (No Officers)

J S Fulton Capt.
for Captain G.S.
29th Division.

12th June, 1916.

HEADQUARTERS.
29th DIVISION.
INTELLIGENCE.
D.S. 70.
13/6/16.

29th DIVISION DAILY SUMMARY.
for
Period from 6 a.m. 12/6/16. to 6 a.m. 13/6/16.

OPERATIONS.

Artillery. During the morning about 70 7.7 cm shells were fired, causing one casualty in FETHARD Street. A few rounds fell in the neighbourhood of PICCADILLY and ST JAMES'S and one round of 15 cm. made a direct hit on a parapet just to the left of the road in Q.16. At 3 p.m. the new fire trench to the right of the REDAN was ranged with percussion and time shrapnel, 7.7 cm. and 10.5 cm. mixed, 12 rounds in all. About 15 rounds were fired on the support trenches in the same area causing one slight casualty. 12 shells fell in KING Street causing some casualties, a few fell in front of "F" Street, BROADWAY, and head of SECOND AVENUE.
Our Artillery shelled some enemy working parties and retaliated with good effect.

Machine Guns. Enemy Machine Guns fired at our aeroplanes during the day.

Patrols. The ~~enemy wire of the~~ Right Sector was patrolled without incident.

Snipers. Snipers report a positive hit at a point in Q.11.c. which will be more accurately given later. Two had exposed themselves as if to look round. They were fired on and one fell appearing to have been hit.
A sniper has been located at Q.5.c.0.55.

INTELLIGENCE.

Enemy Movements. Men were seen in full kit, carrying pick and shovel proceeding north along enemy's third line (R.2.b.5.0. to R.2.a.9.0).
Conditions for observation were unfavourably, but five vans, five limbers, and one wagon were noted entering and leaving BEAUCOURT. One of the limbers was loaded with long planks and was followed by a small fatigue party.
Small working parties were noted on the Railway line in the ANCRE Valley.
The usual Horse Transport was observed on the PYS - GREVILLERS Roads during the day.
Observed on the Road at point G.25.d.2.1. movement of guns or ammunition wagons, three horsemen in front, seven four horse limbers riders on leader and wheeler, four horsemen in rear. This party was proceeding north.
About 7.25 a.m. much transport was observed coming from the direction of PUISSEUX - AU-MONT going towards IRLES.

Enemy Work.
Working parties were seen at Q.5.b.75.50, Q.6.a.30.85, Q.11.a.35.30, Q.11.a.15.20 and were dispersed by our Artillery.
A party of about 20 strong were observed at 7.30 a.m. on the GREVILLERS Road from IRLES at point G.23.b.

Train activities. The following train movements were observed:-
7.50 to ACHIET LE GRAND from BAPAUME.
9.27   ditto
9.48   ditto
10.2 to BAPAUME from ACHIET LE GRAND.
10.33 ditto
10.58 ditto
11.0   ditto
11.27 to ACHIET LE GRAND from BAPAUME.

-2-

```
2.15 to BAPAUME from ACHIET-LE-GRAND.
2.45  "  ACHIET-LE-GRAND from BAPAUME.
4.20  "      "    "    "    "    "
5.40  "  BAPAUME from ACHIET-LE-GRAND.
```

MISCELLANEOUS.

    (a) There is a glass fixed up a tall tree from Q.4.d.9.4.
    (b) More smoke than usual issuing from Q.5.c.5.4.
    (c) Two men were seen observing from trench in front of ~~BEAUCOURT~~ BEAUMONT HAMEL. They were dressed in light blue coloured uniform with black braid on chest. Small round caps with a white band and black top.

    A man reported seen dresses in uniform exactly the same as our R.F.C. including cap approximately Q.5.b.90.50.

    (d) Enemy opposite the right of our right sub-sector appear to be much tanned or slightly coloured. They wear the peakless hats.

    (e) There appeared to be a flag flying near BAILLESCOURT position of flag approximately R.3.c.65.10.

    (f) ~~An aircraft was observed at point X.2.0.~~

W. M. Armstrong

15th June 1916.
                                                      Captain G.S.
                                                      29th Division.

D.S. 71.

HEADQUARTERS
29th DIVISION.
INTELLIGENCE.

14th June 1916.

29th DIVISION
DAILY SUMMARY
Period from 6.0 am. 13/6/16 to 6.0 am. 14/6/16.

OPERATIONS.

Artillery. The enemy continued his registration of our lines being especially active between 2.0 pm. and 5.0 pm. The FETHARD STREET Area is estimated to have received about 140, 7.7 cm. during the day. CONSTITUTION HILL, SHOOTERS HILL, and FRENCH TRENCH were also ranged with percussion and time sharpnel. HORSE SHOE, LANWICK STREET, PILK STREET, HOUNSLOW STREET and Front Line were shelled during the day.

Our Artillery retaliation was prompt.

Machine guns. A gun at Q.4.d.9.5. fired a few rounds on our front line about 9.30 pm.

Trench Mortars. From noon to 1.0 pm. the enemy sent over some five medium sized bombs into the REDAN. They fired four more at 10.30 pm.

Patrols. Listening patrols posted 50 yards in front of the wire had nothing to report.

SNIPERS. The approximate co-ordinates of the spot where the man fell when fired on by one of our snipers as reported yesterday is Q.11.c.6.4. Both men seen wore long blue grey overcoats, caps of same colour and black half boots.

INTELLIGENCE.

Enemy work. Telephone wire was seen laid from Q.6.a.8.3. to Q.5.c.75.50.
New earth has been thrown up around Point Q.6.a.25.95.
The enemy was observed to be throwing up chalk at intervals during the day at Q.17.b.2.4.
A working party was observed at 2.15 pm. about 50 strong, working at a point G.32.c.

Movements. Large parties of men were seen marching North and South along GREVILLERS Road, one party consisted of a strong Company (3 parties of about 80 men) led by mounted officers.
Two parties of troops were observed, each party about 60 strong, proceeding in the direction of GREVILLERS, on the road at point G.22.d.6.7.
Two parties were also observed on this road, each about 40 strong, at 11.15.
Two horse transport wagons were seen coming from PYS on road at point M.1.b.3.2.
Four horse transport wagons were observed, and one four horse limber, on road at point G.25.d.2.1., proceeding North.
At 7.20 am. several transport were observed going and coming from IRLES to GREVILLERS.

Train activity.
The following train movements were observed.
5.55	to BAPAUME	from ACHIET le GRAND.
7.25	to "	from LE SARS.
8.25	to "	from ACHIET le GRAND.
8.50	to ACHIET le GRAND	from BAPAUME.
11.25	to BAPAUME	from ACHIET le GRAND.
12.30	to "	" " "
1.2	to ACHIET le GRAND	from BAPAUME.
2.5	to "	" " "
3.30	to BAPAUME	from ACHIET le GRAND.
4.13	to ACHIET le GRAND	from BAPAUME.

MISCELLANEOUS. (a). Smoke was seen issuing from a ruined house in BEAUMONT (b). Periscope was seen 60 yards in front of enemy's trench in BEAUMONT HAMEL, in grass.   A bombing sap is suspected.

(c). <u>Projectiles.</u>   Nose caps bearing the following marks have been found and can be forwarded if required :-

   K.Z.14°   K.Z.14.   DOPP Z 96 n/A.
  S.W.N. 15.   F.E.A. 15   0   108
    220   364

(d). At 4.30 pm. what seemed to be either an O.P. or a gun pit was observed at M.1.d.84.

W. M. Armstrong Capt.

                                     Captain. G.S.
14th June 1916.   29th Division.

D.S.72.

29TH DIVISION DAILY SUMMARY
for period
from 6 a.m. 14/6/16. to 6 a.m. 15/6/16.

HEADQUARTERS.
29th DIVISION.
INTELLIGENCE.

No............
Date............

OPERATIONS.

Artillery. From 7.30 to 9.30 a.m. support and communication trenches in region of Regent Street, PICCADILLY and CONSTITUTION HILL were shelled with about 35 rounds of 7.7 cm. At 9.30 a.m. MARY REDAN and the front line on its left received a few rounds of the same calibre. At 5.30 p.m. a few rounds of 10.5 cm. fell near PICCADILLY. Our Artillery retaliation was on each occasion prompt. At 6.30 p.m. the BEAUCOURT REDOUBT and communication trench immediately to the north of it was successfully shelled by our heavy Artillery.

Machine Guns. A few rounds were fired from HAWTHORN REDOUBT.

Patrols. A patrol from ROONEY'S SAP went out at 9.45 p.m. heard sounds of working, hammering as if on a metallic substance. Transport was also heard, but lines were quiet and no enemy patrol was seen.

INTELLIGENCE.

Enemy Work. Smoke and steam was seen rising from screen at Q.5.c.3.8.; work is being carried on behind this. Working parties were observed at Q.5.c.1.6., Q.5.c.4.2., Q.5.d.7.7.
New earth has been thrown up from point Q.6.a.25.90. to point Q.6.a.3.8., and also from Q.6.a.27.85 to Q.6.a.15.80.

Enemy Movements. The volume of traffic noted in the vicinity of BEAUCOURT was greater than usual. Seven limbers, eleven transport wagons, two motor cars, seven covered vans, were observed to enter or leave the village. In some cases the limbers were loaded with boards and accompanied by fatigue parties.
Numerous small fatigue parties crossed and recrossed the Railway line at a point approximately R.7.d.3.4.
Transport was seen going from IRLES to PUISIEUX - DU - MONT.
8 transport wagons were observed and a party of men about 10 strong coming from MIRAUMONT and going towards GREVILLERS.
At 4.50 p.m. a party of men about 40 strong were seen on GREVILLERS ROAD moving from ACHIET - LE - GRAND and went into Wood north of IRLES CHURCH.
At 5.10 p.m. 6 transports were observed coming from PYS and going towards IRLES.
A party of troops about 100 strong were seen at 5.25 p.m. marching from PYS in the direction of GREVILLERS.
At 6.0 p.m. a party of about 100 strong were observed marching from IRLES towards GREVILLERS.
A white cloth was seen flapping in the breeze at point Q.5.b.10.25. at 10 a.m.; steam rose from same point at 7.0 a.m.
From 8 a.m. and during the day men could be seen getting out of trench at Q.5.b.95.5. and entering trench at Q.6.a.3.8. and vice versa.
At 4.35 p.m. two parties of men of about 30 strong each party were observed coming from the direction of GREVILLERS on Road at point G.22.d.6.7.

-2-

Train Activities. The following train movements were observed.
8.15 a.m. to ACHIET-LE-GRAND from BAPAUME.
10.15 a.m. to BAPAUME from ACHIET-LE-GRAND.
12.30 p.m.   "   "
1.15 p.m. to ACHIET-LE-GRAND from BAPAUME.
2 p.m. to BAPAUME from ACHIET-LE-GRAND.
4 p.m.   "   "
5.12 p.m. to ACHIET-LE-GRAND from BAPAUME.
5.40 p.m.   "   "
8.45 p.m. to BAPAUME from ACHIET-LE-GRAND.

MISCELLANEOUS.

(a) Pigeons. Two pigeons were seen to cross the enemy's lines and our own flying in the direction of ENGLEBELMER. (Reported by Infantry).

(b) Loopholes. The loophole at about Q.5.c.15.50 has an oblong slit of about 2 feet, which points to it being an O.P. rather than a machine gun emplacement or snipers post.

(c) Gun Emplacements. A flash of a gun was seen just North of IRLES CHURCH.

(d) Signals. A green light and then a white light was sent up opposite HAPPY VALLEY and was followed by Artillery fire on left sub-sector.

W. M. Armstrong.

15th June, 1916.

Captain, G.S.,
29th Division.

D.S. 73.

29TH DIVISIONAL DAILY SUMMARY.

From 6 a.m. 15/6/16. to 6 a.m. 16/6/16.

HEADQUARTERS.
29th DIVISION.
INTELLIGENCE.

No.............
Date............

OPERATIONS.

Artillery. Enemy Artillery searched our communication trenches from BROADWAY to BLOOMFIELD and a few shells fell in the neighbourhood of SECOND AVENUE. At 6.30 a.m. a few rounds of shrapnel were fired on AUCHONVILLERS ROAD and at 2 p.m. six rounds of shrapnel on GABION AVENUE. At 11 a.m. 30 rounds of 7.7. c.m. and shrapnel fell in the left section of our Right Sector.

Our Artillery were registering very effectively on support and communication trenches at "Y" RAVINE.

Trench Mortars. An enemy trench mortar is suspected at Q.17.a.96.99.

INTELLIGENCE.

Enemy Movements. The usual transport was seen along the PYS - LE SARS ROAD.

Six men and apparently an officer were seen building S.E. from "F" STREET. They came out from behind some bushes and extended at about 25 yards apart. They then lay down and passed long planks into a trench. They were dressed in long dark greatcoats with capes over them. At 12 noon a large working party was observed at R.2.d.3.7. The usual enemy movement was observed in BEAUMONT - HAMEL. Men were also seen near BEAUCOURT carrying timber across Railway line.
A working party about 60 strong was observed marching along the road from GREVILLERS to IRLES at 1.10 p.m. They returned at 5.40 p.m.
Working parties were seen at points L.32.b.2.4 and M.5.a.2.1 respectively.
Four motor transports were observed moving from GREVILLERS to IRLES at about 3.10 p.m.

Enemy Work. At 9.10 a.m. the enemy were working at approx. point Q.10.d.65.71 and sounds were heard like that of an excavation. At 10.0 p.m. the enemy were working apparently at their wire near above point till 12.30 a.m. Wiring was also heard in progress at Q.18.c. between the hours of 11.0 p.m. and 1 a.m. New knife rests have been put out at Q.4.d.9.5. On the south side and in front of second and third lines at "Y" RAVINE new wire has been put up. At Q.11.d.4.5 a brushwood screen has been put up in the trees.
At the screen which covers opening in parapet at point Q.5.c.15.65 men could be observed looking through slit and this continued for half an hour.

Train Activity. The following train movements were observed :-
11.30 a.m. To ACHIET-LE-GRAND from BAPAUME.
12.7 p.m. To BAPAUME from ACHIET-LE-GRAND.
12.15 p.m. To ACHIET-LE-GRAND from BAPAUME.
12.55 p.m.   -"-
1.7 p.m.   -"-
4.30 p.m. To BAPAUME from ACHIET-LE-GRAND.
5.13 p.m. To BAPAUME from LE SARS.
5.15 p.m. To ACHIET LE GRAND from BAPAUME.

MISCELLANEOUS. NIL

W. M. Armstrong

HEADQUARTERS.
29th DIVISION.
INTELLIGENCE.

D.S.74.
No............
Date.......... 17/8/16.

29th DIVISION DAILY SUMMARY.
Period from 6.a.m.16/8/16 to 6.a.m. 17/8/16.

OPERATIONS.

ARTILLERY. From 9. to 11. a.m. enemy sent over about 40 shells on St JOHN'S ROAD, CARLISLE STREET and CLONMEL AVENUE apparently for registration purposes. Transport approach to WHITE CITY and 2nd AVENUE was also shelled. The noticeable feature was the number of "blinds". No damage was done.

TRENCH MORTARS.
Between 9.45 and 10.p.m. enemy fired 46 trench mortar bombs some distance on the left of our left sub-sector. They appeared to fire in groups of three.

MACHINE GUNS.
Enemy Machine Guns were quiet during the day but rather active at dusk.
A machine gun emplacement is suspected in the disused chalk quarry North end of the bank which runs parallel with the South face of the BEAUCOURT REDOUBT at Q.12.d.3.4.
A machine gun was firing from "stand to " last night from a point Q.5.c.15.88. It is probable a gune of the Lewis type as there is no emplacement at this point and it appeared to fire a great deal faster than the ordinary German Machine Gun. It is thought that it may be a captured Lewis Gun.

PATROLS.
A listening patrol went out South of the HORSE SHOE at 11.30 p.m. and returned at 2.30 a.m. No enemy patrol was seen or heard.

INTELLIGENCE.

ENEMY MOVEMENTS.
About 10.30 a.m. four bodies of troops of about 80 men each, at intervals, were observed going out of the road away from BEAUCOURT-SUR-ANCRE, point R.8.b.4.8.
At 9.15.p.m. enemy were observed marching down track by light railway at BEAUCOURT-SUR-ANCRE, they were estimated at 800 strong and were marching in the direction of their front line, so possibly they were taking over. They were dressed in full marching order.
At 5.30. p.m. about 30 or 40 men were seen to form up at R.8.b.4.8. It was apparently a party which had been working in the third line. When formed up they marched towards BEAUCOURT-SUR-ANCRE.
At 2.30 p.m. at Q.10.d.7.8. tops of rifles or working impliments could be seen. About 10 minutes later chalk was being thrown up from this spot also a little further ahead.
At 7.40. p.m. timber was seen being carried towards Q. 10.d.6.6.
Two men apparently Officers were seen at 8.p.m. using teliscope at Q.10.d.7.6. 3 mortar and 6 horse transports were observed coming from the direction of GRENVILLERS and horse transport from direction of COURCELLETE. A number of iron knife rests were pushed over the top of the parapet at intervals throughout the day at Q.4.d.9.5. Several Germans seen at this point were wearing blue overalls, and a small round blue cap with white band.

ENEMY WORK.
A small trench has been dug from Q.5.c.40.85 to Q.5.a. 26.60.

More iron stakes and wire have been placed at point Q.4.d.8.6. Also at point Q.4.d.38.50

INTELLIGENCE Contd.

TRAIN ACTIVITY.   The following train movements were observed:-
6.55 a.m. to LE - SARS from BAPAUME.
7.5. a.m.   " BAPAUME from ACHIET-LE-GRAND.
10.15. a.m." ACHIE -LE-GRAND from BAPAUME.
11.35 a.m.   "   "   "   "   "
12.15 a.m.   " BAPAUME from ACHIET-LE-GRAND.
12.45 p.m.   "   "   "   "
12.45 p.m.   "   "   "   LE - SARS.
1.20 p.m.   " ACHIET-LE-GRAND from BAPAUME.
4.55 p.m.   "   "   "   "   "

The 11.35 train to ACHIET-LE-GRAND from BAPAUME was probably carrying a large gun.

MISCELLANEOUS.

BALLOONS.
Three enemy balloons were up yesterday at COURCELLES, South west of LE-SARS, and BOIS-DE-LOGEAST.

SIGNALS.
At 11.p.m. a green rocket was fired but no noticeable result followed.

W.M. Armstrong
                                                Captain G.S.
17th June 1916.   29th Division.

D.S.75
18/6/16.

HEADQUARTERS.
29th DIVISION.
INTELLIGENCE.

No..........
Date..........

29th DIVISION DAILY SUMMARY.
Period from 17/6/16 (6.a.m.) to 6.a.m. 18/6/16.

OPERATIONS.
Artillery.
At 11.15 a.m. 24 rounds were fired on St JOHN'S ROAD but no damage was done. 9 Enemy shells fell in the region of the junction of NEW TRENCH and LONG ACRE. Possibly the digging of a mortar emplacement had been observed. There was no damage done. BLOOMFIELD and BROADWAY received attention from a 7.7 c.m. battery, AUCHONVILLERS Cemetery was also shelled.

Our artillery registered with effective results alon the enemy's front and second line trenches from 'Y' Ravine Q.5.a.25.7.

Machine Guns.
Enemy Machine Guns were quiet. The gun reported yesterday was again seen firing at 'stand to', but appears to be a 'roving' gun as its position was different.

A machine gun emplacement or O.P. is believed to be at Q.5.c.5.9.

Three machine gun emplacements have been observed at R.19.c.6.4.

Patrols.
A listening patrol went out South of the HORSESHOE at 11.30 p.m. and returned at 2.a.m. Nothing to report.

A patrol left Sap at Q.17.9. at 11.p.m. and returned at 1.30 a.m. Nothing was seen or heard of the enemy.

INTELLIGENCE.
Enemy Movements.
Several transports were seen at 5.30 p.m. at R.8.b.4.6. going to and from firing line. Men were also seen at above point as well as 2 men on horseback. At 11.45. a.m. at R.8.b.4.6. a man on horseback followed by a party of 50 men were seen going away from BEAUCOURT-SUR-ANCRE.

A working party was observed in trench at point Q.5.a. 95.40. New earth has been thrown up along the trench on each side of this point.

During the day 16 horse transport wagons were observed, 12 proceeding towards ERLES and 4 at point G.22.b.72 proceeding North.

A German Officer was seen observing on the roof of a house in BEAUMONT HAMEL. Men were seen here wearing blue grey uniforms and small round caps with white bands.

Enemy Work.
Enemy work in field around MIRAUMONT proceeded all day. They were cutting and carrying away fodder.

More wire has been placed at Q.5.a.10.45 and iron stakes and wire at Q.4.d.80.55. More knife rests have been pushed over parapet at Q.4.d.8.95., those reported yesterday have been placed in position.

New wire continues to be put up in front of second line at 'Y' Ravine.

New earth has been thrown up at Q.6.a.3.9.

In several cases were the houses in BEAUMONT HAMEL have been shelled, the holes have been filled up with loose bricks.

Train Activity.
The following train movements were observed:-
10.5. a.m. to ACHIET-LE-GRAND from BAPAUME.
10.20 a.m. " " " " " "
11.40 a.m. " " " " " "
11.42 a.m. " BAPAUME from ACHIET-LE-GRAND.
12.27 a.m. " " " " " "
12.42 a.m. " " " " " "

Train Activity (contd.)

    12.45 p.m. to BAPAUME from LE-SARS.
    1.10 p.m. " " " ACHIET-LE-GRAND.
    5.35 p.m. " ACHIET-LE-GRAND from BAPAUME.
    5.58 p.m. " " " " "

MISCELLANEOUS.

Smoke.

Small puffs of smoke or steam were observed again in enemy salient Q.10.d.7.5. at 9.a.m.

Signals.

At 11.20 p.m. two green lights went up on the Northwest edge of BEAUMONT HAMEL. At 11.35 p.m. - 2 more. At 11.45 - 1 more. No resulting action was observed.

Aeroplanes.

There was considerable aeroplane activity on both sides during the day. At 2.30 p.m. 5 enemy aeroplanes were over our lines for a few minutes but were driven off by our Anti-aircraft guns and aeroplanes. At 7. p.m. they again endeavoured to cross our line but were met by heavy shell fire and our own aeroplanes. They withdrew.

18th June, 1916.
                                Captain G.S.
                                29th Division.

HEADQUARTERS
29th DIVISION.
INTELLIGENCE
D.S.76.

29TH DIVISION DAILY SUMMARY.

Period from 6 a.m. 18.6.16. to 6 a.m. 19.6.16.

OPERATIONS.

Artillery. Enemy again shelled support and communication trenches between BROADWAY and BLOOMFIELD. No damage was done. PILK STREET was lightly shelled and slight damage was done. The ground behind 86th and 88th trenches was searched by their guns during the day and the front line of the Left Sector received attention but no damage was done. About 70 shells came over, several falling in firing line, communication trenches and supports in the Right Sector. Parapets were damaged in two or three places and a bridge smashed in the firing line.
Our Artillery effectively registered on the enemy's wire and trenches. Between Q.5.a.2.6 and Q.5.a.2.56 considerable was done to the wire.

Machine Guns. Enemy machine gun was seen operating at Q.11.c.45.45 firing at aeroplane at 8 p.m. Also one at Q.11.c.2.8.

Patrols. A listening patrol went out from the HORSESHOE at 11.30 p.m. and returned at 2 a.m., sounds of working were heard, but no hostile patrols seen.

Snipers. A German was observed using a telescope at Q.11.c.45.45. Our sniper claims to have hit him, and this was verified by an observer.

INTELLIGENCE.

Enemy Movements. 20 men were observed going towards PYS, three horse transport and two motor wagons going in the direction of GREVILLERS, nine horse transport on Road at G.25.d.2.1 going North.
At Q.5.c.52.80 men were observed during the day preparing an emplacement or observation post, head cover has been placed here and small bushes cover top at this point.
At 9.35 a.m. a part of troops about 40 strong were observed marching from IRLES to GREVILLERS.
Another party of about 30 strong were seen on the right of PYS CHURCH at G.8.b.4.4 carrying sandbags, and at point G.32.a.2.2 another party was observed. New earthworks can also be seen here.
15 transports were seen at 5.50 p.m. coming from PYS, passing IRLES, and going towards GREVILLERS.
Numbers of men, men on horses and transport are reported continually using the road at R.8.b.4.6 going from and coming into BEAUCOURT SUR ANCRE. Quite a number are seen turning off from this point in a North-westerly direction (there is evidently a new road here as traffic is frequently seen turning off in this direction).

Enemy Work. At Q.6.c.70.25 what seems to be a tunnel has been cut in the bank.
Enemy appear to be taking chalk from the well in BEAUMONT HAMEL.
Parties were again seen in the fields behind BEAUCOURT, carting hay.

Train Activity. The following train movements were observed.
7.50 a.m. to ACHIET LE GRAND from BAPAUME.
8.7 a.m.   -"-
8.7 a.m. to BAPAUME from ACHIET LE GRAND.
11.38 a.m. to ACHIET LE GRAND from BAPAUME.
11.55 a.m.   -"-
12.20 p.m. to BAPAUME from ACHIET LE GRAND.
12.28 p.m.   -"-
12.50 p.m.   -"-

Train Activity (continued)
4.15 p.m. to BAPAUME from ACHIET LE GRAND.
4.55 p.m.   -"-
5.4 p.m. to ACHIET LE GRAND from BAPAUME.
5.20 p.m.   -"-

MISCELLANEOUS.

Observation Posts. An observation post is thought to exist at K.36.c.4.5.
At Q.5.c.5.9. reported 17.6.16. as an O.P. or M.G. emplacement, a periscope could be seen.

Aeroplanes. Activity again considerable on both sides. During the day eight enemy machines appeared over our lines flying very high. On each occasion with one exception the enemy planes turned and flew back over their own lines. On one occasion a running fight took place, but no damage appeared to have been done. About 8.15 p.m. an enemy plane over MAILLY appeared to signal ~~what-looked~~ using what looked like "silver tinsel". This appeared to be let down and drawn up twice.

W. M. Armstrong

Captain, G.S.,
19th June, 1916.   29th Division.

29th DIVISION DAILY SUMMARY
for
Period from 6.a.m. 19/6/16 to 6.a.m. 20/6/16.

HEADQUARTERS,
29th DIVISION.
INTELLIGENCE.
D.S.77.
No.
Date.

OPERATIONS.

Artillery.
Enemy Artillery was very active all day from 8.a.m. to about 7.p.m. About 500 shells fell during the day on nearly all front line and support trenches in the Right Sector.

The trenches South of the 'HORSESHOE' and tBe street were shelled. An overhead traverse at MACLARENS LANE was demolished and 5 men wounded. They put 2 H.E. into our wire at Q.10.d.5.7.

Our Artillery retaliated effectively.

Trench Mortars.
Our Trench Mortars fired on BEAUMONT HAMEL last night. The enemy mortars fired twice from a position in front of BEAUMONT HAMEL, each time a gun fired apparently to cover the report.

Snipers.
Enemy's sniping activity has noticeably increased since yesterday morning.

INTELLIGENCE.

Enemy Movements.
At 9.a.m. 2 men were seen walking followed by horse transport wagon at R.8.b.4.6. going away from BEAUCOURT.

6 men were seen walking towards BEAUCOURT at same place soon afterwards.

At different times after 8.45 p.m. 3 or 4 transport wagons were observed leaving MIRAUMONT making North.

7 parties of men about 30 strong each were observed proceeding towards PYS, 5 horse transport and 2 large motor cars proceeding towards GREVILLERS, 11. horse transport wagons proceeding North east from PYS and 6 wagons on road at G.25.b.7.2. proceeding South. Several wagons were observed going to and from IRLES & GREVILLERS.

Enemy Work.
At different times during the day working parties of the enemy's were observed to be hard at work. Much knocking was heard during the night.

More iron stakes and wire have been placed between points Q.4.d.75.45 and Q.5.c.10.75. At 8.15 a.m. a party was working at the Light Railway S.E. of BEAU-COURT apparently repairing line.

Train Activity.

The following train movements were observed :-
8.37 a.m. to BAPAUME from LE-SARS.
9.20 a.m. " ACHIET-LE-GRAND from BAPAUME.
10.55 a.m. " " " " " "
11.0 a.m. " LE-SARS from BAPAUME.
11.3 a.m. " ACHIET-LE-GRAND from BAPAUME.

At 9.30 a.m. a train was seen going away from BEAU- -COURT at R.9.a.5.2..

At 10.15 p.m. smoke from enemy's train clearly visible in the vicinity of Q.18.b.

MISCELLANEOUS.

(a) Balloon rose BOIS DE LOGEAST at 9.30 a.m. and passed from view in mist at 11.a.m.
(b) Enemy Officer and 2 men were seen observing their front line and having the outstanding features of our line, South of the 'HORSESHOE' pointed out to them by another Officer. They were fired on and disappeared.

W.M. Armstrong

20th June, 1916.

Captain G.S.
29th Division.

29TH DIVISION DAILY SUMMARY.

Period from 6 a.m. 20.6.16. to 6 a.m. 21.6.16.

D.S.78.

HEADQUARTERS.
29th DIVISION
INTELLIGENCE.

No.........
Date.........

OPERATIONS.

Artillery. Enemy's Artillery was especially active near the R.E. Dump in ESSEX STREET and a few shells fell near LANSDOWNE PASSAGE on the right of the HORSESHOE.

Machine Guns. A machine gun is thought to fire from Q.5.c.50.65.
At 9.30 a.m. smoke and dust was seen from what appeared to be a machine gun position at about Q.11.c.2.8. A few minutes later after fire had ceased, something which looked like a machine gun was carried along enemy's trench to their left with nearly two feet of it showing above the parapet.

INTELLIGENCE.

Enemy Movements. 100 troops were observed in a field N. left of the PYS ROAD at point G.32.a.2.2.
Four parties of men about 20 strong (each) were seen proceeding towards PYS on road at point M.1.Bx b.2.1. and during the afternoon about 30 men in small parties were also seen at this point going in the same direction.
Five horse transport wagons were observed coming from the direction of GREVILLERS.
Four horse transport wagons with two horsemen in front were seen on road at G.25.b.5.5. going South-East.
Eight motor transport wagons were observed on road in front of BAILLESCOURT.
The usual enemy traffic was observed at R.8.b.4.6.

Enemy Work. Work was going on in communication trench about Q.10.d.8.5.
Knife rests continue to be put out in front of BEAUMONT HAMEL and "Y" RAVINE.

Train Activity. The following train movements were observed.
8.20 a.m. to BAPAUME from ACHIET LE GRAND.
9.40 a.m. to ACHIET LE GRAND from BAPAUME.
12 noon to BAPAUME from ACHIET LE GRAND.
12.5 p.m. -"-
12.30 p.m. to ACHIET LE GRAND from BAPAUME.

10.30 a.m. Train running North from BEAUCOURT.
11.30 a.m. Train running South towards BEAUCOURT.
7.30 p.m. Two trains passed R.9.a.5.2. coming towards BEAUCOURT.
12.5 p.m. Train observed running South towards GRANDCOURT.
1.5 p.m. Train running South towards BEAUCOURT.

MISCELLANEOUS.

Aeroplanes. A sentry reports at about 11.45 a.m. a British Aeroplane passed over our lines and over BEAUMONT HAMEL. At a spot North-West of BEAUMONT HAMEL the plane was heavily shelled and circled three or four times and then dived into the German lines.

Smoke. Smoke was seen at Q.5.c.05.55 during the early hours of the morning, and at Q.4.d.9.5 during the day.

Balloons. Enemy had three balloons up during the day, one S.W. of LE SARS, one over COURCELLES LA COMTE, and one in rear of Wood at point G.34.

D. M. Armstrong
Captain, G.S.,
29th Division.

21st June, 1916.

D.S.79

HEADQUARTERS.
29th DIVISION.
INTELLIGENCE.

29th DIVISION DAILY SUMMARY.
Period from 6.a.m. 21st/6/16 to 6.a.m. 22/6/16.

OPERATIONS.

Artillery. Enemy's artillery was active during the day, registering on trenches South of the 'HORSESHOE' and St HELENS. 1 shell fell into LANSDOWNE PASSAGE and some near the SUCRERIE. AUCHONVILLERS also received attention and some casualties were caused.
Our artillery was active and put a few heavy shells into BEAUMONT HAMEL.

Patrols. The Left Sector posted a listening patrol South of the 'HORSESHOE' in the same place as one was previously posted but had nothing to report.

Snipers. A marked increase in enemy sniping activity was observed.

INTELLIGENCE.

Enemy Movements.
Continuous small traffic has been noticed at R.7.b.0.3.23 entering BEAUCOURT on the BEAUCOURT Road most of it appearing to come and go by way of ARTILLERY LANE. There was also a considerable amount of traffic on the BEAUCOURT-MIRAUMONT ROAD at R.8.b.20.65.
Much transport was observed during the day going between IRLES and GREVILLERS.
A party of 100 troops were seen coming down the PYS Road and going towards GRANCOURT. Another party of about 20 strong were seen going in the same direction.
Two parties of troops each about 50 strong were observed marching across a field and going towards GREVILLERS.
A working party about 10 strong were seen at point M.1.d.2.4.
A party of troops about 40 strong were seen coming from GRANCOURT and going in the direction of GREVILLERS.
At 6.5.p.m. 2 men were seen moving along the railway with 6 large dogs, colour black and white. The dogs were heard barking in BEAUMONT HAMEL at 11. p.m.
4 horse transport wagons and 2 motor wagons were seen coming from PYS. 3 horse transport wagons were seen going towards PYS, and 5 horse transport wagons coming from GREVILLERS.

Enemy Work. A listening party near Mine Head (1st Avenue) heard working apparently at wire to their right front. The enemy were also active on their front line opposite MARY REDAN.

Train Activity. The following train movements were observed:-
8.15 a.m. to ACHIET-LE-GRAND from BAPAUME.
9.30 a.m. " BAPAUME from LE-SARS.
9.40 a.m. " ACHIET-LE-GRAND from BAPAUME.
11.5. a.m. " " " " " "
12. Noon. " BAPAUME from ACHIET-LE-GRAND.
12.15 p.m. " " " " " "
4.15 p.m. " LE.-SARS " BAPAUME.
5.25 p.m. " ACHIET-LE-GRAND from BAPAUME.
A train was heard in BEAUMONT HAMEL at 11.45 p.m. and 1 was also heard at 12.25 a.m. proceeding away from BEAUCOURT.

MISCELLANEOUS.

Balloons. Enemy had 3 balloons up yesterday, 1 South west of LE-SARS BOIS-DE-LOGEAST, and 1 over wood at G.34.

Aeroplanes. Our Aeroplanes were very active all day.

22nd June 1916   Captain G.S.

HEADQUARTERS.
29th DIVISION.
INTELLIGENCE.

No. D.S. 80.
Date.

29TH DIVISION DAILY SUMMARY.

Period from 6 a.m. 22.6.16. to 6 a.m. 23.6.16.

OPERATIONS.

Artillery. Enemy Artillery has been unusually quiet during the past 24 hours, and were chiefly registering behind our lines, and on AUCHONVILLERS, ESSEX STREET, and the HORSESHOE. In the afternoon they appeared to be registering on MAILLY with light shells some of which fell in the Town on the left of MAILLY - AUCHONVILLERS ROAD causing some casualties.

Machine Guns. During the night our Lewis Guns at the HORSESHOE fired and the enemy's guns fired at our parapet.

PATROLS. A patrol of one N.C.O. and one man went out from Sap 7 at 10.30 p.m. with the object of reconnoitring the SUNKEN ROAD to ascertain whether our mining could be heard. Patrol returned at 11 p.m. and reported movement in the long grass which they took to be an enemy patrol about 25 yards from our wire. Patrol went out again at 11.56 p.m. and returned at 1.40 a.m. and reported they could find no trace of the enemy in the SUNKEN and that our mining could not be heard.

INTELLIGENCE.

Enemy Movements. Much traffic was seen during the day at R.8.b.20.65. proceeding between MIRAUMONT and BEAUCOURT. This included numerous horse transport wagons, horsemen, bicycles, etc. and 1 four horse transport wagon which appeared to be very heavy.
In addition to the above two horse teams, one six horse team and one eight horse team were observed at R.8.b.20.65 going away from BEAUCOURT. They both had heavy loads which were covered over with canvas. These may possibly have been guns.
The usual transport and small parties of men were seen during the day moving between GREVILLERS and IRLES.
Several transports and a party of troops about 50 strong were observed going towards MIRAUMONT.
Three motor transport wagons and six horse transports were seen coming from PYS on road at point M.1.b.2.1.
Three horse transports were observed on road at G.26.b.5.5. going South-East, three horse transports at M.2.b. going North-West, and four horse transports coming from GREVILLERS at G.22.d.6.7.
A sniper in the Left Sector reports that he observed what appeared to be four Field Guns moving back at PYS. They were each drawn by four horses and later the empty wagons were seen coming back.

Enemy Work. At 7.30 a.m. a party was observed working on ridge in lines opposite THIEPVAL WOOD.
From what could be heard from our firing line the enemy was particularly busy wiring and digging last night in the vicinity of Q.10.b. and also at Q.17.a.9.7. The wire at the later point appears to be either in the trench, over it, or unusually near the edge of the parapet.
There appears to be a vertical slit in crescent shaped bank about Q.12.b.7.0.
A new trench appears to run apparently from STATION ALLEY South-East to just above Bank North of STATION ROAD.
Digging was heard half right of NEWTOWNARDS, and wiring half left.

/Train Activity.

- 2 -

<u>Train Activity.</u>   The following train movements were observed :-
9.5 a.m.   To BAPAUME from ACHIET LE GRAND.
10.1 a.m. To BAPAUME from LE SARS.
11.0 a.m. To ACHIET LE GRAND from BAPAUME.
11.25 a.m. To BAPAUME from ACHIET LE GRAND.
12.20 p.m. To BAPAUME from ACHIET LE GRAND.
2.50 p.m. To ACHIET LE GRAND from BAPAUME.
4.0 p.m.   To BAPAUME from ACHIET LE GRAND.

MISCELLANEOUS.

<u>Aeroplanes.</u>   At 7.30 a.m. one enemy plane appeared over AUCHONVILLERS and one over Salient. Both were driven back by Anti-Aircraft Guns and failed to get further over our lines.
Our machines were very active. One turned three or four somersaults but righted itself.
One enemy machine is reported to have been hit.

<u>Balloons.</u>   Balloons were observed at the following points :-
1. In the direction of WARENCOURT.
2. In the direction of BAPAUME.
3. Over Wood near BOIS DE LOGEAST.
4. South-West of LE SARS.
5. Point 0.34.

23rd June, 1916.

Captain, G.S.,
29th Division.

D.S. 81.

29TH DIVISION DAILY SUMMARY.

Period from 6 a.m. 23.6.16. to 6 a.m. 24.6.16.

OPERATIONS.

Artillery. A quiet day. At 5.30 p.m. the communication trenches in the MARY REDAN Area were shelled with about six rounds of H.E.
An Anti-Aircraft gun was active from a position in the Northern outskirts of BEAUMONT HAMEL.

Machine Guns. About 11 p.m. an enemy working party wiring East of the REDAN was fired on by our Lewis guns. Several short bursts of hostile machine gun fire were distributed over the front between Q.10.6. and Q.16.4.; otherwise the night was quiet.

Patrols. An officer and a N.C.O. reconnoitred from the Sap at the north end of CHARING CROSS in front of our wire to the tip of the REDAN without incident.

INTELLIGENCE.

Enemy Movements. Seven motor transport wagons were observed coming from the direction of GREVILLERS on Road at point G.22.d.6.7.
Five transport wagons were seen going to GREVILLERS from IRLES.
Several transport wagons were observed coming from IRLES to MIRAUMONT.
At 10.50 a.m. a working party of about 30 strong were seen working in trench in front of IRLES CHURCH at G.31.A.6.6.
The normal amount of transport was heard from the direction of BEAUMONT HAMEL between 10 p.m. and midnight.
Transport was seen during the day going towards PYS, COURCELETTE, and POZIERES.

Enemy Work. During the early morning a working party of about 15 men were seen at point R.22.d.3.1.

Train Activity. The following train movements were observed.
7.15 a.m. To BAPAUME from LE SARS.
8.10 a.m. To ACHIET LE GRAND from BAPAUME.
9.15 a.m. To ACHIET LE GRAND from BAPAUME.
4.45 p.m. To BAPAUME from ACHIET LE GRAND.

MISCELLANEOUS.

Dogs. Six large dogs were seen with one man on the BEAUCOURT ROAD about 2.30 p.m.

Balloons. Enemy balloons were seen at the following points.
1. In the direction of WARENCOURT.
2.   -"-   BAPAUME.
3. Over BOIS DE LOGEAST.
4. point G.34.
5. South-West of LE SARS.
6. Over GREVILLERS.

W. M. Armstrong.

Captain, G.S.,

24.6.16.   29th Division.

D.S. 82.

29TH DIVISION DAILY SUMMARY.

Period from 6 a.m. 24.6.16. to 6 a.m. 25.6.16.

HEADQUARTERS.
29th DIVISION.
INTELLIGENCE.

No.........
Date.........

OPERATIONS.

Artillery. The enemy's Artillery retaliated to our bombardment during the afternoon and the fire was more intense between 10 p.m. and 1.30 p.m. A number of shells fell in our front and support trenches damaging them in several places, few casualties however were caused.
MAILLY was shelled early this morning and a few casualties occurred.
Our Artillery maintained a steady fire along the enemy's wire.
The enemy's wire has been much damaged at points 53 and 41, and in front of Q.6.a.40.00 and Q.6.c.30.00. and between points 27 and 95 and back to 36 and front of 27.

Machine Guns. Machine and Lewis Guns kept up a fire on the enemy's wire during the night.

INTELLIGENCE.

Enemy Movements. 6 horse transport wagons were seen on road at point G.33.b.50.10. proceeding South.
2 parties of men about 40 in all were observed going towards PYS on road at point M.1.b.2.1.
At 2 p.m. a large working party was observed on trench between points O.6 and 38 strengthing earthworks. A party of 25 men left point and proceeded in the direction of BEAUREGARD at 4.45 p.m.
3 horse transports were seen on the road at G.22.d.6.7. coming from the direction of GREVILLERS.
A convoy of about 30 horsed vehicles was seen coming from LOUPART WOOD G.34. and was lost to view just before entering IRLES. This is thought to be have been guns and limbers as there were riders on the leaders and wheelers and men sitting on the front and rear of limbers. There were 2 horsemen in front and 4 in rear.

Enemy Work. The enemy were working on their wire at Q.11.c.72.30. between 0430 and 0500 but ceased work at once before machine guns could be trained on them.
A working party was seen at work on trench between points 06 and 38. (see above)

Train Activity. The following train movements were observed :-
6.35 a.m.   To BAPAUME from ACHIET LE GRAND.
9.15 a.m.   To ACHIET LE GRAND from BAPAUME.
9.35 a.m.   To BAPAUME from ACHIET LE GRAND.
11.30 a.m.   -"-
11.47 a.m.   -"-
11.50 a.m.   -"-
5.0 p.m.   To ACHIET LE GRAND from BAPAUME.
5.25 p.m.   To BAPAUME from LE SARS.
5.33 p.m.   -"-
6.40 p.m.   To BAPAUME from ACHIET LE GRAND.
7.35 p.m.   -"-

MISCELLANEOUS.

Aeroplanes. One of our aeroplanes flew over enemy's trenches very low but no enemy machine gun fired at it. It is thought that their machine guns are either in deep dug-outs or have been removed, as aeroplanes have never previously been permitted to fly so low without being fired on.

MISCELLANEOUS.
(continued)

Gas Shells. A few gas shells were fired on our Right Sector.

Smoke. During the period between 10 p.m. and 11.45 p.m. dense clouds of smoke were observed in front of and over the German lines principally North of MARY REDAN and at Q.4.b.9.9. It was impossible to distinguish whether these clouds were the smoke from bursting shells or gas clouds. They were only visible by the light of the German flares. The red flares did not appear to be answered by enemy's Artillery and were possibly used as gas alarms.

W. M. Armstrong.

Captain, G.S.,

25.6.16.

29th Division.

29TH DIVISION DAILY SUMMARY

from 6 a.m. 25.6.16. to 6 a.m. 26.6.16.

OPERATIONS.

Artillery. Our Artillery has been steadily cutting wire with considerable success. The wire is much damaged at the following points, 53, 41, 98, North and South of 57, between 53 and 78, 36 and 27, 27 and 35, 59 and 35, 86 and 91, Q.5.c.05.60 and Q.5.c.10.70, and in front of 39. Between Q.11.c.00.30 and Q.11.c.15.30 wire was reconnoitred and found to be much knocked about and easily passable by Infantry. There is a clear passage at this point about 8 feet wide.
At Q.17.a.90.60 there are several gaps in the wire.
The enemy's Artillery has replied to our fire, little damage however has been done.
A hostile battery could be seen firing from the front of BEAUREGARD and south of PUISIEUX-AU-MONT about point L.26.b.

Machine Guns. Our Lewis and Machine Guns fired on the enemy's wire during the night.

Patrols. A patrol under 2nd Lieut. CASEBY, 1st Lancashire Fusiliers went out and examined the wire last night in the front of 100 yards across WATLING STREET point 27. They report the wire is about 40 yards deep reaching up to the enemy's parapet. At front edge of the wire large iron knife rests which are unmoved, behind the knife rests the wire is much blown about and there are large holes in it 5 or 6 yards in diameter. There is no clear passage, infantry could work through with little difficulty. The enemy have made no attempt to renew the wire in this sector. The patrol consider the front line to be unoccupied.

INTELLIGENCE.

Enemy Movements.
Five horse transport wagons were seen proceeding towards IRLES point G.34.b.1.7.
Four wagons were observed going towards PYS at M.1.b.2.1.

Enemy Work.
A working party was seen at work at point 06. Owing to the dense clouds of smoke it was impossible to see if anything was going on.

Train Activity.
The following train movements were observed :-
9.27 a.m.   ACHIET LE GRAND to BAPAUME.
11.45 a.m. BAPAUME to ACHIET LE GRAND.
2 p.m.   ACHIET LE GRAND to BAPAUME.
2.47 p.m.   BAPAUME to ACHIET LE GRAND.
4.30 p.m.   BAPAUME to ACHIET LE GRAND.
5.20 p.m.   ACHIET LE GRAND to BAPAUME.

MISCELLANEOUS.

Smoke. From 6 p.m. to 8 p.m. volumes of smoke were observed at the Station (Q.18.b.)

Signals. At midnight 14 star shells were fired from trench immediately in front of BEAUMONT, but all other lights issued from their support and reserve trenches.

MISCELLANEOUS.
(continued)

Balloons.
At 2 p.m. a balloon was seen falling to the ground in flames at the South end of BOIS DE LOGEAST.
A few minutes afterwards another was observed to fall South-West of LE SARS.
At 7.15 p.m. a third balloon was seen to fall near COURCELLES LA COMTE.

Signal Trench. A 5.9" shell hit the signal trench at the western end of GABION AVENUE without damaging the line in any way.

W. M. Armstrong

Captain, G.S.,
29th Division.

26.6.16.

D.S. 84.

HEADQUARTERS.
29th DIVISION.
INTELLIGENCE.

No............
Date............

29TH DIVISION DAILY SUMMARY.

From 6 a.m. 26.6.16. to 6 a.m. 27.6.16.

OPERATIONS.

Artillery. The enemy replied to our bombardment fairly actively. They were particularly active between 11p.m. and 12 p.m. and damaged our trenches in several places in the support and front lines.
Our artillery have damaged the enemy's support line and the houses in BEAUMONT HAMEL. A house at Q.5.c.5.2 was set on fire about 2 p.m. and burnt till dark.
Great damage appears to have been done to the buildings between Q.5.c.5.6. and Q.5.c.5.0.

Machine Guns. Two machine guns were in action last night near BEAUMONT HAMEL sweeping our parapet.
Machine Gun emplacements are thought to exist in the bank running North-West from the new trench at Q.12.d.8.8.

Trench Mortars. Our trench mortars have fired on the wire in the vicinity of BEAUMONT HAMEL with good results.

Wire "A" A patrol of 3 officers and 40 men of the Lancashire Fusiliers went out at 10.30 a.m. to cut gaps in the enemy's wire. Five gaps were cut and completed, and two others were worked on and are easily passable, but still have some loose wire in them.
It was found that Guns and Trench Mortars had cut through the wire to a large extent, but work was required to make gaps quite clear, except at point 27.
The outer edge of the German wire is a row of heavy iron knife rests fastened to each other by very thick wire, and fixed to the ground by strong iron screw staples. These are very difficult to move and are apparently unaffected by anything but a direct hit.

"B" Three officers' patrols went out from the Right Sector. They report that there is a succession of gaps in the enemy's wire between Q.10.d.80.40 and Q.11.c.50.10. Little damage however has been done between Q.11.c.10.30 and Q.11.c.37.18.

"C" The Royal Fusiliers patrolled the wire from point 7828 to point 89. Here however little damage had been done to the wire.

"D" Observers report that the wire is badly damaged between 59, 91 and 86, from 39 to 15, from Q.x.6.x Q.6.c.5.4 to point 57, and from point 59 and Q.5.a.4.3.

The enemy appears to be making no attempt to repair the wire across his front.

The patrols established the fact that while the enemy may evacuate the front line by day, it is fairly thickly held by night by sentry posts and machine guns.

INTELLIGENCE.

Enemy Movements. Two motor transport wagons were observed going towards GREVILLERS on the road at G.22.d.6.7.
Eight transport wagons and five small parties of men were seen going to GREVILLERS.

Enemy Work. No enemy working parties were observed during the day.

/Train

Train Movements. The following train movements were observed :-
11.20 a.m. ACHIET LE GRAND to BAPAUME.
12.55 p.m.   -"-
1.5 p.m.   -"-
6.38 p.m.   -"-
7.23 p.m. BAPAUME to ACHIET LE GRAND.

MISCELLANEOUS.

Signals. The enemy received artillery support on sending up red flares.
A gong was struck in BEAUMONT HAMEL about 4 a.m. followed by three blasts on a horn. This was followed by the enemy shelling our lines.

Smoke. Large clouds of smoke were observed rising East of LOUPART WOOD (G.34)
Dense clouds of smoke were also seen rising from ACHIET LE GRAND.

W. M. Armstrong.
Captain, G.S.,
29th Division.

27th June, 1916.

APPENDIX 6.

Comprises the following :-

Daily List of Casualties during the Preliminary Bombardment i.e. from 24th June to 30th June.

=================

To Gen. Staff. War Diary.

Casualties to 12 noon, June 25th 1916

	KILLED		WOUNDED		MISSING	
	OFFICERS	OTHER RANKS	OFFICERS	OTHER RANKS	OFFICERS	OTHER RANKS
2/Royal Fusiliers	–	–	–	3	–	–
2/South Wales Borders	–	–	–	⊕ 4	–	1
1/K.O.S.B.	–	–	–	⊕ 9	–	–
1/R. Inniskilling Fus.	–	3	–	7	–	1
1/3 Kent Field Coy.	–	–	–	1	–	–
Special Bde. R.E.	–	–	–	1	–	–
88th Field Amblce.	–	–	–	1	–	–
1/Essex Regt.	–	–	⊕ 1	–	–	–
132nd Bde. R.F.A.	–	–	–	2	–	–
147th Bde. R.F.A.	–	–	–	1	–	–
17th Bde. R.F.A.	–	–	–	*2	–	–
	–	3	1	31	–	2

* Includes 1 O.R. of 48th Divn.

⊕ accidentally (bomb)

① S.W.B. " 2 only "

25/6/16.

Casualties during 24 hrs ending noon 24th June.

Unit	Killed		Wounded		Missing	
	Officers	O.R.	Officers	O.R.	Officers	O.R.
1st Lancs. Fus.	0	1	0	1	0	1
2nd Hants Regt.	—	1	—	1	—	1
7th Bde R.F.A.	—	1	—	1	—	1
132nd Bde. R.F.A.	—	1	—	1	—	1
	—	1	—	3	—	1

Appendix 6

Lieut Colonel
Andrews 29 Div.

25/6/16.

To 'Gen Staff'.

Casualties to 12 noon June 27th, 1916.

Unit	Killed		Wounded		Missing	
	Officers	Other Ranks	Officers	Other Ranks	Officers	Other Ranks
2/South Wales Borderers	-	-	-	2	-	-
1/R. Inniskilling Fus.	-	-	-	5 x	-	-
2/Royal Fusiliers	-	-	-	4	-	-
1/Lancashire Fus.	-	-	-	-	-	-
Special Bde. R.E.	-	1	-	8	-	1
29th Divl.Signals Coy.	-	-	-	3	-	-
17th Bde. R.F.A.	-	-	-	-	-	-
Total:-	-	1	-	22	-	1

x Includes 1 self-inflicted

Mitford
B. Colonel,
A.A. & Q.M.G., 29 Div.

27/6/16.

To "G.S."

Casualties to 12 noon 26th June, 1916.

from DAA?

UNIT	KILLED		WOUNDED		MISSING	
	OFFICERS	OTHER RANKS	OFFICERS	OTHER RANKS	OFFICERS	OTHER RANKS
2/South Wales Borderers	-	1	1	1	-	-
1/R. Inniskilling Fus.	-	2	-	5	-	-
1/Essex Regt.	-	-	-	*4	-	-
Special Brigade R.E.	-	-	1	2	-	-
2/Royal Fusiliers	-	-	-	1	-	-
88th Field Ambulance	-	-	1	1	-	-
15th Bde. R.H.A.	1	-	1	-	-	-
17th Bde. R.G.A.	-	1	-	1	-	-
Totals =	1	2	1	16	-	-

* Accidentally, bomb.

Mr Roach
Lieut Col.
actg A.A. + Q.M.G.

26/6/16.

To "Gen. Staff."

Casualties to 12 noon, June 29th, 1916.

Unit	Killed		Wounded		Missing	
	Officers	Other Ranks	Officers	Other Ranks	Officers	Other Ranks
2/Royal Fusiliers	—	1	2	3	—	2
1/Lancashire Fus.	—	1	—	1	—	—
16th Middlesex Regt.	—	✕1	—	✕3	—	—
1/Newfoundland Regt.	—	—	—	1	—	1
2/South Wales Borderers	—	2	—	8	—	—
1/R. Inniskilling Fus.	—	1	—	4	—	1
1/R. Dublin Fus.	—	1	2	3	—	1
	—	5	4	23	—	25
						28

✕ Accidentally, by bomb.

W. Averk
A.A. & Q.M.G. Lt.Col.

29-6-16.

To General Staff.

War Diary.

Casualties to 12 noon 28th June 1916

	Killed			Wounded			Missing		
	Officers	Other Ranks	Officers	2nd Lieut	Officers	Other Ranks	Officers	2nd Lieut	Officers	Other Ranks
1/Newfoundland Regt.	—	3	3	9	—	3
2/South Wales Borders.	—	1	1	1	—	1
1/R. Inniskilling Fus.	—	—	—	2	—	—
2/Royal Fusiliers	—	—	—	4	—	1
1/Lancashire Fus.	—	1	1	6	—	2
29th Divl. Reserve Coy.	—	1	1	—	—	1
16th Sanitary Section	—	1	1	1	—	1
92nd Battery R.F.A.	—	—	—	—	—	1
371st Battery R.F.A.	—	1	1	1	—	1
	1	5	6	25	—	6

1 o.r. of 1/Lancashire Fusrs. reported missing yesterday has since rejoined.

28/6/16.

"Confidential"

Casualties to 12 noon, June 30th. 1916.

Unit	Killed		Wounded		Missing	
	Officers	Other Ranks	Officers	Other Ranks	Officers	Other Ranks
2/ South Wales Borderers	—	1	—	4	—	—
1/R. O. Y. L. I.	—	*1	—	*1	—	—
1/R. Inniskilling Fus.	—	—	—	+3	—	—
1/ Border Regt.	1	1	—	2	—	—
2/ Royal Fusiliers	—	—	—	1	—	—
1/R. Dublin Fus.	—	#2	1	6	—	13
147th Bde. R.F.A.	—	—	—	4	—	—
Total =	1	5	1	21	—	13

* incl. 87th T.M. Battery
+ includes 2 O.R. attd. 87th T.M.B
# 2/29 T.M.B.

[signature]
30/6/16.

[signature]
Lt. Col.
A.A. + Q.M.G.

APPENDIX 7.

Comprises the following :-

       29th Division Dispositions on June 16th and June 24th.

=================

Appendix. 7

29th DIVISION DISPOSITIONS.
at 10.a.m. on June. 16th.

Divisional Headquarters.	ACHEUX.
R.A.Headquarters.	"
15th Brigade R.H.A.	MAILLY-MAILLET.
17th Brigade. R.F.A.	ENGLEBELMER.
147th Brigade. R.F.A.	"
132nd (How.) Brigade.	MAILLY-MAILLET.
Divisional Ammunition Column.	ARQUEVES.
H.Q. Divisional R.E..	ACHEUX.
London Field Coy. R.E.	"
Kent Field Coy, R.E.	ENGLEBELMER.
West Riding Field Coy. R.E.	MAILLY-MAILLET.
H.Q. 86th Brigade.	" "
M.G. Company.	Left Sector,
2nd Royal Fusiliers.	" "
1st Lancs. Fusiliers.	MAILLY-MAILLET.,wood.
1st Dublin Fusiliers.	" " "
16th Middlesex Regt.	Left Sector,
H.Q. 87th Brigade.	LOUVENCOURT.
M.G. Company.	"
2nd S.W.Bs.	"
1st K.O.S. Borderers.	"
1st R. Inniskilling Fusrs.	"
1st Border Regt.	"
H.Q. 88th Brigade.	ENGLEBELMER.
M.G.Company.	Right Sector.
4th Worcester Regt.	ENGLEBELMER.
2nd Hants. Regt.	Right Sector.
1st Essex Regt.	ENGLEBELMER.
Newfoundland Regiment.	Right Sector.
Pioneer Battalion. (Monmouth Regt.)	MAILLY-MAILLET.
87th Field Ambulance.	LOUVENCOURT.
88th Field Ambulance.	ARQUEVES.

89th Field Ambulance. ACHEUX.
Divisional Sanitary Section. "
H.Q. Divisional Train. ARQUEVES.
H.Q. Company Train. "
No.2. Coy. " "
No.3. Coy. " "
No.4. Coy. "
18th Mobile Vet. Section. LOUVENCOURT.
Supply Column. BEAUVAL.

Headquarters,

    VIII Corps.

I.G.39.
16/6/16.

    Herewith dispositions of formations in 29th Division as called for in your G.167 of 31st March.

U. M. a.

Major General.
Commanding 29th Division.

16th June, 1916.

29TH DIVISION DISPOSITIONS
at 10 a.m. on June 24th.

```
Divisional Headquarters                 ACHEUX
R.A.                                      "
15th Bde. R.H.A.                        MAILLY-MAILLET
17th Bde. R.F.A.                        ENGLEBELMER
147th Bde. R.F.A.                         "
132nd How. Bde.                         MAILLY-MAILLET
Divisional Ammunition Column            ARQUEVES
Headquarters Divisional R.E.            ACHEUX
London Field Company R.E.                 "
Kent Field Company R.E.                 ENGLEBELMER
West Riding Field Company R.E.          MAILLY-MAILLET
Headquarters 86th Brigade.                "
M. G. Company                           Left Sector
Royal Fusiliers    2 Coys. Left Sector  2 Coys. MAILLY-MAILLET WOOD.
Lancashire Fusiliers    -"-              -"-
Dublin Fusiliers     )
Middlesex Regt.      )                  ACHEUX WOOD.
Headquarters 87th Brigade.              ENGLEBELMER
M. G. Company                           Right Sector.
S.W.B.'s                )
Inniskilling Fusiliers  ) 2 Coys. in Right Sector 2 Coys ENGLEBELMER.
K.O.S.B.s               )
Border Regt.            )               ACHEUX WOOD
Headquarters 88th Brigade.              LOUVENCOURT
M. G. Company                              "
                         (less 8 guns in Redoubt Line)
Worcester Regt.                         LOUVENCOURT
Hampshire Regt.                            "
Essex Regt.                                "
Newfoundland Regt.                         "
1/2nd Monmouth Regt. (Pioneer Bn.)      MAILLY-MAILLET WOOD.
87th Field Ambulance.                   LOUVENCOURT
88th    "       "                       ARQUEVES
89th    "       "                       ACHEUX
Divisional Sanitary Section                "
Headquarters Divisional Train           ARQUEVES
Headquarter Company Train                  "
No.2 Company                               "
No.3    "                                  "
No.4    "                                  "
18th Mobile Veterinary Section          LOUVENCOURT
Supply Column                           BEAUVAL
```

HEADQUARTERS,
29th DIVISION.
INTELLIGENCE.
No. 9.6.39
Date 24/6/16

W. M. Armstrong Capt.

for Lieut-Colonel, G.S.,
29th Division.

24.6.16.